PILLARS OF POWER
Australia's Institutions

PILLARS OF POWER
Australia's Institutions

David Solomon

THE FEDERATION PRESS
2007

Published in Sydney by:
The Federation Press
PO Box 45, Annandale, NSW, 2038
71 John St, Leichhardt, NSW, 2040
Ph (02) 9552 2200 Fax (02) 9552 1681
E-mail: info@federationpress.com.au
Website: http://www.federationpress.com.au

National Library of Australia
Cataloguing-in-Publication entry
Solomon, David.
Pillars of power: Australia's institutions.

Bibliography.
Includes index.
ISBN 978 186287 645 3 (pbk.).

1. Implied powers (Constitutional law) – Australia. 2. Legislative power – Australia.
3. Delegation of powers – Australia. 4. Legislative bodies – Australia. I. Title.

342.94029

Typeset by The Federation Press, Sydney, NSW.
Printed by Southwood Press, Marrickville, NSW.

Preface

I began reporting national affairs from the Press Gallery in the Old Parliament House in Canberra in the mid-1960s. I have been a keen observer of Australia's political, legal and economic institutions since that time, with an academic as well as journalistic interest in the way they function and in the people responsible for their operation.

In *Pillars of Power* I provide an analysis of where Australia's major institutions stand today, and an assessment of how well (or otherwise) they work. The book draws on the views of many people from within the institutions but importantly, it also tries to provide an historical context, showing how they have developed, and the extent to which they have changed in relatively recent times.

This book is the culmination of a two-year project. It is based on a year-long series I researched and wrote for the *Courier-Mail*, Brisbane, at the suggestion of the newspaper's editor, David Fagan. It was published as a series of articles throughout 2005 under the general title, 'Pillars of Power'. It involved interviewing more than 50 current and former politicians, administrators, public servants, academics and other experts, as well as a study of books, articles, magazines and newspaper records. In 2006, after I retired from full-time journalism, I updated and rewrote the material for this book. I am grateful to David Fagan for encouraging me to undertake the project, for providing the resources that made it possible and for permission to continue to make use of the title. I also thank the many people who made their time available for interviews.

David Solomon
June 2007

Contents

List of figures and tables

Acknowledgments

Figure 1 is reproduced from a research paper 'Trends in Australian Agriculture', Productivity Commission and figures 7.1 and 7.2 are reproduced from 'Structural Reforms Australian-style: lessons for others' by G Banks, Productivity Commission.

Figures 1.1 and 1.2 are reproduced from a Parliamentary Library research paper, 'The 41st Parliament: middle-aged, well-educated and (mostly) male'.

Figures 2.1, 2.2 and 2.3 are from the Treasury's 2006 Budget Papers.

Table 3.3 is from the website of the Governor-General.

Figure 5.1 is adapted from a figure in *Report on Government Services 2005*, Steering Committee for the Review of Government Service Provision.

Figures 8.1 and 8.2 are from the Australian Bureau of Statistics, *Year Book Australia* 2004 and Figure 12.1 from the *Year Book Australia* 2001, 'Centenary Article – a century of population change in Australia, chart C4.15'.

Figure 11.1 is from the Australian Sports Commission's 2006 Budget papers.

All the above are copyright Commonwealth of Australia, reproduced by permission.

Figures 9.1 and 9.2 are from the Australian Vice-Chancellors Committee, adapted from DEST statistics, copyright AVCC and reproduced by permission.

Introduction

Australia underwent massive changes in the last half of the 20th century. Its population more than doubled, increasing from 8.3 million in 1950 to 19.2 million in 2000. This was a faster rate of growth than any other western country, due mainly to a very high rate of immigration – a net intake over 50 years of over 23 per cent of the population.

Its economy, which had stagnated during the first 50 years of the century, matched the overall growth of other developed countries during the second half.[1] However its international economic ranking fell consistently between 1950 (when it was ranked fifth) and the late 1980s (when it was 15th) before putting on a remarkable spurt to take eighth position in 2002.[2]

Over the past 40 years the Australian economy has changed very significantly. Manufacturing and agriculture, which made up almost 40 per cent of the economy in 1963, had less than half that share early in the 21st century. All of the net increase in employment in the past 35 years – over 4.3 million jobs – was provided by the services sector of the economy, including retail trade, property and business services, health and community services, travel and communications (see Figure 1 over page).[3] In 1960 women made up 25 per cent of the workforce. Forty years later they were almost 44 per cent of the workforce.

Before World War II a university education was available only for a privileged elite – slightly more than 10,000 students were enrolled at the six universities based in the State capitals. Sixty years later there were 38 universities, with about three-quarters of a million students.

In the early 1950s it went largely unremarked that the Prime Minister, Mr Menzies, was able to travel to England by boat with the Australian cricket team, stay for a month or so and watch the cricket, and then return by boat, taking another six weeks to do so. 'Such conduct is inconceivable today. Not even our present Prime Minister could restore the pace of that era in this regard'.[4]

In sport, half a century ago amateurism was the rule in most areas. Professionals were banned from the Olympic Games, the Davis Cup was restricted to amateurs, and international cricketers were paid relatively frugal living allowances when they travelled overseas. These days most elite sportsmen (and some top sportswomen) are full-time professionals.

Figure 1: Agriculture has declined in *relative* terms

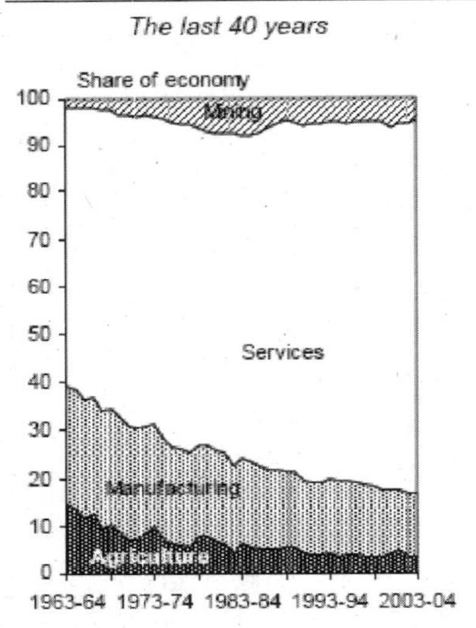

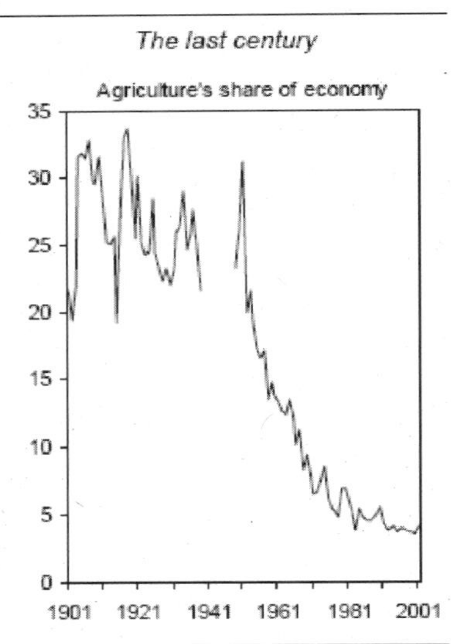

Source: Productivity Commission.

But the basic structure of most political and legal institutions in Australia has remained relatively unchanged. Australia remains a monarchy. It retains the federal structure introduced when it achieved nationhood in 1901. At the national level and in the States, it employs the same system of responsible, cabinet government that was introduced when the New South Wales, Victorian, Tasmanian and South Australian colonies achieved self-government in 1856. The first Supreme Court was created in 1823, under an Act of the British Parliament. As with all subsequent superior courts at the colonial, State and federal level, the legislation created an independent judiciary, presiding over the rule of law.

And during this period, 'save in England and North America the institutions of governance in virtually every part of the world went through numerous fundamental transformations'.[5] NSW Chief Justice Jim Spigelman says:

> Australians should appreciate the longevity of our fundamental institutions. We should long have abandoned that national diffidence which made us act as if history was something that happened somewhere else. Our own history is long and remains of fundamental significance in our day to day lives.

But important changes in those institutions are occurring, particularly those of governance. In the past generation – 25 to 30 years – there have been significant changes in the relative powers of the Prime Minister, Cabinet and Parliament and in the operation of the public service. The Commonwealth has greatly expanded its powers at the expense of the States. The economy has been subjected to national regulation by a small group of largely autonomous Commonwealth-appointed agencies, including the Reserve Bank (that sets interest rates) the Australian Competition and Consumer Commission, the Australian Securities and Investment Commission and the Australian Prudential Regulatory Authority.

Some institutional changes have been prompted by external events. The terrorist attacks on the United States of 11 September 2001 and on Bali on 12 October 2002 have prompted a massive change in defence and security arrangements within Australia. In a more benign way, international competition prompted government intervention to change the way in which sport is organised. Technological change is affecting the media, political decisions have changed industrial relations and may reduce the power of the trade union movement.

Many of Australia's institutions are evolving at a rapid rate. This is a snapshot of many of the more important ones, taken in 2006.

Notes

1 Tiffin and Gittins 2004: 42-47.
2 See Chapter 7, page 127.
3 Productivity Commission 2005c: xviii.
4 Spigelman 2004: 1.
5 Spigelman 2004: 3.

1

Government and Parliament

Prime Minister, Cabinet, Parliament – the principal institutions of Australian government – are in a process of rapid evolution.

Two generations ago, when political scientists and historians described the Australian political system, their starting point was the British system, the Westminster system of responsible cabinet government. The Australian system of government differed from the system it inherited from Britain in relatively few ways, and mainly as a result of the way the local political institutions developed in the colonies before federation. The Australian ethos, for example, had quickly rejected the notion of an appointed upper House, modelled on the House of Lords. And Australian parliamentary parties, unlike those in Britain, became highly disciplined at a very early stage, and discouraged their MPs from voting independently: this was true even of the conservative parties which condemned the Australian Labor Party's decision, taken soon after it was formed, to tightly discipline its MPs and require them to vote the party line in the Parliament.

But one generation ago, students of the Australian political system were being encouraged to take much more notice of the influence of American processes on the way we were governed. In 1980 Dr Elaine Thompson coined the word 'Washminster' to help describe the Australian system as a blending of the Westminster system of parliamentary, cabinet government, with an important contribution from the American system, a formal separation of the powers of the executive, the legislature and the judiciary, that was written into the Australian Constitution.[1]

Prime Minister and cabinet

However in the late 20th and early 21st century Australia moved beyond both Westminster and Washminster. In essence, it developed a far more presidential system of government, though one without the built-in constitutional safeguards of the American system. There are fewer inherent limitations on the power the Australian Prime Minister may exercise than there are on an American President. The checks and balances that restrain an American President are either not present, or of little importance, in the case of an Australian Prime Minister.

The Prime Minister and the President are the respective heads of the executive government. They are responsible for the administration of the laws. Both also have a role in making law. The president may send proposed laws to Congress for approval and may veto laws that Congress passes, though Congress can overrule his veto if it can muster a large enough majority. The Prime Minister does not have or need a veto power. His party controls the House of Representatives and the Parliament will not pass laws of which he disapproves. And the laws he and his government proposes are almost guaranteed passage through the House of Representatives, and most will also pass the Senate.

The President nominates the Federal judges, but all have to be approved by the Senate. The same is true of the members of his cabinet, the most senior public servants and all ambassadors. But the Prime Minister's nominations of judges, senior public servants and ambassadors, after approval by cabinet and executive council, do not face scrutiny by either House of Parliament. Under Coalition governments, the Prime Minister also decides who his Liberal Ministers will be, and what positions they will hold. Labor ministers are chosen by the Caucus (the whole parliamentary party), but the Labor Prime Minister decides what portfolios they will hold. Unlike the situation in the US these Cabinet appointments are not subject to parliamentary approval.

The President has a decisive role in the determination of American foreign policy. But decisions involving war and peace have to be approved by the Congress. The Australian Prime Minister is not so limited. For example, in deciding to invoke the ANZUS Treaty (see Chapter 6) to support the United States following the 11 September 2001 terrorist attacks on New York and Washington, Prime Minister John Howard did not need to be concerned about whether his actions would be supported in the Parliament: it was enough that the Cabinet would approve whatever he did. This was true also of his decision to commit Australia's armed forces to support the Americans in trying to defeat the Taliban in Afghanistan and in invading Iraq in 2002.

Formally, the executive power of the Commonwealth is exercised through the Federal Executive Council, which acts on decisions taken by the cabinet. But the cabinet in modern times rarely if ever makes decisions that are not those desired by the Prime Minister.

The pre-eminent and predominant position of the Australian Prime Minister and his increasing power are the consequences in part of the way elections are fought, and the way the last four Prime Ministers have used the cabinet system of government to advance their own supremacy in government. This is the view of Dr Neal Blewitt, a former Professor of Political Science who served as a senior Cabinet minister in the Hawke Government. He says the way television covers Australian elections has turned them into a presidential-style contest. 'You scarcely see most other ministers – even the Treasurer – getting much attention', he says. 'Perhaps the media is to blame. The media have allowed this to occur in a system where, theoretically, responsibility is collective'.[2]

Former head of the Prime Minister's Department, Dr Michael Keating, and Professor Pat Weller from Griffith University, agree that the media had contributed to the increasing importance of the Prime Minister. In a chapter they jointly wrote on cabinet government in Australia, they say that developments in technology mean that the media now demand an immediate response from governments as events unfold. They say, 'Typically, only the Prime Minister is sufficiently across all aspects of the more significant policy issues to meet these media demands. Conversely, Prime Ministers cannot allow one of their political rivals to be seen to speak for the government as a whole lest their own position is undermined'.[3] They say there is a view that the increase in prime ministerial power is an inevitable reaction to the various pressures to which cabinet government is having to adapt. But they say there are others who believe the growth of prime ministerial power should be resisted or it will undermine the basic rationale for cabinet government, which is to act as a collective forum for decision-taking, particularly because tight party discipline means that Parliament is no longer seen as an effective check on executive power.

No-one disputes the claim that the power exercised by Australian Prime Ministers has increased substantially over the past 30 years. The last four Prime Ministers – Malcolm Fraser, Bob Hawke, Paul Keating and John Howard – have all dominated their cabinets and their governments. Contrary to popular belief, between 1972 and 1975 Gough Whitlam, Fraser's immediate predecessor, was unable to assert any direct authority over his cabinet, particularly in crucial areas of economic management, nor was he able to influence the policies or conduct of many of his senior ministers.[4] The only area where Whitlam's power was unchallenged was in formulating and administering foreign policy. Hawke says bluntly that Whitlam's relationship with his cabinet was a total disaster. Ministers could argue their case in cabinet and if they did not get their way could go back and argue in Caucus to try to overturn the cabinet's decision.

Hawke says when he became Prime Minister in 1983 he made it clear from the very first that cabinet decisions would be binding on ministers: they could not try to change them in Caucus. However he told ministers they would have every opportunity to argue their case and there would be no situation where people could claim they were rolled. 'It led some to say it was cabinet by exhaustion at times but it was deliberate', he says. 'And it worked. For the whole of my nine years as Prime Minister there was never any going back. They knew they had a complete opportunity to present their case'. Yet at the same time, Hawke says his ministers always took the position that ultimately his (Hawke's) own view as Prime Minister would prevail:

> Even towards the end, on Coronation Hill [a decision to ban uranium mining of a productive area in the Northern Territory], I didn't have the numbers but they said, 'that's the old bloke's view; that's what its got to be'.

He says the same occurred over the draft Antarctic treaty where he rejected the views of Foreign Minister Gareth Evans and Environment Minister Graham Richardson, the two ministers responsible for the cabinet submission that would have allowed mining in the Antarctic: 'I was in a clear minority, but they said, "Alright, if that's what you think"'. Hawke says: 'It made for good government because I didn't abuse that knowledge (that Cabinet would ultimately bow to his wishes). There were discussions where I changed my mind'.[5]

Malcolm Fraser used a different technique to get his way. According to Professor Weller, his biographer, Fraser also ran long cabinet meetings, and allowed a great deal of discussion. But he often preceded a cabinet meeting by resolving issues with a small group of ministers and then gradually expanded their number so that everyone was tied into his own views. Fraser was concerned to get his cabinet to acquiesce with his views.[6]

Subsequently Prime Minister Howard formalised the rules that bind ministers into the decision-making process. As Dr Keating and Professor Weller explain:

> [T]he first essential of cabinet government is *collective* government. Ministers discuss government policy, determine the choices, and jointly take responsibility for those decisions they helped to make, even if for some that is only by way of acquiescence. Indeed, occasionally they are committed to decisions they had no part in determining, but which were announced by the Prime Minister, or perhaps the Treasurer. While there is a substantial debate about what cabinet does, should do and might do, this feature of collective responsibility is common to all accounts. In every case it is the prime minister who decides exactly how that rule should be applied in detail.[7]

The supremacy of the Prime Minister is made bluntly clear in the official *Guide on key elements of ministerial responsibility*. This is published by the Prime Minister's Department.[8] It states, for example, that the Prime Minister sets out his priorities and strategic direction for each portfolio in a letter he sends to ministers after he appoints them. It says cabinet and its committees meet as and when required 'consistent with the Prime Minister's wishes' and decisions on whether an item should be considered in cabinet and what business would be considered at a particular meeting are taken by the Prime Minister.

When John Howard became Prime Minister he introduced new bureaucratic arrangements that bolstered his own power as Prime Minister. He decided to replace the career public servant who had been secretary to cabinet with his own political appointee, a former bureaucrat who had worked with him in the lead up to the election. The new Cabinet secretary was made head of a new Cabinet Policy Unit, again staffed by political appointees, to provide him with advice and a political perspective on Cabinet business.[9] Howard also removed six heads of public service departments and brought in an outsider as head of the Prime Minister's Department. And he increased the size of his own personal staff to around 40.

Like Dr Blewitt, Senate Clerk Harry Evans is concerned that the system has become presidential without the requisite safeguards. He likens the system under Prime Minister Howard to a monarchy, with the Prime Minister's office acting as a royal court. Everything depends on who has the King's ear, who has influence at court. 'It is very obvious that cabinet counts for very much less than it used to and the government party room counts for much less than it used to'.[10] He says another sign of change is that where once the heads of the various public service departments were appointed by the Governor-General, they are now appointed directly by the Prime Minister and contracted to him. 'It is a very significant symbolic change. It is clear you are now a servant of the PM'.

Prime Minister and Parliament

In February 2006 the Liberal and National Party members of Parliament were allowed a 'conscience' vote on whether the Minister for Health should continue to determine the availability to medical practitioners of the abortion pill, RU486. The Prime Minister granted his MPs and Senators this free vote after it became public knowledge there was significant backbench unrest over the Minister's refusal to lift his ban on the pill. This event was hailed by many of the MPs and Senators who spoke on the issue as a proud moment for the Parliament. It was, rather, an indication of the extent to which they had for the most part surrendered, in the interests of their party and the government, their freedom to determine how they should vote.

Some months later, several backbenchers in the Liberal Party and one National Party MP either voted against or abstained from voting on government legislation to send all asylum seekers detected arriving in or headed for Australia to overseas detention camps, established by Australia, for processing. When the Prime Minister recognised after speaking with relevant Senators that the legislation would be defeated in the Senate, he withdrew it before a vote was taken. This was taken by media commentators to be a significant defeat for the Prime Minister, an extremely rare instance of a public revolt by a small but significant number of his backbenchers.

Such events were more common in earlier times. Coincidentally, the Parliamentary Library published a research paper in October 2005 entitled *Crossing the floor in Federal Parliament 1950-August 2004*.[11] It reported that during the 54-year period under review, there were more than 14,000 divisions but an MP or Senator voted against their party in only 3 per cent of those divisions. Of the 28 people who had crossed the floor 10 times or more only one, Senator Robert Hill, was still in Parliament when the statistics were compiled. Most floor crossings took place in the 1960s. The study found that when a Coalition Government controls the Senate, instances of floor-crossing increase. It also found that the effect of floor-crossing was 'largely symbolic' because it rarely affected parliamentary outcomes.

The reversal of roles

In the 21st century instances of floor-crossing by backbenchers are so rare that Bob Hawke considers Parliament has become 'a charade, where everything is preordained'.[12] He says there is scepticism and cynicism, if not contempt, about Parliament and the way it is conducted. Malcolm Fraser takes a similar view. He complains there is an iron-clad control over both parties in today's world, with monolithic control and discipline far greater than in his time in Parliament, more than 20 years ago.[13] David Hamer, a Liberal backbencher who served in both the House of Representatives and the Senate, has written that the House has developed into 'an elective party dictatorship'.[14] Dr Neal Blewitt similarly describes the House of Representatives as an elective dictatorship. He says it has been turned into a rubber stamp for the actions of the executive.[15] As Senate Clerk Harry Evans puts it:

> Instead of executive governments being responsible to parliaments, parliaments have become responsible to executive governments. The body which is supposed to be scrutinised and controlled by parliament has actually come to control the body which is supposed to be doing the scrutinising and controlling – a reversal of roles.[16]

All commentators agree that the main reason for this development has been the ever-increasing rigidity and discipline of the major parties that dominate the House of Representatives. According to a recent study published by the Australian National University as part of a project called the Democratic Audit of Australia, our main political parties are often described as the most disciplined in the world. An audit team led by Professor Dean Jaensch of Flinders University says the Labor Party is the only major party that applies formal party discipline but the cohesion of the Liberal Party is as complete as that of Labor, and while the National Party was often critical of Labor's discipline, it also manages a high degree of cohesion. The team's report points out that both non-Labor parties have used 'the power of pre-selection as a potent means of enforcing cohesion and punishing dissension'.[17]

Malcolm Fraser agrees. He says that in his time there were a number of Victorian and Tasmanian Liberals who were prepared to get up and cross the floor on an issue of principle. They could do so because their party branches were prepared to support them. But now the pre-selection system had changed to give the head office more power.[18]

According to David Hamer, the dominant activity of the House of Representatives after each election is to begin electioneering for the next. He points out that the House of Representatives, through its majority, selects the government. Given the existence of tight party discipline, there is a fundamental problem about expecting that majority then to be an effective critic and scrutineer of that government.[19] As Harry Evans puts it, 'Members of Parliament no longer see themselves as the scrutineers and controllers of executive power, but as either the supporters of the government or the supporters of the would-be government'.[20]

Dr Blewitt says of the three major functions attributed to a modern Parliament – remonstration of individual grievances, scrutiny of legislation, and rendering the executive responsible to Parliament – only the first is performed with any distinction by the House of Representatives. He says there is no effective scrutiny of legislation – the House simply rubber-stamps the legislative wishes of the government. 'The principle that the executive has the right to use its majority to get its legislation through the House has made a farce' of the subtle procedures the Parliament inherited from Britain for passing legislation. He also says the House plays little effective role in scrutinising the general operations of government, to assert the control over the executive that is supposedly the essential characteristic of the Westminster system:

> In the parliamentary system, the accountability of the executive to parliament, the principle that ministers are responsible to parliament for their actions, are lofty ideas with grand traditions, but today they are little more than hollow shams. Provided the cabinet retains the loyalty of the majority party it cannot be made accountable, nor its ministers made responsible.[21]

The Clerk of the Senate is even more critical. He says responsible government has disappeared, or at least developed into something different. Even the term 'responsible government' has been dropped. Instead we settle for something less, called 'accountability'. Government, it is now said, should be accountable to Parliament, that is, obliged to give account of their actions to Parliament and through Parliament to the public. But he says the system of government in Australia has moved on even from this notion:

> Governments now expend a large part of their time and energy suppressing parliamentary accountability, seeking to ensure they are not held accountable by parliament, that the old accountability mechanisms do not work and that new ones are not introduced. Just as the party system developed to ensure that governments formed by the majority party are never overthrown by parliament, the system has developed to ensure that governments are not held

> accountable by parliament, so they are less likely to be overthrown by the electorate at the next election.[22]

While 'accountable' government may have replaced 'responsible government' individual ministers have largely ceased to be either 'accountable' or 'responsible' to Parliament. The relevant section in the *Prime Minister's Code of Conduct for Ministers* is headed 'Accountability'. It says in part:

> Ministers do, however, have overall responsibility for the administration of their portfolios and for carriage in the Parliament of their accountability obligations arising from that responsibility. They would properly be held to account for matters for which they were personally responsible, or where they were aware of problems but had not acted to rectify them.[23]

However the dismissal of a number of ministers at the beginning of Mr Howard's prime ministership demonstrated that the responsibility and accountability of ministers is best understood as being not to the Parliament but to the Prime Minister, who will decide, according to his appreciation of the political situation, whether a minister will survive or be required to resign if an accountability problem becomes public knowledge and a political liability.

Control of Finance

An important and central aspect of the relationship of government to Parliament concerns the control of finance. The government needs parliamentary approval to raise and spend money, and it is accountable to the Parliament for what it does. However according to Senate Clerk Harry Evans 'Such is the current financial system that the Parliament does not effectively control either the amount of money available to the government or the purposes on which it may be expended'.[24] He points out that money is now appropriated within departments for 'outcomes', but 'the outcomes are so nebulous and vaguely expressed that the purposes of expenditure are unknown until the expenditure occurs'.[25] This system was introduced by the Howard Government.

Dr Blewitt says Question Time often provides fine political theatre but rarely much substance.[26] He says one of the problems is that the rules are written by the executives of the government and the opposition and they have a joint interest in ensuring that Question Time doesn't embarrass government. He says the standing orders say an enormous amount about what is a proper question, but scarcely a word about what constitutes a proper answer. 'That means ministers can get away with long and irrelevant answers, just to fill up time'. He says another concern is that the Prime Minister and the Leader of the Opposition dominate Question Time, taking a significant proportion of time and contributing to the shift away from a collective cabinet to a presidential system. Former Liberal cabinet minister Jim Carlton likens Question Time to feeding time at the zoo and says it gives a totally wrong impressions of what parliamentarians do and how hard they work.[27] However the parliamentary workload of the Commonwealth Parliament, although substantially greater than that of Parliaments in the States, is considerably lower than its overseas counterparts. In 2005, for example, the House of Representatives was scheduled to meet on just 64 days. The British House of Commons met for 164 days, the Canadian House of Commons for 134 days and the New Zealand Parliament, 90 days.

The Senate

Since the late 1960s the Senate has replaced the House of Representatives as the more effective functioning parliamentary chamber in the Commonwealth Parliament. While the House provides the central stage for the media and the politicians of the political battle between government and opposition, the Senate has taken on the other functions that Parliament is supposed to perform in a Westminster system – and particularly, the legislative and accountability functions. The House retains its primary role: determining which party or parties should form the government. But that is normally a role performed by the electorate at the time (normally once every three years) when the House is elected. The electoral returns show which party or coalition has a majority. There is no need for a vote by the House itself – though from time to time the House will debate and vote on no-confidence motions, which normally are rejected by the governing party.

Until the 1960s, the Senate played a relatively smaller role in the parliamentary process. Although sharing almost equal power with the House of Representatives (it could reject any proposed law, but its ability to amend some financial measures was, in theory, limited: it could not make amendments, but it could make requests) it had not lived up to its supposed role as a protector of the States, despite the fact that each State elects the same number of Senators (MPs in the House represent electorates with relatively equal numbers of electors – the unequal distribution of the Australian population between the States means that, for example, while New South Wales has almost five times as many members of the House of Representatives as Tasmania, New South Wales and Tasmania have the same number of Senators.) From the very beginning, party politics, not State interests, determined the way Senators would vote. But for almost 50 years, representation of the parties in the Senate was often very different from in the House. This was partly because Senators are elected for six years, rather than the three years for MPs. More important, however, was the fact that the various electoral systems used for selecting Senators tended to exaggerate majorities. A majority party could have up to 33 of 36 Senators. When the government lacked a majority in the Senate it could force a double dissolution – a dissolution of the House of Representatives and the whole of the Senate (instead of just half the Senate, as would occur at a regular election) – and the new government (either the government that obtained the double dissolution, or, if it had been defeated at the election, its successor) would have obtained a Senate majority. However the electoral system for the Senate underwent a major change in 1949, with the introduction of proportional representation. That had the effect of allowing Labor and the Coalition parties to have almost equal representation in the Senate much of the time, with the balance of power frequently held by minor parties (first the Democratic Labor Party, then the Democrats and the Greens) that normally were unable to win seats in the single-member constituencies in the House of Representatives.

The Coalition was in government from the time the Senate voting system changed in 1949 until the election of the Whitlam Labor Government in 1972. In the mid to late 1960s, the preparedness of some Liberals to cross the floor and vote with Labor on some issues, and then the election of Democratic Labour Party Senators holding the balance of power, opened the way for those who wanted to boost the Senate's parliamentary role. A key development was the Senate's decision in 1969-1970 to experiment with a series of standing committees to look at policy issues and budget estimates across the whole range of government activities. The estimates committees' detailed review of the Budget and financial statements took the Senate into the one area where the House of Representatives had a privileged constitutional position – it has a special role in passing revenue and spending laws. Yet from this time on, it was the Senate that was to subject the Budget to the intense scrutiny that ought to have been the role of the lower house.

Crossing the floor

The Senate's role did not change significantly after the Fraser Government defeated Labor in 1975 and was returned with a majority in both Houses. This was because there remained a small number of Liberal Senators who were prepared to vote against the government on issues they considered important. Senate Clerk Harry Evans says that in April 1976, shortly after the Fraser Government took power, the government was defeated in the Senate on a social services bill that would have taken funeral benefits away from pensioners. Evans says it was widely believed at the time 'that half a dozen Liberal Senators were really sending the Prime Minister a message: "Don't assume that we're going to do what we are told – don't assume that you control the Senate". And they did cross the floor on a few other occasions subsequently in the life of the government. But the government did get the message'.

He notes that Fraser did not even attempt to dismantle the Senate committee system – 'They had a gang of Senators they knew wouldn't stand for it'.[28] Fraser agrees that despite the numbers, he didn't control the Senate, saying his 'majority' included a number of 'independent-minded' Liberals from Victoria and Tasmania.[29]

The Senate's committee system developed further under Labor and Liberal governments through the 1980s and 1990s when once again those governments were dependent on Senators from minor parties to build majorities to pass their legislation. As well as estimates committees, the system included legislation committees (chaired by government senators) and reference committees (chaired by non-government Senators). Senate Clerk Evans says the estimates hearings 'allow apparent problems in government operations to be explored and exposed, and give rise to a large amount of information that would not otherwise be exposed. They have come to be recognised as a major parliamentary institution of accountability'.[30]

In July 2005 the Howard Government became the first in 25 years to have a majority in the Senate. Slowly over the next year it set about reducing the ability of the committees to set their own agenda for examining what the government was doing, and reducing the power of the estimates committees to question and demand answers from officials and ministers. The Senate's legislative role was also reduced. According to Labor Senate Leader Chris Evans as a result of the changes that were introduced 'The Howard Government will now control not only the matters that are referred to Senate inquiries, but also who chairs those inquiries, where and when they meet, the subjects they consider, the witnesses they heard and the content of the reports they provide'.[31] Senator Andrew Murray, Australian Democrats spokesperson on accountability, says as a result of the government achieving a Senate majority there was routine rejection of non-government amendments to bills, reduced time for committees to consider bills, reduced sitting times, greater use of the gag to pass legislation and increased refusals to answer question in estimates hearings. He says during 2005-2006 the Senate rejected 16 references to reference committees (three in 2003-2004), it rejected 636 non-government amendments to bills and accepted just three (in 2003-2004, 456 were accepted and 721 rejected), it approved just one (out of 11) resolutions ordering the production of documents (compared with 33 requested and approved in 2003-2004).[32]

In 2003 the Howard Government floated a different way of reducing the Senate's power: it proposed making it easier to resolve (in the government's favour) conflicts between the Senate and the House. It suggested joint sittings of the two Houses without a double dissolution (as is required under the current constitution).

The proposal was dropped after an inquiry by an expert group found there was no substantial measure of support for it. Senate Clerk Harry Evans says it was amazing that a Liberal Prime Minister could have put forward such a proposition. 'In the Liberal Party, traditionally, the constitution is sacred, federalism is sacred, the role of the Senate has been sacred'. He says in recent times the only way the government was compelled to account to Parliament was through the non-government majority in the Senate. 'If the government has a majority, chances are there will be no inquiries a government doesn't like, no inquiries into things which might be awkward, embarrassing, difficult for government'.[33]

Members of Parliament

In 2002 John Button, a member of the Hawke Government in the 1980s and 1990s, argued that the Federal Parliamentary Labor Party had become a 'cloistered profession'. He pointed out that during the Whitlam years, Labor MPs and Senators had come from a broad spectrum of backgrounds, and had included farmers, lawyers, businessmen, medical doctors, policemen, tradesmen, public servants and teachers, as well as trade unionists. By the late 1990s, this mix had been replaced by 'a new class of political operator who had been filtered through the net of ALP machine politics'.[34] He pointed out that of the 96 Labor MPs and Senators in 2002, 76 had tertiary qualifications while a mere two had trade qualifications. Of the 96, 53 had gone into Parliament from jobs in party or union offices, while another 10 were former members of State Parliaments and nine described themselves as political consultants, advisors or lobbyists.

Button's critique was seized on by Labor's political opponents. Health Minister Tony Abbott said every Labor MP was a union or party official, parliamentary staff member or public sector employee before entering Parliament (except for one executive of a government-funded community organisation and two lawyers with union practices). He contrasted this with the occupations of Coalition MPs, who included a cane cutter, wool classer, crocodile shooter, milkman, fitter and turner, boilermaker, slaughterman, fencing contractor, carpenter, policeman, professional fisherman and nurse, as well as the Coalition staple of lawyer, farmer and business executive.[35] However Prime Minister John Howard doesn't think it is just a Labor phenomenon. He warns of the 'danger to both parties' of a 'narrowing of the gene pool' for political candidates to those 'whose only life experience has been working in politics'.[36]

An analysis of the 41st Parliament (elected in 2004) by the Parliamentary Library concludes that MPs and Senators 'tend to be middle-aged, well-educated men, who are likely to have been employed in politics-related occupations, business or law before entering Parliament in the last decade'.[37] It says that the high proportion from politics-related backgrounds suggests that those who argue that the professional political class has taken over the national Parliament may be correct. It says that while nearly 70 per cent of Labor's parliamentary members held politics-related jobs immediately before entering Parliament, whereas less than 20 per cent of Coalition members did, there may not be a great deal of difference between Labor and the Coalition if the whole career pattern of parliamentarians is taken into account (see Figure 1.1).

Figure 1.1: Occupation, by party

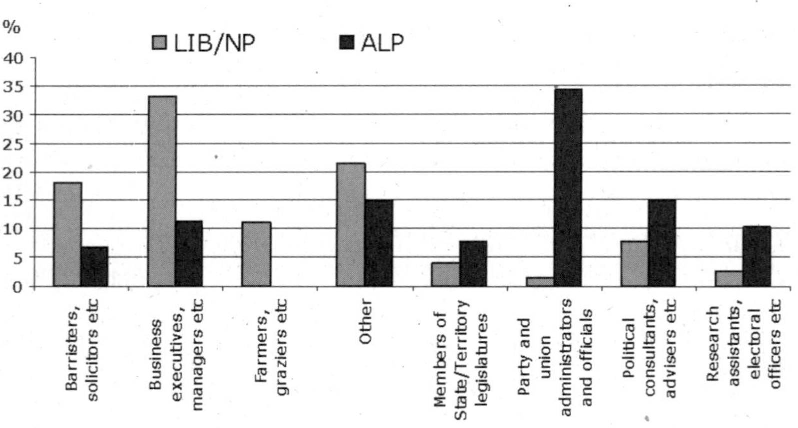

Source: Parliamentary Library.

The other significant change in parliamentary membership is the increasing number of women who are elected. It was not until 1943 that women were first elected to the Federal Parliament – Enid Lyons in the House, Dorothy Tangney in the Senate. By 2004 the 64 women made up 28.3 per cent of the Parliament – there were 49 men and 27 women in the Senate and 113 men and 37 women in the House. In State and Territory Parliaments women occupy 32.7 per cent of parliamentary places.

Figure 1.2: Total MPs in each age bracket

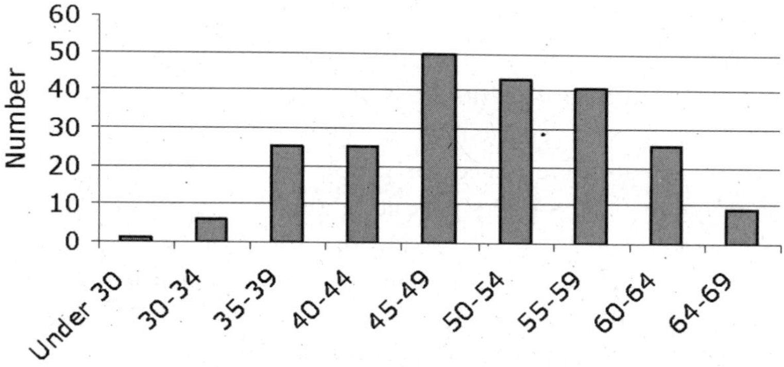

Source: Parliamentary Library.

Voting

Australians have an extraordinarily proud democratic history and tradition. Australia pioneered such fundamentally important aspects of electoral best-practice as the secret ballot (introduced in Victoria and South Australia in their first elections in 1856), preferential voting, permanent electoral offices and continuous electoral rolls, and it was the second (after New Zealand) to give women the vote. It was also the first to introduce and nationally adopt compulsory voting (first in Queensland in 1915 and then in Commonwealth elections in 1924). There is a significant element in the Liberal Party, including senior Ministers, who believe that reform should be reversed as it would (arguably) increase the conservative share of the vote by up to five per cent.

Other changes to the electoral system to improve equity (particularly, 'one person, one vote') took much longer. A bias in federal elections favouring rural electorates (they could have 20 per cent fewer electors than metropolitan seats) was not removed until the 1970s.

Recent changes in the electoral system

Recently, however, changes to the electoral system have been undermining its fairness and even corrupting it, according to some academic and other expert commentators. In 2006 the government used its Senate majority to introduce changes that had been opposed by the Labor Party, the Democrats and independents. The most important resulted in the closure of the electoral rolls on the evening of the day when electoral writs are issued. The previous law (and the practice before it was enacted) was to allow at least seven days after the election writs were issued for people to enrol or change their electoral details. According to calculations by Professor Marian Sawer, based on evidence provided by the Australian Electoral Commission, the new law will disenfranchise about 80,000 people and impact particularly on young people. It will also cause difficulties for another 200,000 people who may have changed their address since they last adjusted their enrolment details.[38] Professor Colin Hughes, who was the first Australian Electoral Commissioner from 1984 to 1989 and Professor Brian Costar say the 2006 legislation 'was motivated by the desire for partisan advantage'. They claim 'that the purported rationale for the changes to the electoral laws is so flimsy that only misleading evidence can be deployed to support it'.[39]

Professor Sawer, a political scientist who heads the Australian National University's Democratic Audit of Australia program, says the current rules of the election game in Australia are:

> stacked against the principles of political equality and popular sovereignty. Australia still has a system of electoral administration that is the envy of the world but we have fallen well behind other democracies when it comes to regulating political finance and restricting the role of private money or government advertising in electoral politics.

Professor Barry Hindess, also of the ANU, has expressed concern at electoral campaigning conducted by governments at public expense and the use for 'manifestly partisan purposes' of funds intended to serve the day-to-day business of government. He describes this as a prima facie instance of institutional corruption, a form of corruption in which the gain is political rather than personal. But he says the line between acceptable and unacceptable conduct is difficult to draw, and because Opposition parties make use of the same largesse 'we can hardly expect them to pursue the issue too vigorously'.[40]

The complaints can be made, however, by independent MPs. Peter Andren, for example, has expressed concern that Australia is heading towards becoming the second-best democracy (after the US) that money can buy. The difference between the two countries, he says, is that in Australia the cost is mainly met by taxpayers, who face an ever-increasing bill to help re-elect MPs both at election time and between elections.[41]

Public funding of elections

Institutionalising the purchase of votes by the governing parties with the voters' money was, in one sense, begun by Labor in 1983 when it copied some overseas precedents and introduced the public funding of elections – or, more accurately, public funding of candidates. The main aim of public funding was to help the Labor Party to get close to matching the spending by the Liberal Party on election campaigning – particularly expensive television advertising. The system introduced in 1983 provided government funding for candidates who achieved more than four per cent of the votes cast in an election. Candidates in House of Representatives elections received 60 cents for each vote they were given while Senate candidates received 30 cents a vote. These amounts were to be indexed to the cost of living. By 2006 the rate had increased to 204.904 cents a vote. At the 2004 election total public funding amounted to just over $41.9 million. The Liberal Party received almost $18 million, the Labor Party over $16.7 million and the Greens $3.3 million. The highest amount paid to an individual candidate was just under $200,000, paid to Senate candidate Pauline Hanson. Successful independents in the House of Representatives election, Bob Katter, Peter Andren and Tony Windsor, received between $63,000 and $90,000.

But these rewards for candidates who get four per cent and more of the vote are dwarfed by the amounts now paid in various allowances to MPs and Senators. In 2005 the Howard Government increased the stamp allowance for MPs from $27,500 a year to $45,000 a year and $27,500 a year for Senators. In 2006 it increased the printing allowance from $125,000 a year to $150,000 a year for MPs while Senators who previously were entitled to 10 reams of paper a month were given a $20,000 a year printing allowance. Both these allowances can be carried over from year to year, and may be used for blatant electioneering. As Norm Kelly of the ANU's Democratic Audit puts it:

> Unfortunately, such increases blur the boundary between the legitimate needs of being an effective member of parliament, and the illegitimate use of incumbency to further partisan ends. In other democracies there are strict controls over the use of parliamentary allowances of this kind.[42]

All told the cost to the taxpayer of these two allowances is about $300 million over the three-year election cycle.

In 2007 the Government announced a further measure that would increase the ability of MPs and Senators to conduct election campaigns. All were to be provided at public expense with an additional staff member. For most backbenchers that meant an increase from three to four. This move was of somewhat more benefit to the government than to the Opposition, as 126 of the 226 members of the federal parliament were in the government's ranks.

Another incumbency benefit – available only to governments, and used in a partisan way against the interests of Opposition parties and independents – is government-funded advertising. Professor Hindess says:

> The use of government advertising for electoral campaign purposes skews the electoral system in favour of incumbent governments. It is also an abuse of public resources for political gain and one which is now practised on a very large scale.[43]

Its extent has been documented by Professor Sawer and by Dr Sally Young, from the media and communications program in the political science department at the University of Melbourne. Professor Sawer says there are spikes in government advertising in periods immediately before elections. In 1996 the Keating Labor Government spent $9 million in the three months before the elections while in 1998 the Howard Coalition Government spent $29.5 million in the three months before the elections. In 2001 the Howard Government spent roughly $78 million in the four months before the election.[44] In 2004-2005 the Federal Government advertising bill was $137.7 million. In the following year it was $208.5 million.

Dr Young says in 1999 the Federal Government ranked as the ninth largest national advertiser in Australia below such commercial groups as Telstra, Coles-Myer, Unilever, Nestlé, Woolworths, Toyota and McDonalds. But by 2000 it was the largest advertiser and in 2001, with spending of $160 million, it was spending $30 million a year more than the next largest advertiser, Coles-Myer. Dr Young says Australian politicians, unlike those in countries such as Britain, New Zealand, Canada and the US, have set up an extraordinary system of public funding of election campaigns, unlimited access to paid advertising, no caps on election expenses and no limits on private donations. Combined with these, incumbents have turned to using other State-subsidised outlets to give them a massive advantage over challengers:

> In a mediated political system where 'getting the message out' is crucial, incumbents are using the perks of office – including government advertising, printing and communication allowances, electoral databases, media advisers, government communications units and MPs' offices and staff – to secure their re-election chances.[45]

As an adjunct to the introduction of public funding the government set strict limits on the amounts that private individuals and corporate groups could donate to political parties without their names being publicly disclosed. In 2006 the Howard Government made changes to these rules to make it easier for individuals and corporations to make secret political donations. The non-disclosure limit for individuals was increased from $100 to $1500 and for corporations from $1500 to $10,000. In a federal election a corporation could make donations to the State, Territory and Federal branches of a political party of almost $90,000 without its name ever being made public.

Reputations

Young people in Australia frequently characterise politicians as liars and promise-breakers. A survey conducted for the Australian Electoral Commission in 2004 found that only half the respondents to the survey agreed that parliamentarians could be trusted to do what was right for the country, while barely a quarter agreed that parliamentarians were honest.[46] The survey found that a major disincentive for young people to participate, through voting, in Australian democratic practices, was 'the lack of trust in political leaders'. The findings echo public opinion polling of the general Australian population showing a continuing decline in the reputation of Australian politicians for ethics and honesty. According to Professor Murray Goot, from Macquarie University, the data 'suggest an increase in electoral cynicism around the credibility of election promises and they document a weakening of attachment to party'.[47] He points out that between 1976 and 1981, 19 per cent of people rated State MPs high or very high for honesty and ethics while 17 per cent thought Federal MPs should be so judged. By 2000 this had dropped to 11 per cent for State MPs and 10 per cent for Federal MPs.

Politicians are conscious of their low standing and frequently promise action to try to improve their reputation. At the federal level, however, they have resisted institutional action that would make them more accountable for their actions. In 1978 a committee on public duty and private interest established by Prime Minister Malcolm Fraser and headed by Federal Court Chief Justice Sir Nigel Bowen (a former Liberal Attorney-General) recommended the establishment of a code of conduct for ministers, all MPs and public servants, administered by an Integrity Commission. While the government was inclined to adopt the proposals, Liberal backbenchers voted against the scheme because of their concern that an independent body would be able to hear complaints against MPs.

Political power in the 21st century

The past three decades have seen a decided shift in the way power is exercised in Canberra. Parliament's ability to question and restrain ministers has been reduced, compromised by the willingness of government MPs and Senators to put their political commitment to keeping their government in office as their first priority. Ministers have in turn conceded more and more power to the Prime Minister – so long as he appears to retain the ability to deliver success when an election is held. Prime Ministers have become increasingly presidential in the way they conduct themselves. They have increased their ability to provide leadership within the government, strengthening their personal power over the bureaucracy. They have also increasingly used government resources to try to maintain the government's standing with the electorate, for example through taxpayer-funded advertising aimed at popularising government policies. The electoral system has been 'reformed' for the sole purpose of improving the government's electoral prospects.

Notes

1 Thomson 1980: 50.
2 Blewitt 2005.
3 Keating and Weller 2000: 58.
4 See the author's analysis of relevant Cabinet archives, in the *Courier-Mail*, 1 January 2005 and 1 January 2006.
5 Hawke 2005.
6 Weller 2005.
7 Keating and Weller 2000: 47 Original emphasis.
8 Available on the Prime Minister's Department website.
9 Tiernan 2006: 312.
10 Evans, H 2005b.
11 McKeown and Lundie 2005.
12 Hawke 2005.
13 Fraser 2005.
14 Hamer 1994.
15 Blewitt 2005.
16 Evans, H 1992: 22.
17 Jaensch, Brent and Bowden 2004: 21.
18 Fraser 2005.
19 Hamer 1994.
20 Evans, H 1992: 22.
21 Blewitt 2005.
22 Evans 2000: 52.
23 Cabinet Secretariat 2004: 13.
24 Evans, H 2006a: 1.
25 Evans, H 2006a: 2.
26 Blewitt 2005.

27 Carlton 2005.
28 Evans, H 2005b.
29 Fraser 2005.
30 Evans, H 2006b.
31 Evans, C 2006.
32 Murray 2006.
33 Evans, H 2005b.
34 Button 2002: 23.
35 Abbott 2004b.
36 Howard 2003.
37 Miskin and Lumb 2006: 1.
38 Sawer 2006: 5.
39 Hughes and Costar 2006: 91.
40 Hindess 2004: 47.
41 Andren 2004: 1.
42 Kelly 2006: 2.
43 Hindess 2004: 45.
44 Sawer 2004: 4.
45 Young 2003.
46 Print, Saha and Edwards 2004.
47 Goot 2002: 50.

2

Federalism and the States

The federal balance – the weighting of the respective powers of the Commonwealth and the States – has been constantly changing since the Commonwealth was inaugurated. The change has been in just one direction, towards a greater concentration of power at the centre. The Constitution contains no hint that this would happen. It carefully sets out the limited powers the new Commonwealth Parliament would be able to exercise. Most of these are enumerated in 39 parts of s 51 of the Constitution, and they include powers over defence, taxation and immigration. Some involved a direct transfer of responsibility from the States (for example, running posts and telegraphs, and levying customs duties). Others were not taken up by the Commonwealth for many decades (for example, the power to make laws covering marriage and divorce).

Yet the new States found themselves dominated by the Commonwealth from the very beginning. A year after the Commonwealth came into being one of the Convention delegates, P McM Glynn, who had been elected to the first Commonwealth Parliament, wrote in his diary that if Federation were to be put to the people again, it was likely the vote would go against it. Five years after Federation the Chief Justice of South Australia, Sir Samuel Way, in a letter to the Governor-General, Lord Tennyson, described Federation as 'like a foreign occupation'.[1]

In 1901 the new national Parliament attracted most of the best and ambitious of the colonial politicians, including many of those who had taken part in the conventions that helped draft the new constitution. Once in Parliament and in government, they tended to favour the adoption of policies that pushed the powers of the new national government well beyond what they had earlier thought likely or desirable. As early as 1902 Alfred Deakin, soon to become Prime Minister, predicted in an anonymous article in an English newspaper that 'the independence of our states is doomed'.[2] Within a few years he was in a position to help make his prediction a reality. The Constitution included a carefully devised compromise scheme (in s 87) to pay to the States for the first 10 years of the Commonwealth at least three-quarters of the net revenue from customs and excise duties. Only a quarter was to be available to the Commonwealth and any money it did not spend was to be provided to the States or used for their debts. Deakin devised a scheme to divert the surplus Commonwealth funds that would otherwise have gone to the States into a trust fund for the eventual use of the Commonwealth; a device the High Court decided was quite valid.[3]

This was the first of many moves by the Commonwealth that strengthened its own financial resources at the expense of the States and which eventually made them financially dependant on the Commonwealth. The most important of these was the introduction of a national uniform income tax scheme during World War II that included the takeover by the Commonwealth of income tax collection from the States, and of the State tax offices. This had a devastating effect on the States, which at that stage relied on income tax for 60 per cent of their revenue. The Commonwealth returned some of the money as grants to the States. While introduced as a war-time measure, the uniform tax scheme was continued in a modified way after the war, and two State challenges were rejected by the High Court. A further financial blow to the States came in 1997 when the High Court decided the States could no longer tax petrol, tobacco and liquor because it decided that these were 'excise' taxes that the Constitution said could only be levied by the Commonwealth.

The High Court had much earlier given the Commonwealth one of its most powerful weapons to intrude on the independence of the States when it decided that the power in s 96 of the Constitution for the Commonwealth to make grants to the States on such terms and conditions as the Parliament thought fit, meant that the Commonwealth could (in the 1924 test case) give money to the States to carry out specified road construction, even though the Commonwealth had no constitutional power itself to build roads in the States. Later Commonwealth governments were able to use their financial muscle coupled with the grants power to dictate State policies in a multitude of areas outside its own constitutional ambit, including health, education, housing and transport.

A further weapon used by the Commonwealth to dictate to the States was its 'external affairs' power. The High Court in a series of cases in the 1930s and 1980s held the Commonwealth could rely on its power to enforce its international obligations to establish control over air traffic and airlines, to ban racial discrimination and to enforce environmental laws in world heritage areas.

Transformation of the federal balance

The transformation of the federal balance occurred because federal politicians sought to increase their ability to determine national policies. They were adept at using and apparently expanding what seemed to be the limited powers available under the Constitution to the Commonwealth, and successive High Courts normally ruled in their favour. On the other hand, the route for changing the constitutional power balance dictated by the Constitution itself (in s 128) proved extraordinarily difficult. This section allowed the Commonwealth Parliament and the Australian people to change the wording of the Constitution through a referendum process. In the first 50 years of the Commonwealth governments tried on dozens of occasions to get approval for new Commonwealth powers in areas such as monopolies, corporations, industrial relations, industry and commerce, aviation, marketing and rents and prices, but the people said 'no'. In most of these areas the Federal Parliament subsequently passed valid laws, frequently relying on the existing corporations power in the Constitution.

Sir Robert Menzies, during his Prime Ministership between 1949 and 1966, was responsible for some of the significant changes in the federal landscape. He rejected requests by the States to return the taxing powers and instead set about increasing the Commonwealth's intervention in their affairs, first through the provision of substantial federal finance for the State universities, then by providing money for private and public schools (initially for science blocks and libraries). During the 23 years the Liberal-led coalition was in power from 1949, the relative influence of the Commonwealth increased hugely and all attempts by the States to improve their own financial resources were rebuffed by the Federal Government. On several occasions the Commonwealth told the States that if they persisted with particular new taxes they had devised, the Commonwealth would penalise them by reducing their federal grants by the amounts they were raising for themselves. As Prime Minister John Gorton told the premiers at the 1968 Premiers Conference:

> I think you have the legal and constitutional right to do what you have said you will do: but I think it can only be helpful if, in deciding whether to exercise that legal and constitutional right and how far to exercise it, you know the Commonwealth Government's attitude.

The States surrendered to the Commonwealth's superior financial power and did not proceed with their new taxes and charges.[4]

Gough Whitlam was elected in 1972 on a platform in which Labor committed itself to implementing many programs that would dictate to the States or override their policies in areas such as education, housing, transport, the environment and off-shore resources. He also tried to make grants directly to local government, rather than through the States (a policy rejected by the Liberal Party at the time, but later enthusiastically endorsed and expanded by the coalition government under John Howard) and to fund unemployment relief works. It was under Whitlam that that the Federal Government tried to use the external affairs power to extend the Commonwealth's power in State areas of political responsibility. Its main success was in passing the *Racial Discrimination Act*, but this was not used to overturn a State activity (Queensland discrimination against Aboriginal people) until 1983. The same law prevented Queensland from resisting the Mabo claim for native title over part of the Murray Islands.

The next Liberal-National Party government, under Malcolm Fraser, also experimented with expanding the Commonwealth's powers, as in its use of the Corporations power to outlaw secondary boycotts by trade unions. However Fraser also offered to return some taxing powers to the States, an offer none of them sought to take up because they decided it would have been unpopular with the voters.

Then under the Hawke Government, the external affairs power was again used to implement federal policies – this time involving the environment – against the wishes of a State Government. The government introduced legislation to prevent the construction of a dam in a World Heritage Area in Tasmania.

Under the Howard Government, the centralisation of power continued apace and some of these developments are discussed below. Throughout the period since the end of the Fraser Government, the relative power of the Commonwealth to the States continued to increase, though in some cases this occurred with the co-operation of the States. For example, when the High Court ruled invalid much of the Corporations Law passed by the Commonwealth the States agreed to bring in uniform legislation to replace it, while demanding some small input into its contents. Mostly, however, the Commonwealth has increased its control by providing the States with funding to implement policies devised exclusively by the Federal Government.

Philosophy

Historically, the Labor Party favoured centralising power in Australia and used its best endeavours when in government to increase the Commonwealth's power. The Liberals until recently expounded the virtues of federalism. Sir Robert Menzies, the party founder, was a proud and committed federalist, and a reluctant (though successful) centraliser. In a series of lectures he gave in the United States following his resignation as Prime Minister Sir Robert Menzies repeatedly insisted, 'I am a Federalist'.[5] He explained, 'I believe … that in the division of power, in the demarcation of powers between a Central Government and the State governments, there resides one of the true protections of individual freedom'.[6] Yet he had to defend the fact that his own government advanced the centralist cause:

> I subscribe to the sound political principle that governments exercising independent powers should, if possible, have the responsibility for raising the revenues needed for such exercise. Uniform taxation ... cuts across this principle.[7]

But uniform taxation became entrenched in peace time under his government because, he explained, the States could not agree on the terms of a transfer back to them of some taxing powers.[8] And he acknowledged that the grants his government inaugurated to support State universities was a development not foreseen when the Constitution came into force or even at a much later date:

> The whole development is one which has affected what was then thought to be the federal distribution of powers between the national Parliament, which had been granted no general power over education, which remained a State function, and the Parliaments of the States. But it undoubtedly has had the effect of saving the State universities from financial disaster, and of enabling new universities to be established. The whole matter is a very good illustration of how something which was not anticipated in the Constitution when it was first enacted can come into existence by judicial interpretation and the inexorable demands of new circumstances.[9]

Malcolm Fraser, like Menzies, offered the States the opportunity to impose some form of income tax, but his offer was similarly rejected. He says he very much regrets that none of the States had the political courage to pick up the proposal.[10] 'It would have made the States responsible for their own affairs in a way in which they were not, and are not'.

Fraser says federalism was a distinguishing feature of Australian liberalism. The Liberal Party rejected socialism and nationalisation and centralist philosophies:

> A dispersion of power from the outset was seen as important, and the more time has gone on, the more important I believe it to be. I believe in the dispersion of power, the dispersion of authority, for a number of reasons. Governments need to be close to where the people are. The Liberal Party never believed that all power should reside in one place. We often thought it would be more convenient,

> it would be easier, if we had more power in this matter or that, but we also believed it would be wrong for Australia. The Liberal party was federalist for a whole host of very good reasons, based on high principle and in a division of power.[11]

He rejected the argument (in effect, put by John Howard – see below) that Canberra needed more power to make people freer. 'You can't be freer if you are more beholden to Canberra, you really can't. I don't want to see all power in one place'. Government, he says, is about diversity, not uniformity.[12] Fraser reflects official Liberal Party policy. The party's federal platform includes the statements:

> We believe … In the separation and distribution of powers as the best protection for the democratic process.
>
> In a federal system of government and the decentralisation of power, with local decisions being made at the local level.[13]

The platform contains a special section on federalism. It says:

> Australian federalism reflects the fact that, while some tasks of government are best performed nationally, many responsibilities are better carried out by other spheres of government. Liberals strongly support federalism.
>
> Federalism, including the territories and local governments established under state legislation, takes government closer to local people, creating higher levels of democratic participation and government more closely reflecting the people's wishes and regional needs. Federalism reduces the chance of laws appropriate only to one area being imposed on another.
>
> Federalism allows for policy experiments, so that governments can compete with each other for citizens and business by offering the best possible policy frameworks.
>
> A strong federal system requires commitment from the governments of the States and the Commonwealth. Responsibilities should be divided according to federal principles, without the Commonwealth taking advantage of powers it has acquired other than by referendum. All spheres of government should possess and exercise taxing powers commensurate with their responsibilities.[14]

However John Howard and his ministers have moved a long way from these principles, philosophically as well as in practice. In April 2005, in a prepared speech delivered at a Liberal think-tank held at the Menzies Research Centre, Howard said:

> There has been some commentary of late that my Government has discarded its political inheritance in a rush towards centralism …

> These fears of a new centralism rest on a complete misunderstanding of the Government's thinking and reform direction. Where we seek a change in the Federal-State balance, our goal is to expand individual choice, freedom and opportunity, not to expand the reach of the central government.
>
> For example, the desire to have a more national system of industrial relations is driven by our wish that as many businesses and employees as possible have the freedom, flexibility and individual choice which is characteristic of the Liberal Party's workplace relations philosophy. This can only be achieved by removing the dead weight of Labor's highly regulated State industrial relations systems. The goal is to free the individual, not to trample on the states.

Howard said he was, first and last, an Australian nationalist:

> When I think about all this country is and everything it can become, I have little time for state parochialism ... I have never been one to genuflect uncritically at the altar of States' rights. Our federation should be about better lives for people, not quiet lives for governments.

Howard said the dispersal of power that a federal system promotes, together with its potential to deliver services closer to peoples' needs, 'are threads of our political inheritance that I have always valued and respected. The trouble is that, in practice, there is often less to these arguments than meets the eye'.[15]

In an earlier speech to mark his first 30 years in Parliament, Howard referred to the 'increasingly dysfunctional character of our federal system'. Health Minister Tony Abbott, who has proposed a total Commonwealth takeover of health, has called the current system 'feral federalism'. In 2004 he wrote a chapter in a book in which he said:

> Federal Governments will try to put their policies into place, as far as they constitutionally can, because that is what people who voted for them have a right to expect. A century after Federation, Australians' governmental loyalties lie with the nation, rather than the state.

He also said that, historically, the Liberal Party had seen centralism as a species of big government but over time Liberals had come to realise that lots of governments do not necessarily mean small government. He said, 'Under the pressures of globalisation and modern democracy, the States are likely to shrink but not disappear'.[16]

Another senior minister, Attorney-General Philip Ruddock, has said effective national government requires a re-evaluation of the institutional roles of various governments. 'Co-operative efforts work, but sometimes the states and territories need to be goaded into action'.[17]

Federalism under Howard

In his first decade as Prime Minister, John Howard presided over a number of significant changes to the federal balance, further increasing the power of the Federal Government at the expense of the States. One of the more far reaching was the government's introduction of A New Tax System in 1999 involving the abolition of the wholesale sales tax and its replacement with a Goods and Services Tax (GST) at a rate of 10 per cent. The plan was hailed by the government as a bonus for the States, because all the net revenue (after the expense of collection) would be paid over to the States and Territories (see figures 2.1, 2.2 over page). In return, the States were required to abolish a series of taxes, such as financial institutions duty, stamp duty of share transfers and debits tax, over time. Prime Minister Howard, in announcing the scheme on 13 August 1998, described the plan as:

> the biggest single remake of the Australian taxation system since Federation. It involves some historic changes in relations between the Commonwealth and the States ... What [the GST] will do will be to give the states far greater freedom and far greater resources over time.

The resources available to the States did increase, as predicted, however they soon found this gave them no greater freedom. In early 2005, for example, Treasurer Peter Costello warned those States that had not fully complied with the plan to cut States taxes and charges could suffer by having the GST moneys reduced. He also said:

> The states have got to understand that accountability goes two ways. If they are going to have to take $35 million of GST revenue, they need to be held accountable – accountable for their hospital systems, for their infrastructure.[18]

The Howard Government also made increasing use of special purpose payments to the States to dictate not only how the federal grants

Figure 2.1: Australian Government payments to the State/ local sector in 2006-2007 (estimated)

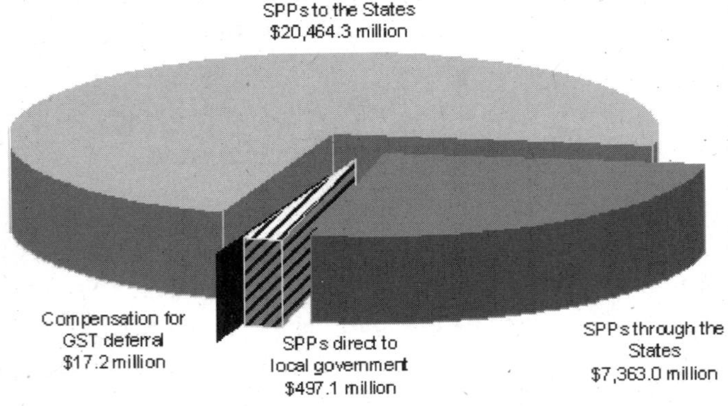

Note: SPPs through the States are payable to State governments to be passed on to local governments and others.

Figure 2.2 GST revenue provision to the States in 2006-2007 (estimated)

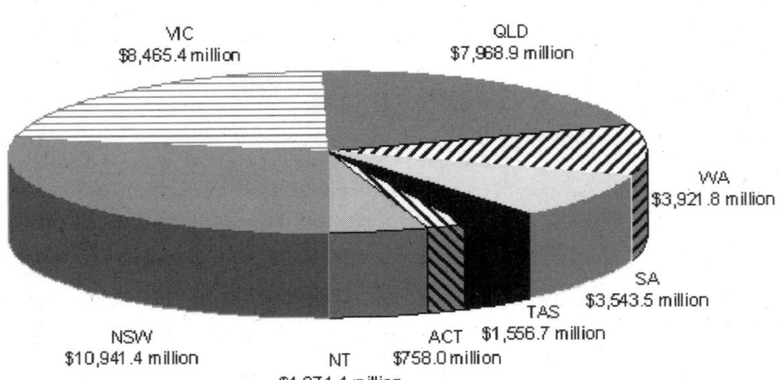

Source: Australian Government 2006a.

should be spent, but also how matching State funding would be spent on projects specified by the Commonwealth and in some cases run by the Commonwealth. A funding agreement for training, for example, established a national strategic initiatives fund that would be administered by the Federal Government, but would require contributions from the States. This was probably the first time any Federal

Government had found a way to force the States to contribute to a federally determined and administered policy project, in an area where the Commonwealth had no constitutional responsibility.[19]

The Federal Government was very active across a whole range of education issues outside the range of its responsibilities. The Professor of Public Administration at the University of Queensland Business School, Professor Kenneth Wiltshire, gave this summary:

> In schools, literacy and numeracy, assessment, teacher training and curriculum; in Vocational Education and Training with the establishment of [24] new Commonwealth colleges and the abolition of the Australian National Training Authority which as a joint Commonwealth-state body gave the states (which provide the majority of VET funding) some leverage; and universities where more Commonwealth powers have been mooted.[20]

He might have added direct federal support for parents groups at schools, provided the schools comply with other federal requirements, such as flying the flag.

The legislation authorising the creation of the new colleges makes it clear they must operate outside the State education systems. And the teachers may not rely on trade unions in negotiating individual contracts.

The area of greatest controversy was the introduction of a new industrial relations law, designed to reduce the power of the unions to influence workplace relations, and to displace the role of State industrial relations commissions. It also greatly limited the role of the Australian Industrial Relations Commission to intervene in industrial disputes, and handed over to a newly created statutory body the power the Commission had exercised for almost a century to set the minimum wage. The proposals were challenged in the High Court by all the States and Territories and by some leading unions.

By a 5-2 majority, the High Court upheld the validity of the Work Choices legislation.[21] One of the major arguments concerned the way the legislation would change the federal system. The two dissenting judges, Justices Michael Kirby and Ian Callinan, complained that the majority decision would improperly change the balance required by the Constitution. Justice Kirby said that under the

Constitution the position of the Federal Government was necessarily stronger than that of the States but 'it would be completely contrary to the text, structure and design of the Constitution for the States to be reduced, in effect, to service agencies of the Commonwealth by a sleight of hand'.[22] Justice Callinan said 'The federal balance is not to be maintained as a matter of political or social preference, but as a matter of constitutional imperative'.[23] But the joint judgment of the majority judges rejected these arguments. They pointed out that references to the 'federal balance' erroneously 'carry a misleading implication of static equilibrium'[24] and they refused to read any limitation on the corporations power (on which the legislation was based) to protect the States.[25]

The majority also rejected submissions accepted by the minority judges based on the fact that the Australian people had on four occasions in referendums rejected attempts by different federal governments to increase the Commonwealth's industrial relations powers. Justice Callinan said the court should not disregard the history of the referendums. To do so would be to treat s 128 of the Constitution (which allows changes to be made through referendums) as irrelevant and '*also* for the Court to subvert democratic federalism for which the structure and text of the Constitution provide'.[26] Justice Kirby said amendments to the Constitution that have been repeatedly rejected should not be lightly cast aside as irrelevant. The majority said the failure of the referendums provided 'no assistance' in determining the issues.[27]

The Work Choices cases was a rare example of unanimity among the States and Territories in trying to resist centralising changes proposed by the Howard Government. Not all its reforms have been resisted by the States. Attorney-General Philip Ruddock's threat to use the Commonwealth's power to make laws affecting corporations to pass a national defamation law affecting all the media proved sufficient to end a 20-year debate among the States and persuade them to enact uniform defamation laws, fairly much along the lines Ruddock had proposed. He has similar plans to force unified standards on the states for a national conveyancing system and personal property securities and other ways in which the legal system can be 'harmonised'.[28]

Federal mechanisms

Over the past century, Australian Governments have devised a number of mechanisms to assist the operations of the federal system. Premiers Conferences pre-dated Federation and were then used after the Commonwealth was inaugurated to try to find solutions to the many problems that arose in the creation of Commonwealth control over activities that had been separately managed by the former colonies.[29] After Federation the Premiers Conference (which then included the Prime Minister) became an annual event at which the Commonwealth was inevitably dominant, because of its financial position relative to the States. In 1928 the Constitution was changed to give effect to a financial agreement made the previous year for the Commonwealth to take over and manage the debts of the States. That resulted in the creation of the Loan Council, consisting of representatives of the Commonwealth and the States (normally the Treasurers or Premiers), which formally considered government borrowing programs, but usually only to endorse the Commonwealth's prior decisions.

Another longstanding element of the federal relations equation is the Commonwealth Grants Commission. This was created in 1933, several years after the people of Western Australia voted to secede from the Commonwealth (legally, this could not happen). The Grants Commission was designed to assess claims by States for special financial assistance, claims made at some time or other by all except the major States. After the introduction of uniform income taxation in 1942, the commission became involved in determining general revenue assistance to all States. Its role was further expanded after the introduction of the GST. The commission's advice on grants is based on the principle of fiscal equalisation which states:

> each state should be given the capacity to provide the average standard of stat-type public services, assuming it does so at an average level of operational efficiency and makes an average effort to raise revenue from its own sources.[30]

Reviews normally occur every five years. New South Wales and Victoria frequently complain they have to subsidise most of the other States, and particularly Western Australia and Queensland.

However as a former member of the Commission, Professor Kenneth Wiltshire, has pointed out:

> In intergovernmental funding, through the horizontal equalisation process, some states receive less than their per capita share because their capacity is greater than other states. This is the price of nationhood. It seems well worth paying.[31]

In 1990 Prime Minister Bob Hawke proposed a closer partnership between the Commonwealth and the States. Instead of the Commonwealth dictating how the States should spend the federal grants they received, there would be a more genuine effort to reach agreement with the States and to avoid overlap and duplication, and to improve efficiency. His ideas were welcomed by the States, and after a series of Special Premiers Conferences, the Council of Australian Governments (COAG) was created (under Hawke's successor, Paul Keating) to replace the annual Premiers Conferences.

COAG had important successes, though for a time under John Howard, it met only as required to ratify agreements or appointments. Its great achievement, and this was confirmed under Howard's leadership later, was in implementing the national competition policy recommended in a report prepared in 1993 by a committee headed by Professor Fred Hilmer. This resulted in the creation of the Productivity Commission which set the detailed reform agenda, which the States were persuaded to implement (to a large extent) through the payment of incentives in the form of competition payments, to return to the States and Territories part of the fiscal dividend from their implementation of agreed reforms (those grants were withheld where a State did not implement the relevant policy).

According to the Productivity Commission the implementation of the national competition policy reforms was a major contributor to a productivity growth rates in the late 1990s that were the highest for at least 40 years.[32] It said the changes had increased Australia's gross domestic product by 2.5 per cent or $20 billion.[33] In 2005 COAG adopted further recommendations made by the Productivity Commission for its national reform agenda.

Figure 2.3: Composition of Specific Purpose Payments to and through the States in 2006-07 (estimated)

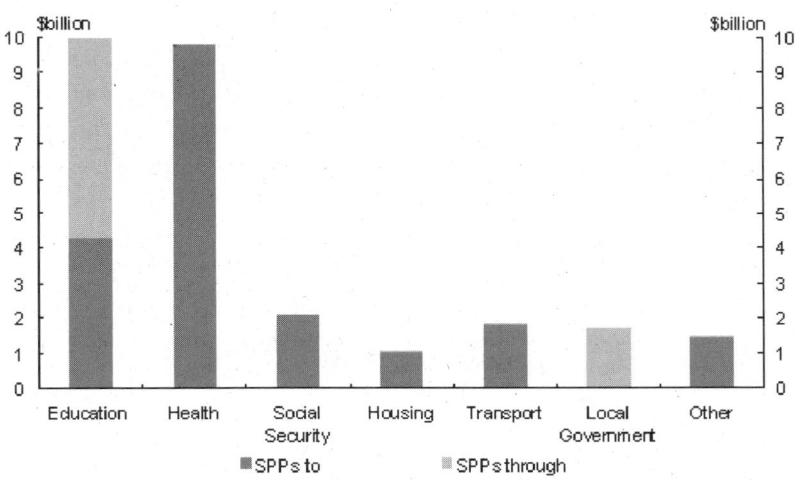

Source: Australian Government 2006a.

New States, altered States, no States

The Commonwealth Constitution contains a permanent reminder of the strength of the new State movement in Queensland at the time of Federation. The framers included a special and unique provision to allow Queensland to be divided into a number of divisions for the purposes of Senate elections. This was a concession to the strong movement in tropical north Queensland for the State to be divided into three parts. It helped persuade people in the north to support Federation: a majority of voters in Brisbane would have kept Queensland out of the Commonwealth.

The Constitution also contains a number of provisions that deal with the possibility of new States being created (in Chapter VI). The possibility of new States – either created from Commonwealth territories, or from an existing State or States – has excited the attention of many activists in different parts of Australia over a long period. A significant movement to create a new State in the New England district of New South Wales has existed for at least half a century (a referendum was conducted in the area and 54 per cent rejected the proposal). Local politicians from time to time promote the idea of a new tropical State in northern Queensland. The people of the Northern Territory rejected statehood in a referendum in 1998, by a relatively small margin – 51.3 per cent voted against.

Advocates of changes to the existing system include politicians and academics. Former Labor Minister Chris Hurford has produced a plan for Australia to have 51 separate regions to replace the existing States and Territories and take over responsibility for local government. He says:

> in designing the regions, the balance to be achieved is between providing geographic areas on the one hand small enough to undertake the function of local government and facilitate people involvement in decision-making, and on the other hand large enough in resources to be sub-national units in a federation with their own taxing powers.[34]

Professor Geoffrey Blainey also wants more sub-national units, but rather than abolishing the States he would want to see more of them. He says:

> the whole purpose of a federal system is that, in general, the matters of national or shared concern can be handled by the federal government, and that the distinctive regional interests can each be handled by state government. In a huge continent the argument for a federal system is double powerful.

He points out that the United States when it held only four million people was divided into twice as many States as Australia possesses today. Since 1859, when Australia reached its maximum of six States, the US has created another 20 new States. 'By having too few States, we miss one of the advantages of federalism'.[35] He particularly favours the creation of two new States in northern Queensland and northern Western Australia. Professor Victor Prescott argues the number of States should remain the same, but there should be a radical re-alignment of boundaries. He proposes incorporating Victoria into Tasmania (he prefers the name of the island State for a new entity that would be dominated by its capital, Melbourne). He would incorporate tropical Queensland north of

Cairns and Western Australia north of Port Headland, into a new State including the Northern Territory to be called Northern Australia. He would also move South Australia's eastern boundary to include some of the western areas of New South Wales.[36]

Another advocate for a regional system to replace the States is author Rodney Hall. In his book, written before the republican referendum, he proposed the States and local governments be replaced by 30 to 40 regions.[37] His book included statistical research by Mark Drummond suggesting that a two-tier system such as that Hall proposed would save, conservatively, $30 billion a year.[38] Drummond later pruned his estimate severely, calculating the saving would be $13.5 billion a year, $2.4 billion of which would be in the areas of education and health.[39] No mainstream political party currently supports changes to the federal system. However research conducted by Griffith University suggests less than a third of Australians support the current system. It suggested 31 per cent favoured a two-tier system – national plus regional governments – 15 per cent favoured the present three-tier system, but with more States, 16 per cent wanted a four-tier system, with regional governments as well as States and local government, while 29 per cent wanted the present system.[40]

Reform

The High Court's decision in the Work Choices case 'will have profound consequences for the residual legislative and governmental powers of the States' according to Justice Michael Kirby's dissenting judgment.[41] He instanced among those State activities where the Commonwealth could use the corporations power to intrude: education, health town planning, security and protective services, local transport, energy, environmental protection, aged and disability services, land and water conservation, agricultural activities, corrective services, gaming and racing, sport and recreation and fisheries.[42] Justice Ian Callinan said 'The reach of the corporations power, as validated by the majority, has the capacity to obliterate powers of the State hitherto unquestioned. This Act is an Act of unconstitutional spoliation'.[43]

Even if the Commonwealth resists the temptation to explore the ways it can exploit the corporations power in the areas nominated by Justice Kirby, it will continue to gradually expand its influence. As senior Labor MP Lindsay Tanner wrote in November 2005:

> Bit by bit, as Australia's economy and society continue to outgrow our colonial origins, the States are shrinking in scope and significance. Uniform national regulatory schemes in areas as diverse as road rules, competition regulation and defamation laws are slowly reducing the individuality of state regulation. Economic realities are eroding the ability of particular states to run radically different tax regimes from their neighbours. State industrial relations systems are about to be swallowed by a national scheme.[44]

He claims the dominance of the Labor Party at the State level accelerated the trend – for most of the Howard Government's term, Labor held office in every State and Territory. He says the conservatives have 'happily abandoned decades of devotion to States' rights and used their control of the Federal Government to impose an unprecedented level of national interference and regimentation upon the states'.

From a conservative point of view, these developments are deplored by Professor Greg Craven, Professor of Government and Constitutional Law at Curtin University. He points out that while Labor had had a traditional enmity towards the notion of federalism as a form of government, conservatives had always defended the constitution (as their own handiwork) and federalism as a matter of principle.[45] He says:

> Australia's conservatives historically have understood and accepted federalism as a means of achieving their fundamental goals of dividing power, making power accountable and limiting power. Consequently they have been temperamentally supportive of federalism, even when they found it irritating.

Professor Craven says the central conclusion of his lecture was:

> that the historic alliance between Australian conservatism and Australian constitutional federalism is over, and that after a century of ideological convergence, we now face the spectacle of an ostensibly conservative government in Canberra waging war on federalism. In suggesting this, I am not naively asserting that Australian federalism has been in robust good health for the past one hundred years. We all know of the progressive decline of Australian federalism and the states.[46]

He says:

> the ultra-centralism of the Howard Government – more correctly its power monopolism – is in reality of enormous significance in Australia's constitutional history. This is because for the first time in that history, there is no Australian party of federalism, in the sense that there is no political party fundamentally, philosophically committed to federalism as a political ideal.[47]

Justice Michael Kirby says the High Court and the Commonwealth need:

> to rediscover the federal character of the Constitution. It is a feature that tends to protect liberty and to restrain the over-concentration of power which modern government, global force, technology, and now the modern corporation, tend to encourage.[48]

Fixing federalism

Even before the Howard Government, people in the States lamented the transfer of power to Canberra and the 'de facto abolition of the States', as then Queensland Premier Wayne Goss put it in a speech in 1994 entitled 'Re-inventing the States'. He proposed more cooperation and a radical carve-up of existing State and federal powers and a review of the way the Senate functions. Other Premiers have agreed radical changes are required. In 2004 NSW premier Bob Carr offered to hand responsibility for hospitals to the Commonwealth, in return for State control of schools and technical education.[49] Both Victorian Premier Steve Bracks and Queensland Premier Peter Beattie launched initiatives aimed at re-invigorating the COAG process and improving federal-state cooperation.

Professor Patrick Weller, in a book published in 2000, wrote:

> The federal structure distributes power in a way that arguably no longer corresponds with the original intentions. The structure was determined at a time before modern technology either created new powers or reduced the requirements for territorial provision of services. Gradually the application of those powers has changed, creating a situation that every level of government regards as inadequate. The question is not whether the power of government should be divided, but how those divisions should take place. Federalism can respond to and encourage diversity, providing multiple points of influence and veto. But it can also reduce accountability, divide responsibility and make solutions more complicated to deliver.[50]

In 2006 Federal Treasurer Peter Costello put 'fixing federalism' as the first of a series of achievements that would make the person who did it one of the most influential Australians in a list to be compiled in 2100.

> The person who can solve the problem bedevilling Australian political life in every area, the problem of federalism, will be there. In 1900 Federation was a great success, the coming together of colonies in a customs and economic union within an empire. But the empire has faded and the nation has consciousness of itself. We are no longer dealing with self-governing sovereign colonies. I believed that by giving the States a revenue base – a financial free kick – we would restore that sense of sovereignty. It was a failed hope. States are moving towards the role of service delivery more on the model of divisional officers than sovereign independent governments. Legally, constitutionally and practically we must fix the problem of federalism.[51]

In so far as federalism is a problem, it may be that the answer can be supplied by the Federal Government. This is what is implied in the 2006 review of Australia by the Organisation for Economic Co-operation and Development (OECD). The report acknowledges that the present state of federalism:

> undermines the accountability to taxpayers for expenditure decisions; creates duplication and overlap in the provision of services; constrains beneficial tax competition across jurisdictions; and weakens incentives for tax and microeconomic reform.

But it points out that the 'need for specific-purpose payments provide the Federal Government with a lever with which to pursue national objectives'. It concludes:

> If some increase in the revenue-raising capacity of the states to meet their expenditure responsibilities were considered warranted, *the most direct solution would involved broadening the states' land property and payroll tax bases. A less direct option would be to allow the states to 'piggy-back' on the personal income tax levied by the Commonwealth, with the centre making 'tax room' by lowering its personal income tax.*[52]

These suggestions attracted no comment from the Federal Government or State Governments. However in October 2006 the States held their own summit on federal issues, excluding the Federal Government. To avoid confusion they did not call it a Premiers Conference (though that is what it was) preferring instead to call it the Council for the Australian Federation. The Premiers met for the first time under this new banner in October 2006. Their intention was to complement COAG by working on issues that affect the States, but do not require the involvement of the Commonwealth – or where it has declined to take a role. They promoted the Council as instituting a new era of collaborative and co-operative federalism, saying the council would recognise that federalism is based on shared principles, including respect for constitutions and the division of powers.

Immediately before the inaugural meeting Queensland Premier Peter Beattie called for a constitutional convention to consider a change in the composition of the Senate, removing 'party hacks' and replacing them with State government representatives, including Premiers, an idea based on the German upper house, the *Bundesrat.* Beattie proposed that the Constitutional Convention should also consider Commonwealth and State duplication in health, education, infrastructure, power and water. Federal Attorney-General Philip Ruddock responded saying, 'Australia's constitutional arrangements have served us well'.[53]

Professor Greg Craven considers the High Court's decision in the Work Choices case as:

> the greatest constitutional disaster to befall the states in 80 years … The court's interpretation of the Commonwealth's corporations power is positively contemptuous of any notion of a federal balance of power. This effectively means that the Commonwealth has an open cheque in almost any area of power that catches its eye, from higher and private education, through every aspect of health, to such matters as town planning and the environment. The court has given Canberra the key to the Constitution.[54]

And Canberra, whichever party is in power, seems likely to use that key whenever it seems there may be a political advantage that might be gained. This has dismayed at least some Liberals. Peter Coleman, a former leader of the Opposition in NSW, wrote during the 2007 NSW elections that there was a crisis in the Liberal psyche as a result of the Howard Government's denunciation of 'the states and their powers', of it brushing aside federalism and espousing a new Whitlamism, and the fear that 'Federalism may have become non-core Liberal belief'.[55]

According to Professor Craven, the only hope for the states is unity and a constitutional convention and 'even the people might be asked their opinion'.[56]

What is clear is that Australia would not have come into being in 1901 if the people who voted for the new constitution had been told that the federal system was to be so changed in little over a century.

Notes

1 Wright 1970: xiv.
2 Solomon 1999: 63.
3 Solomon 1999: 63-64.
4 Solomon 1971: 198.
5 Menzies 1967: for example, 3, 24 and 89.
6 Menzies 1967: 24.
7 Menzies 1967: 89.
8 Menzies 1967: 90-92.
9 Menzies 1967: 88-89.
10 Fraser 2005.
11 Fraser 2005.
12 Fraser 2005.
13 Liberal Party of Australia 2006.
14 Liberal Party 2006: 3 and 12.
15 Howard, J 2005.
16 Abbott 2004b:190.
17 Ruddock 2005b.
18 Costello, P. 2005b.
19 Nelson 2005.
20 Wiltshire 2005: 32.
21 *New South Wales v The Commonwealth* [2006] HCA 52 (14 November 2006).
22 *New South Wales v The Commonwealth*, at para 549.
23 *New South Wales v The Commonwealth*, at para 797.
24 *New South Wales v The Commonwealth*, at para 54.
25 *New South Wales v The Commonwealth*, at paras 183-208.
26 *New South Wales v The Commonwealth*, at para 732. Emphasis in original text.
27 *New South Wales v The Commonwealth*, at para 135.
28 Ruddock 2005a.
29 Wright 1970: xiii.
30 Grants Commission 2006.
31 Wiltshire 2004: 14.
32 Productivity Commission 2005b.
33 Productivity Commission 2005b: xvii and xviii.
34 Hurford 2004: 50.
35 Blainey 2004: 29.

36 Prescott 2000: 112.
37 Hall 1998.
38 Drummond 1998: 97-109.
39 Drummond 2005: 5.
40 Hudson and Brown 2004: 40.
41 *New South Wales v The Commonwealth*, at para 451.
42 *New South Wales v The Commonwealth*, at para 539.
43 *New South Wales v The Commonwealth*, at para 794.
44 Tanner 2005.
45 Craven, G 2006c: 136.
46 Craven, G 2006c: 137.
47 Craven, G 2006c: 137.
48 *New South Wales v The Commonwealth*, at para 612.
49 See, for example, *Sydney Morning Herald*, 20 October 2004: 1, and 21 October 2004: 8.
50 Weller 2000: 2-3.
51 Costello, P 2006.
52 OECD 2006: 8. Emphasis in original text.
53 Beattie 2006.
54 Craven 2006d.
55 Coleman 2007.
56 Craven 2006d.

3

Vice-regal institutions

Under the modern British and Australian systems of government, the activities and conduct of the Monarch and her vice-regal representatives are supposed to be uncontroversial. In Britain, following the abdication of Edward VIII in 1936, King George VI provided an outstanding demonstration of the way the head of state is supposed to act in a constitutional monarchy where government is theoretically and in practice in the hands of politicians elected by the people. His daughter, Queen Elizabeth II, has similarly behaved in an exemplary manner. While some members of the Queen's immediate and extended seemingly dysfunctional family have attracted public attention for many of the wrong reasons in the past half-century, their behaviour generally has not detracted from the way in which the Queen carried out her own duties – though they may have affected the way many people regarded the monarchy as an institution and encouraged those who wish to replace it with a republic of some kind.

In Australia the Queen's representatives have not always lived up to the standards she has maintained in Britain. Controversy has dogged a number of Governors-General and Governors. Sometimes problems have arisen over the use of the so-called reserve powers – the power of the Governor-General or Governor to dismiss an elected government, to refuse a request by a Prime Minister or Premier for an early election or to sack one or more ministers. In other cases the problem has concerned the personal conduct of the vice-regal representative, either while in office or before his appointment, activities resulting in a loss of public or government support for the Governor-General or Governor.

History

The offices of Governor-General and Governor went through significant and substantial changes as the Australian colonies were created, gradually achieved self-government and then federated and later still as Australia itself became a fully independent nation. The first Governors of New South Wales were appointed by the British Government to rule the new colony. Their powers were extraordinarily wide. They were appointed as Governor-in-Chief and Captain-General with authority to pardon all offences other than treason and murder, to levy armed forces, to proclaim martial law, control public moneys and commerce, to impose duties, to grant lands, and to issue colonial regulations, subject only to the instructions the Governor received from the British Government on his appointment, and others that might arrive subsequently. They were also empowered to establish courts with the Governor or Lieutenant-Governor sitting as a court of appeal. It wasn't until 1823 that the British Parliament passed its first law for the governance of the colony, and that, in addition to creating Supreme Courts in New South Wales and Van Diemen's Land and allowing for the appointment by the Crown of Chief Justices, established a small Legislative Council, whose members were appointed by the Governor, to consider legislation given to it by the Governor. Over the next three decades the powers of the Legislative Councils were increased and their membership reformed until self-government was finally achieved in most of the colonies in the 1850s. Even then, Governors continued to be appointed to represent the interests of Britain in the respective colonies and were equipped with powers to ensure that colonial laws and policies did not conflict with those of Britain. They were required to send dispatches regularly to the Colonial Office in London, reporting on their activities and those of their governments. The Governors were empowered to refuse to act in accordance with the advice given to them by their local ministers in exceptional circumstances.

It was much the same when the Australian colonies federated and the Commonwealth came into being on 1 January 1901. The first Governor-General, Lord Hopetoun, acted primarily as an agent of the British Government, though he was personally responsible for his first and most famous action – known as the Hopetoun blunder – when he chose the wrong colonial politician to be the first Prime Minister (before the holding of an election): he asked the New South Wales Premier to form the government, but the Premier was unable to get sufficient support from his fellow leading politicians, and had to decline the offer.

Until World War I, any communications the Commonwealth Government wanted to have with foreign governments had to be channelled through the Governor-General and then via the Colonial Office through the British diplomatic service. This reflected the fact that internationally Australia was still regarded as part of Britain's empire and it was incapable of speaking for itself or in a different way from Britain.

That began to change in 1910 when Australia sent a High Commissioner to London. But during World War I the Governor-General, Sir Ronald Munro-Ferguson, still asserted a general supervisory role over the activities of the Australian Government on behalf of the British Government.

Prime Minister Billy Hughes tried, however, to establish direct links with the British. Hughes sought a formal change in the arrangements which the Governor-General believed would transform 'the representative of the Crown into a social figurehead' and he would have 'less than ambassadorial responsibility … which must necessarily diminish his power of usefulness, both as the official head of the government in Australia and as a factor in maintaining the unity of the Empire', He reported the changes would lower his status and restrict his sphere.[1]

However the conduct of the war promoted the changes that Hughes wanted. The substantial role the Dominions played in the war effort strengthened their voices in London and gave them seats at the Versailles Peace Conference. In 1920, at Hughes' insistence, the British Government allowed the Federal Cabinet to determine who would be the next Governor-General – from a short-list of three Britons, nominated by the British Government.

The rights of the Dominions to more independence were pushed by Canada, South Africa and Australia at Imperial Conferences through the 1920s. In 1930 the Scullin Labor Government decided to recommend that the Chief Justice of the High Court, Sir Isaac Isaacs, be appointed as the first Australian-born Governor-General. The British Government – and later, the King – objected to the Australian Government having the power to determine who the Governor-General should be, but eventually they conceded. The appointment of Isaacs signalled the end of the idea that the Governor-General was an officer of the British Government, responsible to it for his administration of the office.

In 1947, under the next Labor Government, another Australian was appointed as Governor-General. However when Sir Robert Menzies became Prime Minister he continued to recommend the appointment of superannuated British generals and politicians. Menzies finally ended this practice in 1975 when he recommended the appointment of Lord Casey, a former Minister for External Affairs in the Menzies post-war cabinets. All subsequent Governors-General (and almost all Governors) have been Australian.

The final change in the status of the vice-regal offices came in 1986 with the passage of the *Australia Acts*. Although the Statute of Westminster in 1931 had freed the Commonwealth from the possibility of British legislative intervention in its affairs, the States were not given a similar degree of constitutional independence. The State Governors continued to be appointed by the Queen on the recommendation of the British Secretary of State for Commonwealth Relations, and contact between State Premiers and the Queen had to be conducted through the British Minister, rather than through diplomatic channels.

However the *Australia Acts*, passed by the British, Commonwealth and State Parliaments, gave the States full legislative independence from Britain and provided that the powers of appointment and dismissal of Governors should be by the Queen on the direct recommendation of the relevant Premier. Constitutionally and politically the Governors are now in the same position as the Governor-General: they represent the Queen but their appointment and dismissal are solely in the hands of the various Premiers or the Prime Minister, and they owe no duty or responsibility to the British Government.

Powers

Australia's Constitution begins with a recital that the people 'have agreed to unite in one indissoluble Federal Commonwealth under the Crown of the United Kingdom of Great Britain and Ireland'. The Crown is an integral part of the constitutional system: the Federal Parliament is defined in s 1 of the Constitution as consisting of 'the Queen, a Senate, and a House of Representatives', while the executive power of the Commonwealth is vested (by s 61) in the Queen. But the Queen's powers are mainly to be exercised by 'a Governor-General appointed by the Queen'. The monarchical system extends to the governments of the States, where the Queen's representative in each case is a Governor appointed by the Queen.

The powers assigned to the Governor-General by the Constitution appear to be very extensive. There are almost two dozen separate sections of the Constitution empowering the Governor-General in some way, including the power to appoint Ministers and to dissolve the House of Representatives or both Houses of Parliament. The constitutional authority in almost half these provisions is limited by the requirement the Governor-General must act 'in Council' – that is, with the approval of the Federal Executive Council (of which they are President). But from the beginnings of the Commonwealth it has always been understood that the fact that a power is assigned directly to the Governor-General rather than to him 'in Council' is (mostly) irrelevant: it is the very essence of the Westminster system of responsible government – and that is the system of government the Constitution is meant to create – that the head of government exercises power on the advice of the Prime Minister and ministers who have the confidence of (that is, majority support in) the House of Representatives.

Reserve powers

While that is the general rule, there is a limited number of exceptions that are referred to as the 'reserve' powers. These refer to those rare occasions when the Governor-General may act without or even contrary to the advice of responsible ministers, or not act despite advice that he should act. Section 5 of the Constitution gives the Governor-General power to dissolve the House of Representatives. In the first 10 years of the Commonwealth (in 1904, 1905 and 1909), several Governors-General refused the advice of their Prime Ministers to dissolve. Each case resulted in the resignation of the Prime Minister and a change of government, without an election. Section 64 includes a power to appoint and dismiss ministers (they hold office 'during the pleasure of the Governor-General'). In 1975 the Governor-General dismissed Prime Minister Gough Whitlam despite the fact he and his party had a majority in the House of Representatives. Section 57 provides for dissolution of both Houses of Parliament. In 1975 the Governor-General exercised this power on the advice of Malcolm Fraser who he had appointed as Prime Minister even though he knew he did not have the confidence of the House of Representatives. Similar powers – of dismissal of a Premier, of refusal to grant dissolutions of Parliament, and of refusal to dismiss ministers contrary to advice of a Premier – have been exercised (or not) by Governors of some of the States at various times.

The existence and exercise of the reserve powers remain controversial among academic commentators (they were controversial when exercised, for example, by Governor Phillip Game when he sacked the NSW Lang Government in 1932, and by Governor-General Sir John Kerr when he sacked the Whitlam Government in 1975). They became a public issue again during the republic debate in 1999, when there was considerable argument about whether the powers should exist, whether they should be limited, and whether they should be spelt out in detail in legislation or the constitution.

In 1987 the advisory committee on executive government of the Constitutional Commission formulated a lengthy detailed statement of the circumstances in which a Governor-General might exercise the reserve powers. The committee, chaired by former Governor-General Sir Zelman Cowen, and including constitutional lawyers, former politicians and political scientists, was not unanimous on every point, but agreed it was highly desirable the issues should be settled. However at the Constitutional Convention held to consider the republic in 1998, the majority thought the problem was too difficult to resolve. Former Governor-General Bill Hayden shares that view. In his autobiography he points out that the only way codification of the reserve powers could be reached:

> would be through bipartisan endorsement of a set of proposals, which would be most unlikely given their provocative and potentially explosive nature. More importantly, there are so many imponderables possible in the course of experience that codification would most likely build in the kind of rigidity which would have the potential to hinder flexible and practical handling of some complicated and unanticipated considerations bound to arise in our political system.

Hayden says that if the reserve powers had been codified in 1975, but contained no specific provision for resolving such an affair, the country might have 'been truly seized by the impasse, as no-one would have had the power or authority to resolve it'.[2]

Another former Governor-General, Sir Paul Hasluck, writing while in office in 1972, seems to suggest that the vice-regal role in unusual circumstances might be to bring matters to a head:

> In abnormal times or in case of any attempt to disregard the Constitution or the laws of the Commonwealth, or even the customary usages of Australian government, it would be for the Governor-General who could present the crisis to Parliament and, if necessary, to the nation for determination. It is not that the Governor-General (or the Crown) can over-rule the elected representatives of the people but in the ultimate he can check the elected representatives in any extreme attempt by them to disregard the rule of law or the customary usages of Australian government and he could do so by forcing a crisis.[3]

This is the script Sir John Kerr followed in 1975, and it was what Sir Phillip Game did in 1932 when he sacked the Lang Government for refusing to make payments due to the Federal Government. What is missing from these analyses and these cases is any suggestion that resort might be had to the courts (particularly the

High Court which has the power to issue various writs against an officer of the Commonwealth, including ministers, to prevent anything illegal from happening). As the Constitutional Commission's advisory committee pointed out, there are many cases where the courts could be used instead of the reserve powers.

The way the reserve powers have been used in Australia demonstrates that its vice-regal officers stand in a very different position from that traditionally ascribed to the Crown in Britain. The classic formulation is that of Walter Bagehot in 1867, 'To state the matter shortly the sovereign has, under a constitutional monarchy such as ours, three rights – the right to be consulted, the right to encourage, the right to warn'.[4]

Role

Sir John Kerr's sacking of the Whitlam Government on 11 November 1975 gave the position of Governor-General a public presence and sense of importance that it had never previously enjoyed. Sir Zelman Cowen, the man appointed to replace Kerr when he resigned his office in 1977, saw his role as trying to heal the wounds and damage to the institution caused by Kerr's actions. He later wrote:

> The governor-generalship has a visibility that it did not have before that time; it is now associated in the public mind with political power. Appointments to the office are now made, I believe, with this in mind and certainly with the recognition that the governor-generalship is a visible and controversial office within the Australian community.[5]

That community is now better informed about what Governors-General and Governors actually do, thanks to the willingness of most office holders since the time of Sir Paul Hasluck (who retired in 1974) to write or speak about their experiences. Hasluck delivered an important lecture in 1972, while he was still in office, about how he saw the role of the Governor-General. He was the first to describe in detail the way he dealt with matters in the Federal Executive Council. Hasluck said in presiding over the Executive Council the Governor-General was both a watchdog over the Constitution and laws for the nation and a watchdog for the government – regardless of the party in power:

> He does not reject advice outright but seeks to ensure that advice is well-founded, carefully considered, and consistent with stable government and the established standards of the nation …
>
> Various steps are open to him. He can ask questions. He can seek full information. He can call for additional advice on any doubtful issue. In a matter of major importance he may suggest to the Prime Minister that an augmented meeting of Executive Council be held to consider all aspects of a question or, perhaps better still, suggest that the matter be discussed in Cabinet, if there has been no discussion already, so that the recommendation to Executive Council is certain to be the agreed view of his Executive Councillors.[6]
>
> He can himself question a conclusion, seek to know the reasons for it, draw attention to relevant considerations to ensure they are taken into account, and satisfy himself that the proposal does express the single mind of his advisers, but he himself, while influencing the outcome of the discussion in this way, needs to be careful not to be an advocate of any partisan cause. In doing this he has two dominant interests – one is the stability of government … and regard for the total and non-partisan overall interests of the people and the nation.[7]

Hasluck later said that in the course of five years under three different Prime Ministers (John Gorton, William McMahon and Gough Whitlam) there were four or five occasions on which a major issue arose in Executive Council and as a result of discussion in the Council, 'a government eventually acted more wisely than was at first proposed'. He said he found that two or three items in every 100 were deferred for reconsideration on one point or another and the standard of government was improved as a result.[8] The picture Hasluck painted was of a Governor-General taking an active role – he wrote, 'I fervently hope that Australia in the future will never have the misfortune to have an inactive one'.[9]

He clearly disapproved, however, of Governors-General or Governors taking an active political role – one deliberately favouring a particular political party. This becomes apparent from his recording in his personal minute book (while he was Governor-General) of several conversations with the Governor of Western Australia Sir Douglas Kendrew. One concerned a scheme Hasluck thought had been devised by the Liberal Opposition Leader in Western Australia, Charles Court, to force an election through the refusal of the Legislative Council to grant supply. He quotes Kendrew talking about the parlous state of the nation (under Whitlam's Government) and the only way to meet the Whitlam threat was to get Court into office in Western Australia to join the other non-Labor premiers to fight against the Whitlam Government. 'It was clear', Hasluck noted, that Kendrew's 'whole sympathy was with Court and he hoped Court would find a way of becoming Premier … It was a strange conversation and revealed much of the state of Kendrew's mind'.[10]

But his criticism of the 1975 crisis was different. Stipulating that he offered no comment about who was right and who was wrong, he said:

> I suggest that if there had been more talking and a higher measure of confidence between Governor-General and Prime Minister it is probable that no crisis would have arisen. The role of the Crown (and hence the Governor-General) to be consulted, to encourage and to warn can only be fulfilled if they talk to each other in terms which reflect that they have respect for each other.[11]

The lessons about keeping the vice-regal office well informed appear to have been learned by most if not all governments. In 2003 a former Governor of Queensland, Major-General Peter Arnison, told a meeting of the Australasian Study of Parliament Group in Brisbane that for a decade and a half, Queensland Governors had received copies of all cabinet papers so they would be informed of what would be coming to meetings of the Executive Council. Those meetings provided the Governor with an opportunity to meet with ministers, to discuss broader matters than those that arose formally, and 'also to have a quiet influence'. He saw it as his role to write to the Premier when he regarded things as not particularly good or right. He gave as an example an aged care facility he visited in 1998 on Palm Island that was the worst he had seen anywhere (and he had been to Somalia, Rwanda and Vietnam). The government, he said, picked it up and sorted it out.

Arnison had the unique experience, for a Queensland Governor, of dealing with two successive minority governments. In 1998 an independent gave her support to the creation of the National-Liberal Coalition Government, under Rob Borbidge. Two years later another independent decided to support a Labor Government, under Peter Beattie. Arnison said he decided after the 1998 election when it appeared the Labor Party would have more seats than the Coalition, but the balance of power could be decided by one of several independents, he would not deal directly with the independents, but only with the two possible Premiers. He declined to accept Borbidge's resignation until he had established that Beattie had the support of two independents. He told Beattie he wanted the independents to state clearly the conditions under which they would support him, and that the information should be made public so that the electorate knew. After that had happened, Beattie suggested that Borbidge should remain as a caretaker Premier over the weekend, until a Caucus meeting could be held to decide on the new ministers in the new Labor Government. Arnison said no. He insisted on following the precedent set when Whitlam was elected in 1972, when Whitlam and his deputy were sworn into all the ministerial positions pending the Caucus meeting and the allocation of portfolios.

Constitutional and political duties are not, however, the main occupation or preoccupation of those who hold vice-regal appointments in Australia. As Sir Zelman Cowen acknowledged, the Governor-General is seen by most primarily as a bestower of medals and a cutter of ribbons – a remark he attributed to a parliamentary critic of the office. Cowen defended this formal, ceremonial role as important, in supporting the idea of national identity. He said he believed that through such work, through travel and participation in such activities, the Governor-General offered encouragement and recognition to many Australians who might not be very powerful or visible in the course of everyday life, and to the efforts of those individuals and groups who work constructively to improve life in the nation and the community. The Governor-General, like the Monarch, he said made 'his greatest contribution through the continuing and committed performance of these duties'.[12]

Problem areas

One other aspect of the Governor-General's duties is relatively new, and potentially raises difficulties for the relationship between governments and the vice-regal personage. Sir Ninian Stephen when Governor-General claimed it was the Governor-General's role to interpret the nation to itself.[13] This had begun with Sir Zelman Cowen. As part of the healing process following the departure of Sir John Kerr, he travelled extensively within Australia, making many speeches, attending meetings and pursuing community activities. Sir Ninian Stephen helped cement the new tradition. Another former High Court judge, Sir William Deane, expanded it during his tenure as Governor-General, between 1996 and 2001. He expressed strong and controversial views on issues such as reconciliation with the Aboriginal people that would have been lauded by Paul Keating, the Prime Minister responsible for his appointment, but were something of an embarrassment for the Howard Government, which was in power for most of the time he was in office. Greg Craven, Professor of Government and Constitutional Law at Curtin University, has analysed the political and practical difficulties raised as a result of a Governor-General venturing into public debate on issues that have serious political implications.[14] He concludes:

> that if one wishes to maintain the office of Governor-General (or its republican successor) as one that embodies a subfusc focus of apolitical unity, there is very little room for a Governor-General to act as a statesperson. On balance, if the nation really wants itself interpreted to itself, it probably would be better investing in mass psychiatric analysis than in an adventurous surrogate head of state.

To avoid such difficulties, Prime Ministers and Premiers must consider whether an appointee will be 'safe' – whether their social and political views will generally coincide with those of the government under whom they take office. In the past, this has led some Prime Ministers to recommend the appointment of former politicians. This may itself create some immediate political tensions and controversy, but this tends to pass unless the new Governor-General displays partisanship while in office. In fact the four ex-politicians appointed as Governor-General – former Liberal cabinet ministers Lord Casey and Sir Paul Hasluck, former Labor Premier Sir John McKell and former Labor Minister Bill Hayden – served in the office both uncontroversially and well. Their performance was as exemplary as that of most of the former judges and military men who have usually been favoured for the post because they were supposedly apolitical.

Figure 3.1: Governors-General since 1901

	Term of		Place of birth
23	*2001-2003*	Hollingworth, The Right Reverend Dr Peter, AC OBE	Adelaide, SA
22	*1996-2001*	Deane, The Honourable Sir William Patrick, AC, KBE	Melbourne, VIC
21	*1989-1996*	Hayden, The Honourable William George, AC	Brisbane, QLD
20	*1982-1989*	Stephen, Rt Hon. Sir Ninian, KG, AK, GCMG, GCVO, KBE, QC	Oxford, England, UK
19	*1977-1982*	Cowen, Rt Hon. Sir Zelman, AK, GCMG, GCVO, QC	Melbourne, VIC
18	*1974-1977*	Kerr, Rt Hon. Sir John Robert, AK, GCMG, GCVO, QC	Sydney, NSW
17	*1969-1974*	Hasluck, Rt Hon Sir Paul Meernaa Caedwalla, KG, GCMG, GCVO	Fremantle, WA
16	*1965-1969*	Casey, Rt Hon Richard Gardiner, Baron Casey, KG, GCMG, CH, DSO, MC, PC	Brisbane, QLD
15	*1961-1965*	De L'Isle, Rt Hon William Phillip Sidney, Ist Viscount De L'Isle, KG, VC, GCMG, GCVO, PC	London, England, UK
14	*1960-1961*	Morrison, Rt Hon William Shepherd, 1st Viscount Dunrossil, GCMG, MC, QC, PC	Argyll, Scotland, UK
13	*1953-1960*	Slim, Field Marshal Sir William Joseph, KG, GCB, GCMG, GCVO, GBE, DSO, MC	Bristol, England, UK
12	*1947-1953*	McKell, Rt Hon Sir William John, GCMG, PC	Pambula, NSW

11	*1945-1947*	Henry, Duke of Gloucester, HRH Prince Henry William Frederick Albert, Earl of Ulster and Baron Culloden,	Sandringham,
10	*1936-1945*	Hore-Ruthven, Brigadier General the Rt Hon Alexander Gore Arkwright, Ist Baron Gowrie, VC, GCMG, CB,	Windsor, England, UK
9	*1931-1936*	Isaacs, Rt Hon Sir Isaac Alfred, GCB, GCMG, PC	Melbourne, VIC
8	*1925-1931*	Baird, Rt Hon John Lawrence, 1st Baron Stonehaven, GCMG, DSO, PC, JP, DL	London, England, UK
7	*1920-1925*	Forster, Rt Hon Henry William, Ist Baron Forster, GCMG, PC, DL	Kent, England, UK
6	*1914-1920*	Munro-Ferguson, Rt Hon Sir Ronald Craufurd, GCMG, PC	Fife, Scotland, UK
5	*1911-1914*	Denman, Rt Hon Thomas, 3rd Baron Denman, GCMG, KCVO, PC, JP	London, England, UK
4	*1908-1911*	Ward, Rt Hon William Humble, 2nd Earl of Dudley, GCB, GCMG, GCVO, TD, PC	London, England, UK
3	*1904-1908*	Northcote, Rt Hon Henry Stafford, 1st Baron Northcote, GCMG, GCIE, CB, PC	London, England, UK
2	*1903-1904*	Tennyson, Rt Hon Hallam, 2nd Baron Tennyson, GCMG, PC	Twickenham,
1	*1901-1903*	Hope, Rt Hon John Adrian Louis, 7th Earl of Hopetoun, KT, GCMG, GCVO, PC	Hopetoun, Scotland,

Source: Government House.

In fact, those who have quit the office early because of public controversy were not regarded as political figures when they were appointed. The circumstances of three relatively recent vice-regal episodes should be mentioned, those involving former Governor-General Dr Peter Hollingworth and Governors Richard Butler and Sir Brian Murray. In each of these cases their departure from vice-regal office was due to what they said or did while they held that office. In each case the occupant brought his office into some form of public disrepute and in so doing damaged the office to some (generally limited) extent but, more important, embarrassed the government of the day.

Butler's sins were many, according to his detractors. Butler had been a public servant in the Foreign Affairs Department, private secretary to Gough Whitlam when he was Leader of the Opposition in 1976-1977, and later an international diplomat and head of the United Nations team supervising Iraqi disarmament. He took his appointment as Governor of Tasmania as an invitation to speak out on national and international issues he regarded as of concern. However his speeches were politically provocative, so much so that Premier Jim Bacon who was responsible for his appointment was forced to gag him. Butler refused to follow tradition when he decided not to wear a poppy to Remembrance Day celebrations and he refused to talk to Vietnam veterans. He cancelled a commitment he had given to attend a National Trust function so that he could attend a concert. Other allegations included him misusing his position to try and get a free upgrade on a honeymoon flight to Singapore. He was allegedly extravagant and arrogant in his use of Government House in Hobart for his personal needs. The charge levelled against him was that he did not take into account the sensibilities of the community.

The same might be said of Governor-General Peter Hollingworth. His main sin was to appear on an ABC television program, 'Australian Story', and suggest that a 14-year-old girl, rather than a married clergyman, was responsible for the sexual relationship that had developed between them. Hollingworth was also plagued by arguments about whether he had acted appropriately before his appointment as Governor-General in decisions he had taken as

Anglican Archbishop of Brisbane in relation to allegations of sexual abuse at an Anglican private school. A public opinion poll found that 63 per cent thought Dr Hollingworth should resign, while 66 per cent thought he was not a suitable person to hold the position of Governor-General.[15]

In Victoria, Governor Sir Brian Murray was required to resign in 1985 because he too failed to take public sensibilities properly into account. He and his wife accepted what amounted to free, first-class return tickets to the USA and Britain at a time when the Victorian community had been outraged by revelations that cheap or free airline tickets were being provided to politicians, judges, police and public servants, and the government had established an official inquiry into the scandal.

After Dr Hollingworth resigned, a leading constitution lawyer, Professor George Winterton, wrote that the principal lesson from the affair was 'that a Governor-General cannot survive in office without the confidence of the Australian people'. He said:

> Australians regard the Governor-General as their effective head of state, partly due to the populist activism of Hollingworth's predecessor, Sir William Deane, and monarchist arguments that the Governor-General is Australia's actual head of state. The office is regarded as socially important and receives increasing media scrutiny, which helps make it accountable to the people. Hollingworth's defenders claimed he was the victim of a media "witch-hunt" but on this occasion the media reflected widespread community sentiment …
>
> There are two reasons why a Governor-General cannot survive in office against overwhelming public opposition. Probably the lesser reason is that a Governor-General cannot fulfil the office's role of national unifier and conscience without public support. The principal reason is that since the Governor-General's tenure lies in the Prime Minister's hands, public opposition to the Governor-General's continuance in office will eventually rebound on the Prime Minister, who will ultimately be forced to urge the Governor-General to resign'.[16]

In the 21st century a new problem may be emerging for the Governor-General: relevance. Professor Craven says that since the mid-1980s all Prime Ministers 'seem to have been equally guilty of elbowing the Governor-General from centre stage' and undertaking great ceremonial functions of state that previously had been discharged by the Governor-General. He gives two examples – Prime Minister Howard presiding over the Bali remembrance ceremonies and over the opening ceremony of the Rugby Union World Cup in 2003:

> It was, of course, one of the great traditional advantages of the office of Governor-General that where an event was one of deep national, rather than merely political importance, it was performed by the apolitical Governor-General as a national focus. … The very positive effect of this traditional understanding was to limit any identification between a politician as a repository of power with the profound interests, achievements or griefs of the nation.[17]

Appointment

In May 1973, Governor-General Sir Paul Hasluck wrote a 'Personal and Confidential' note for Prime Minister Gough Whitlam, offering 'some general observations' about the requirements of the office that should be considered in recommending the name of his successor.[18] Hasluck said it was his experience during the Menzies and Gorton Governments that the Prime Minister 'took the responsibility on himself of choosing a nominee' after making discreet and limited soundings among a very small number of senior colleagues, having already discussed the matter directly with the Queen.

As for the qualifications for office, Hasluck said it was his view that the climate of opinion in Australia (in 1973) was unfavourable to the appointment of anyone other than an Australian, and there was also a feeling against a military governor-general, no matter how distinguished. He thought the following categories of people should be excluded from consideration:

(a) Governors of the States – he disapproved of the idea of a vice-regal career service and also of the awkward precedent that such an appointment would create.

(b) Retired Admirals, Generals and Air Marshals – 'They are a class, their political sensitivity is often dull and their social attitudes stereotyped'.

(c) The wealthy or socially privileged – as 'They attract envy and this sets the office further apart from the general community'.

Hasluck said:

> If these exclusions are accepted we come to a position where a Governor-General will be
>
> (a) An Australian.
>
> (b) A civilian.
>
> (c) A person of recognised distinction who has made his mark without being ostentatious in wealth or social pretension or linked with a privileged group.
>
> (d) A person who will be trusted as 'a good Australian' with a national outlook.

He also thought it was essential the person have some knowledge and experience of the working of the machinery of government in Australia and a good appreciation of the constitutional position, as well as personal dignity, speaking ability, the ability of him and his wife to receive guests, be physically fit, and probably be a man of about 60. He did not rule out politicians so long as they were capable of a non-partisan approach to the office. He told Whitlam:

> In short, I suggest that you look first among those persons who have had experience in politics or public administration and, failing the appearance of a suitable nominee in that field, Among Australian citizens of distinction who have had close experience of the workings of government.

Hasluck later sent Whitlam a handwritten list of possible successors. Two were members of the Labor Cabinet, another was secretary of the Australian Council of Trade Unions (ACTU), two were academics, two were 'big business' (one of whom Whitlam approached, but who declined) while the other was Sir John Kerr, then Chief Justice of New South Wales.. Whitlam later offered him the position and, after some negotiations, he accepted nomination.[19]

Subsequently, Prime Ministers have continued to make recommendations for the appointment of Governors-General without taking the matter to a full Cabinet. John Howard was responsible for two appointments that would not have met Hasluck's criteria: former Anglican Archbishop of Brisbane Dr Peter Hollingworth, and former Western Australia Governor and retired Major General, Philip Michael Jeffery.

During the republican debate in 1999, Queensland Premier Peter Beattie suggested he might radically change the way his State appointed its Governor, by involving the people in an election for the post. In 2003, when he had a vacancy to fill, he adopted a very different approach: having selected the incoming Governor and had them confirmed by the Queen, he took the nomination to the Parliament for a vote to give parliamentary recognition to the appointment. He said this was a 'tentative step' in involving the people in the selection of the Governor. He said he hoped that next time he could go further, by calling for people to come forward and then doing it in a different way.[20]

Cost

In 2005 the Federal Government adopted a $15 million, 10-year heritage property master plan for the repair, maintenance and development of the two vice-regal properties, Government House at Yarralumla in Canberra, and Admiralty House, at Kirribilli on Sydney Harbour. This is in addition to the $14 million annual cost of maintaining the buildings and paying the salaries and administrative costs of the Governor-General and his official establishment. Almost $5 million of this is required to run the Australian honours systems – the Order of Australia and other defence and civilian honours, including bravery awards – and that cost is certain to continue to increase to meet an ever-increasing volume of nominations for awards.

Subjects or citizens?

Following the defeat of the Republic Referendum in 1999, the Queen published a special message to her Australian subjects in which she said:

> I have always made it clear that the future of the Monarchy in Australia is an issue for the Australian people and them alone to decide by democratic and constitutional means. This decision has now been reached by way of the Constitutional Convention in 1998 and subsequently by this referendum … For some while it has been clear that many Australians wanted constitutional change. Much of the debate has been about what the change should be.

While the referendum was overwhelmingly defeated in every State with a national 'yes' vote of just 45 per cent, an Australian Election Study showed that 55 per cent supported a republic with a directly elected president, 21 per cent wanted a president elected by the Parliament (the model actually put in the referendum) while 24 per cent supported the retention of the monarchy. More than half those who wanted a president directly elected by the people voted for no change rather than support the model developed by the Australian Republic Movement and the Constitutional Convention.[21]

Subsequently, support for a republic may have waned somewhat. A Newspoll published on Australia Day 2005 showed support for a republic had dropped to 46 per cent, its lowest mark for five years. In two interviews for British television when the Queen was in Australia for the Commonwealth Games in March 2006, Prime Minister John Howard predicted that Australia would not become a republic while the Queen remained on the throne – and he indicated he thought she would remain there for a considerable further time.[22]

In one of those interviews, with Nicholas Witchell of the BBC, the Prime Minister produced a common sense answer to one of the peripheral arguments that arose out of the republic debate as to whether the Queen or her vice-regal representative was Australia's head of state. The term does not appear in the Constitution. It is a term of art in political science. But it is important in ceremonial matters – particularly in an international context, because heads of state take precedence over all others, including heads of government (who normally exercise real power). The issue became important in Australia because one of the arguments used by republicans was that Australia should have its own head of state, not the Queen, while monarchists argued the Governor-General was the head of state, and who for more than 40 years had been an Australian. Prime Minister Howard said in his interview (the Monarchy) was 'a very good institution for delivering a non-political head of state'. Then, when asked had not Australia reached the point where an Australian should be its head of state he replied, 'Well the effective Head of State of Australia is the Governor-General who's been an Australian since, what, 1965'.

The official answer, it seems, is that the Queen is the 'titular' head of state, but the Governor-General the 'effective' head of state.

Notes

1 Cowen 1985: 135.
2 Hayden 1996: 538
3 Hasluck 1979: 14.
4 Bagehot 1967: 111.
5 Cowen 1985: 145.
6 Hasluck 1979: 18.
7 Hasluck 1979: 20.
8 Hasluck 1979: 41.
9 Hasluck 1979: 22.
10 M1767 Folders of copies of papers maintained by Governor-General, 1969-1974, National Archives of Australia, Canberra, headed, 'Governor of Western Australia': 1-6.
11 Hasluck 1995: 187.
12 Cowen 1985: 142-144.
13 Stephen 1989.
14 Craven 2004: 281-290.
15 Roy Morgan Poll, conducted 20-22 May 2003.
16 Winterton 2003.
17 Craven 2004: 289-290.
18 Hasluck had made it clear he and his wife did not want his five-year term of office extended despite Whitlam's request that he should stay on. The letter and other relevant notes are contained in Hasluck's personal papers as Governor-General, in the National Archives.
19 The list is reproduced and discussed by Whitlam in the 3rd edition of *The Truth of the Matter*, MUP 2005: xxii-xxiii.
20 Queensland *Hansard*, Legislative Assembly, 11 March 2003: 369-375.
21 Manne 2004: 26-27.
22 For text of the interviews on 14 March 2006 see <www.pm.gov.au>.

4

The Public Service

In a period of just 21 years, between 1984 and 2005, the proportion of the workforce employed in public services in Australia was dramatically reduced, from 26 per cent to 16 per cent. The main reason for the change was the privatisation by both Federal Government and State Governments of many of their activities, including banking and insurance, electricity and gas, and telecommunications. Others reasons or explanations include increased rationalisation and outsourcing of services, improved productivity and the use of contract rather than direct employment.[1] Over the 21-year period, public sector employment in the electricity, gas and water supply industry fell from almost 96 per cent to under 55 per cent, in communications services from 88.9 per cent to 39.1 per cent in finance and insurance from 26.1 per cent to 2.8 per cent and in cultural and recreation services from 23.8 per cent to 10.1 per cent. At the end of the period 79 per cent of public sector employment was concentrated in just three industry sectors: government administration and defence, health and community services, and education. Commonwealth public servants made up 2.7 per cent of the Australian workforce in 1976, but just 1.3 per cent in 2005.

The Commonwealth Public Service has changed significantly in the past 10 or 15 years – even excluding from consideration those parts that were privatised. Very few people under the age of 25 are now employed in public service – 4.0 per cent in 2005 against 6.3 per cent in 1996. The median age of the public service in 2005 was 42, compared with 39 just 10 years earlier. The 'typical new starter' in the public service is now a 32-year-old woman with graduate qualifications. Less than one per cent of people in the public service are at the lowest salary level.[2] A long-term reduction in the number of ongoing employees at the two lowest levels and the increasing number at higher levels is due to changes in the nature of the work undertaken in the public service, changes in job design and the need for a more highly skilled workforce. In June 2005 half the Australian Public Service (APS) employees had university degrees, compared with one-third just 12 years earlier.

It is not just the composition of the public service and its work that have changed. There has been a deliberate, major shift in the nature of the relationship of the public service with government. Changes in the way government is conducted have also impacted on the public service, through the growing use by ministers of political and other advisors who are not public servants but who interact directly with the public service. Another significant development is that public servants, rather than their political masters, are more likely to be in the firing line when things go wrong, as they have been doing in a more public way in recent years.

Responsive but impartial

Andrew Podger retired in 2005 as the Commonwealth Public Service Commissioner. He earlier served as a departmental secretary (that is, as the head of a public service department) under both the Keating Labor Government and the Howard Coalition Government. He first joined the public service in 1975. He says in the 1970s and 1980s there was a bipartisan political view that the public service was too independent and not as 'responsive' to the elected government as it should have been.[3]

He says:

> [T]he changes in the 1980s and early 1990s, while generating some debate, have generally been accepted by both sides of politics. For example, the current Prime Minister, John Howard, observed in

> 1996 that the service was working more cooperatively with ministers and ministerial staff than had been his experience when Treasurer in the Fraser Government and, of course, he has built on the earlier changes, for example, by introducing performance pay for Secretaries.
>
> I doubt there would be many today, however, who would argue that the Public Service needs to shift the balance further towards responsiveness. The more serious questions today concern our professionalism and our impartiality, and whether our clear obligation to be responsive has caused some of us sometimes to be too concerned to please.

Two former Prime Ministers are quite definite that the answer to that last question is 'yes'. Bob Hawke says one of the real tragedies of the Howard Government is:

> that what was a very good public service which did give frank and fearless advice no longer does. I think it is a tragedy that that attitude has not been continued. When I came into office [in 1983] I had all the heads in and I said I want you people to put what they think is right, not what they think I want to hear. I want it hard and straight. That wasn't a moral position: that was a self-interested position. There was a very great pool of talent in that public service, but many have left and those that stay tend to be looking over the shoulder thinking, 'what do they want to hear from me'. Its bad for government.[4]

Malcolm Fraser also says the public service is giving governments the sort of advice they want to hear:[5]

> In so many ways the public service now operates as gate-keepers, as an extension of the government. In my day the Prime Minister's office was political but the Prime Minister's Department wasn't. Now, in my view, the Department is totally political and is there to do what the Prime Minister wants. It is there to protect the Prime Minister and there to stop uncomfortable information getting anywhere near him.

Michael Costello, who headed the Industrial Relations Department and then Foreign Affairs and Trade during the last four years of the Keating Government and was sacked, along with five other secretaries, when the Howard Government was elected, says the public service has been 'a bit' politicised. '[B]ut much more important, it has become widely intimidated'.[6]

He says there were systemic changes made under Labor governments in the 1980s and 1990s that removed the legal foundations that made it realistic for public servants to give frank and fearless advice to ministers or government even if they did not want to hear it. The first and most important was the decision in the *Public Service Reform Act 1984* to remove permanency for secretaries of departments, allowing them to be sacked without cause or explanation. Then in 1994 the government decided that all departmental secretaries should be appointed on fixed-term contracts. Costello says Prime Minister Howard has taken full advantage of this systemic weakening of the position of secretaries:

> [T]hroughout the public service in Canberra it is widely known that it is a good idea to keep one's head down, rather than express one's professional views firmly when they are in opposition to the government of the day. Governments of both political persuasion have a natural tendency to not want to hear advice that does not suit, and certainly not in writing when it can be leaked or recovered under freedom of information legislation.

The extent and nature of the power to remove Departmental Secretaries was tested in 1999 when the Minister for Defence, John Moore, decided he could no longer work with the Secretary of his Department, Paul Barratt. Barratt went to the Federal Court seeking injunctions to prevent the various steps prescribed in the *Public Service Act* for the dismissal of a secretary from being put into effect. The matters were eventually determined on appeal by a unanimous bench of three, Justices Beaumont, French and Merkel.[7] Barratt succeeded only in establishing that a Secretary was entitled to written notice of the grounds and reasons on which a recommendation might be made by the Secretary of the Prime Minister's Department for his removal, and that he or she must be given a reasonable opportunity to make submissions. Some 'ground' must be established but it could involve 'political and policy considerations'.[8] In Barratt's case the grounds were:

1. that the Minister has lost trust and confidence in Mr Barratt's ability to perform the duties of Secretary of the Department of Defence; and
2 'that this lack of trust and confidence is detrimental to the public interest, because it is prejudicial to the effective and efficient administration of the Department.

This is a formula that could easily be applied whenever a Minister decides to dispose of his departmental secretary.

Dr Peter Shergold, who became Secretary of the Department of Prime Minister and Cabinet in 2003, denies that senior public servants have as a result become 'supine lackies and obsequious toadies'.[9] He says:

> You would expect me to argue that courage is a quality of character not of contract and I do. But, and perhaps you will find this more persuasive, I challenge you to tell me what daring-do is required to be honest to Ministers. Sitting behind closed doors, criticising a policy proposal or (equally likely) having one criticised, requires little more than a mastery of the arguments, an understanding of the alternatives and a relatively tough hide. All ten Ministers I have served – of very different political persuasions – have welcomed policy advice as long as it is provided in confidence (a crucial ingredient of trust) and is proffered in the clear understanding that it will be the Minister (not the public servant) who is responsible for deciding whether it is accepted. Rarely is the 'frankness' of policy advice delivered through heated confrontation. More typically the public servant will seek to persuade the Minister through argument, persistence and guile. In my experience the most effective quality of advice is not that it is 'fearless' but that it is convincing.
>
> Of course a public service should seek to provide frank advice based upon its considered assessment of what is in the public interest. It does. But the task has become harder for a good reason, namely that the making of public policy has become increasingly democratic. There is more competition in ideas than ever before. Think-tanks, research institutes, consultancy companies, private sector lobbyists and community advocates each pursue their particular interests with increasing professionalism, vying with public servants for the ear of ministers and their political advisors. To my mind that's beneficial. Why would one want public servants to have exclusive access to a minister? Why would public servants not themselves want to listen to the views of those who share an interest in the outcomes of public policy?
>
> But, to clothe an old concept in the new management jargon, a professional public service can 'add value'. It can transform information into knowledge with a public purpose. A well-educated public service, with a wealth of collective experience and corporate memory, trained to evaluate the costs and benefits of a range of policy options, should always seek to identify the national interest in the diversity of particular interests that seek – quite legitimately – to influence government. Its views should be conveyed, behind closed doors, robustly. In my experience that is what happens.

> But .the role of the public service is to inform decision-making not to seek to impose its will. It must never, ever believe it has an intellectual or moral superiority over those who have been chosen to govern. It is entirely appropriate – indeed it is fundamental to democratic processes – that elected government collectively may come to a different assessment of the national interest than the public service. Indeed it may come to an equally considered judgement that on some matters it is necessary to give priority to a particular interest – to provide assistance to car workers facing redundancy, drought-stricken farmers, Veterans needing health care or struggling single mothers, for instance. As long as the decision is lawful (an important protection provided by an independent public service) then the officials' task becomes one of vigorous implementation.
>
> So is the role of the public servant, no matter how fierce the private discussion, always to conclude the discussion with 'Yes, Minister'? With regard to the determination of policy, it is. But the professional public servant also has other obligations which may on occasion mean that the answer will be in the negative. Ministers, far from being omnipotent, are constrained by law, Parliamentary process and precedent. Ministers cannot change the outcome of a tender process which has been delegated to a public servant, or use public funds in ways for which they have not been appropriated, or ask to see the advice that their departments have provided to a previous government, or tell a public servant how to respond to an FOI application, or – without the agreement of the Opposition – commit a future government during an election caretaker period, or decide on which senior executives are appointed to their departments. In these, and many other ways, power is balanced between the Australian government and its public administration so that, on occasion, the only possible response will be 'No, Minister'.

Andrew Podger expressed similar views when he retired as APS Commissioner. He says he rarely found it particularly challenging to offer policy advice that was not welcome:

> Where courage was needed was when advising on due process, on releasing documents under FOI, on making corrections in the Parliament, on tender processes, on publishing performance data in the Annual Report, on giving an individual or an organization opposed to the Government fair treatment, and not giving favoured treatment to advisers seeking jobs in the department.[10]

To the list of systemic changes designed to improve public service 'responsiveness' given by Costello involving removal of 'permanency' for Secretaries, followed by term appointments of Secretaries (see above), Podger adds:[11]

- developing and expanding the role of ministerial advisors to complement the role of the public service, providing increased political support to the government;
- strengthening the authority of ministers over the administration of their departments;
- reducing the influence of public service commissioners in the appointment (and termination) of secretaries and other agency heads;
- the introduction of term contracts for secretaries and other agency heads; and
- the introduction of performance pay for secretaries and certain other agency heads (in most jurisdictions).

Podger says:

> There are considerable benefits in most of these developments and any opposition I have to one or two of them (such as performance pay) is very much an on-balance judgment. But I am concerned that the changes, particularly when considered cumulatively, have not been sufficiently balanced by some constraints that would protect the emerging system of public administration from losing its apolitical, professional role that remains essential in a parliamentary democracy.
>
> Protections I believe need to be considered carefully across Australian jurisdictions in the modern era include:
>
> - some codifying of the role of ministerial advisers who are now an important part of the landscape …
> - a clearer role for public service commissioners in the process of appointment, termination and performance appraisal of secretaries and other agency heads …
> - a third and related measure is to strengthen the role of commissioners in Senior Executive Services (SES) appointments below the secretary level.

Of these changes, the most controversial concerns the growth and role of ministerial advisors.

Ministerial advisors and the public services

Dr Glyn Davis, former head of the Premier's Department in Queensland, then Vice-Chancellor of Griffith University and subsequently Vice-Chancellor of the University of Melbourne, says the greatest change in the running of government in Australia in the past 25 years has been the growth of ministerial advisors, their accumulation of power and their impact on who is in charge.[12] He believes ministerial advisors have brought about a fundamental change in the system of government, a one-off transformation that won't be reversed. 'They allow activist ministers to exercise real authority'. Michael Keating, Secretary of the Prime Minister's Department under both Paul Keating and John Howard agrees that probably the most important change over the past 30 years has been the growth in ministerial private offices, both in number of staff and influence. He says the Prime Minister's office staff now act as his alter ego and have greatly expanded his reach in coordinating the government's political activity.[13] Professor Patrick Weller says ministers now have staff that:

> are large, aggressive and policy oriented. When they started, the staff may well have been concerned primarily with organising the minister's diary, but that's clearly no longer true. It's created a couple of fairly dramatic problems. One is that there is often somebody between the secretary or advising officer of the department, and the minister – somebody who is sitting in the minister's ear, giving second advice, and somebody who is often talented and may often be a public servant on secondment, who can put an alternative view and an alternative spin ... It is also true that those staff are, in effect, unaccountable. There are two conventional myths that exist: one is that anything told to staff is told to the minister, and the other is that anything requested by the staff has been requested by the minister. Neither myth currently prevails in practice. They *can't* prevail in practice, when large numbers of ministerial staff ask for information across a whole range of issues in anticipation of what the minister might like. Then they are accountable to nobody; not to the minister, because the minister cannot know, and not to Parliament, because they are meant to be beyond the scope of Parliament.[14]

The change has been rapid and is apparently continuing. Its implications have been assessed and partly addressed by the Public Service Commission. The Commission's *State of the Service Report* in 2002-2003 and again in 2003-2004 reported on surveys the Commission had conducted among public servants to explore the nature of the contact between ministerial staff and public servants, and to quantify it. Subsequently the Commission issued a guide – *Supporting Ministers,*

Upholding the Values – to help public servants in their dealings with ministerial staff, and to ensure that the public service system was not misused.

Prominence of ministerial advisors

In its 2003-2004 report, the Commission reported there were 391 ministerial personal staff employed as at 1 May 2004, compared with 207 21 years earlier – an 89 per cent increase from the beginning of the Hawke Government. It says large increases had also occurred in the number of advisors in New Zealand, Ireland and the United Kingdom, but the 'number of advisers in those jurisdictions remains significantly lower than in Australia'. It concludes 'there is an international trend among Westminster systems for ministerial advisers to play a more substantial role in public administration'.[15] It says its survey showed that one in five APS employees had been in direct contact with Ministers or their advisors during the previous 12 months and showed that where direct contact occurred 'it was overwhelmingly in relation to matters of substance (such as the provision of advice and factual information rather than administrative support)'. The survey showed that about 35 per cent of staff that had contact with ministers or their advisors said they had faced a challenge in balancing the requirement to be apolitical, impartial and professional against the demands from ministers' offices.

Paul Barratt, who was dismissed from his position as secretary of the Department of Defence in 1999 (see above), echoes the concerns expressed by Professor Weller about the role and lack of accountability of ministerial staff.[16] He too says ministerial staff are now successfully competing with Departments for the Minister's ear:

> Regrettably, they are not subject to satisfactory public accountability procedures. The single most important measure to improve the accountability of ministerial staff would be to return to a system where all substantive communication between the Minister, Ministerial staff and the Department is in writing. Reliance upon oral communication exposes the nation to three principal areas of risk:
>
> - Authority: who is actually issuing this instruction? Is it the Minister or is it someone else?
> - Accuracy: who is being asked to do what, for what purpose, with what resources, and by when, and what is the

response of the Minister or Department to these communications?
- Accountability: who did what, for what purpose, and on what authority?

He says all these areas of risk seem to have been present in the 'children overboard' affair (see below). Barratt gives a personal example of the way ministerial staff can use the present system to enhance 'plausible deniability' for their minister. He says in late 1998 he was directed by the Defence Minister to give him a comprehensive report of the Collins Class submarine, a report to be signed by both the Secretary of the Department and the Chief of the Defence Force (CDF). In early December he rang the Minister's office to advise the signed joint statement would be sent to the Minister in that morning's deliveries. Barratt continues:

> I was asked not to. 'Why not?' I asked. 'Because it mightn't be what we wanted, and if it got out that we had received it and sent it back to be changed, that could be embarrassing for everyone. Just send it over 'informally' and we'll have a look at it, and if we need any changes we will get back to you'.

Barratt says he told the CDF of this and said he was not prepared to play this sort of game. He waited till the Minister visited the department two days later, on 16 December 1998, and in the presence of the CDF and the Minister's Chief of Staff handed the advice personally to the Minister. On 21 January 1999, as part of the lead up to Barratt's sacking, the Minister told the Secretary of the Prime Minister's Department he was still waiting for the report and on 7 February 1999 the Age said the report was 'soon due to be delivered'.

Barrett concludes:

> The rationalisation for this position can only be that the advice was not sent through the Department's Ministerial Correspondence Unit, and was therefore provided 'informally'. So signed written advice handed from Secretary to minister in the presence of the CDF can still leave the Minister able to say that he has not been told.

One aspect of the accountability of ministerial staff that has attracted attention and some criticism is their apparent immunity from attendance at parliamentary committee inquiries – both major parties have voted against summoning such staff to committee inquiries. The Clerk of the Senate, Harry Evans, has made it clear that ministerial advisors and ministers' personal staff have no personal immunity.[17] He says, however, there is a case that such persons should not be summonsed because this would tend to destroy the trust and confidentiality which is essential to the performance of their advisory and personal assistance roles, and would discourage frank advice. But he says in appropriate cases the legislature may want to uncover problems with the way in which ministers are advised and assisted:

> In any event their role is not confined to advice and personal assistance. There is ample evidence that they:
>
> - control access to ministers
> - determine the information which reaches ministers, particularly from departments and agencies
> - control contact between ministers and other ministers, other members of Parliament and departments and agencies
> - make decisions on behalf of ministers
> - give directions about government activities, including directions to departments and agencies
> - manage media perceptions and reporting.
>
> They are virtually assistant ministers and participate in government activities as such. On the one occasion in 1995 on which the Senate directed a ministerial staffer to appear, he was in charge of a government agency. Ministers no longer necessarily accept full responsibility for the actions of their staff, as has been demonstrated on several occasions. In these circumstances, it is appropriate that legislative inquiries into the actions of government be able to summon these staff and to require them to explain their part in those actions.

Systemic failures

Prime Minister's Department Secretary Dr Peter Shergold acknowledged in his Press Club speech in February 2006 that the Public Service has to do more – 'always more' – to make itself more productive, more effective, more connected and more committed to service:

> Nor am I blind to our mistakes. The 'children overboard affair' and the appalling mistreatment of Cornelia Rau and Vivian Solon are two incidents which are portrayed as bespeaking a Service in crisis. I

> do not seek to defend these lapses of standards and judgement. Nor even, although it would be easy, do I intend to put these blemishes within 'the context' of millions of decisions made every day by Centrelink, the Australian Taxation Office, Medicare (and, yes, the Department of Immigration) with an astounding level of accuracy and efficiency and delivered with fairness and courtesy. Rather I acknowledge these mistakes for what they are, and seek to learn from them and – with the strong support of government – to rectify them. However it is equally important to identify what has not gone wrong. The foundations of Westminster have not subsided.
>
> The failures were ones of inadequate managerial control, weak direction and poor organisational communication exacerbated by an unacceptable tardiness in acknowledging and correcting the mistakes that had been made. In the first matter there was a failure to balance carefully the twin demands of timeliness and accuracy – information was passed from public servants to ministers before it had been adequately corroborated. In the second instance relatively junior officers were not adequately trained or supervised to exercise appropriately the considerable powers that they wielded. Worst by far, failures in both instances were compounded by organisational silos, poor record-keeping, a reluctance to clarify the record and, in a few instances it would seem, attempts to cover up the initial mistakes. I deeply regret these instances in which the normal standards of the Australian Public Service have not been upheld. I apologise for them.
>
> But I do not accept that the failures represent the collapse of the Westminster tradition or the diminution of public service values or a sad decline in ethical standards. More profoundly, the mistakes are failures of public administration not instances of government conspiracy. The government did not direct public servants to provide false information or fail to correct the record or act outside the law. Nor did it intimate that such behaviour was acceptable. Nor did Ministers put impenetrable barriers around themselves.
>
> The idea that public servants have become part of a network of 'deniability' is a product of conspiratorial imagination. It may be convenient for retired public servants and journalists, for quite different motivations, to attribute blame to vague notions of 'the politicisation of the public service' but it is wrong. It is a cop-out. From my perspective it stands in the way of addressing the problems. We need to accept these as serious public service failures from which we can and must learn.

The 'children overboard' affair occurred during the 2001 federal election campaign when 'border protection' – stopping asylum seekers arriving by boat – proved to be a central issue. Government ministers claimed that some of these people had threatened to throw their children overboard in an attempt to stop the navy turning back their boats. Photographs were made available that purported to support this account. However as Senate Clerk Harry Evans wrote:[18]

> Only after the election was it established that, not only was this story false, but it was known before the election to be false by various people in the government apparatus, including ministerial staff and probably at least one Minister. The tangled and murky story of how the correct information came to be concealed during the election campaign was explored at some length in a special Senate committee. The government's cooperation with the inquiry was partial and grudging. Apart from the impression that a great deception had been perpetrated, the inquiry drew attention to the sorry state of the public service (characterised by inefficient communication or telling the government what it wants to hear, or both) and the somewhat sinister role of ministerial staff (intervening between public servants and ministers and providing 'deniability' for politically inconvenient information).

Andrew Podger, then Public Service Commissioner, told a senior executive service breakfast meeting in April 2004:

> However I look at it now, I do not believe the children overboard case was the service's finest hour. Whatever the circumstances in the lead up to the election – and I am still uncomfortable with what happened over that period – the reluctance by officials to face up to the facts over the subsequent months is extremely difficult to defend.[19]

The Rau/Alvarez (Solon) affairs concerned the illegal detention of Australian citizens, and eventually led to the discovery that at least 200 citizens had been wrongly detained by officials of the Department of Immigration and Multicultural and Indigenous Affairs (DIMIA). In the Vivian Alvarez (Solon) case, a citizen was wrongly deported to the Philippines in 2001 after having been held in immigration detention. Although DIMIA officials became aware in 2003 and 2004 that she had been wrongly deported, nothing was done to correct the problem. Cornelia Rau was held in the women's prison in Brisbane for six months and then four months in the Baxter detention centre before her identity was established.

Former Victorian Police Commissioner Neil Comrie investigated the Alvarez case. His report says:

> DIMIA officers, from field level to senior executive, seem to have had little understanding of their responsibilities under the Act – other than a mistaken belief that they must detain a person and when the person is detained the detention is absolute. The seriousness of taking a person's liberty did not seem to be reflected in their actions ... These attitudes seem to have been nurtured by a cultural environment in which the detention of suspected unlawful non-citizens was viewed as paramount.

Former Federal Police Commissioner Mick Palmer, who investigated the Rau affair, says:

> DIMIA officers are authorised to exercise exceptional, even extraordinary, powers. That they should be expected to do so without adequate training, without proper management and oversight, with poor information systems, and with no genuine quality assurance and constraints on the exercise of these powers is of concern. The fact that this situation has been allowed to continue unchecked and unreviewed for several years is difficult to understand ... There are serious problems with the handling of immigration detention cases. They stem from deep-seated cultural and attitudinal problems within DIMIA and a failure of executive leadership in the immigration compliance and detention areas.

The government subsequently committed $230 million to introducing new systems, procedures and training and changing the management and culture of the department.[20]

Accountability and integrity

Dr Shergold said in his National Press Club speech that the public service was now more accountable than it ever had been before:

> The Westminster tradition has evolved considerably in the last thirty years: there is now much greater scrutiny of public service decision-making than in the past through Parliamentary committees, the Audit Office, and the Ombudsman; through legislation which, within limits set by Parliament, provides freedom of information to the public; and the opportunity, through an extended panoply of administrative law, for citizens to have decisions reviewed. There is now a network of integrity which did not exist 30 years ago.[21]

As the 'children overboard' and wrongful detention cases show, that scrutiny is not always effective in delivering desirable outcomes. However Ombudsman John McMillan believes there have been considerable improvements in the 30 years since the establishment of his office. Huge sea changes have occurred in the public service, he says. 'They are much more open and much more attuned to what is happening outside. They are more responsive to change and much more committed to improving service delivery. I think the levels of performance in the service are very high'.[22] Professor McMillan says the biggest problem areas involving his office concern Centrelink payments, child support payments and the tax office and mostly involve money:

> They are all highly complex legislative schemes that are not easily understood, even by those administering them. They all involve people who have an on-going relationship with an agency, so that if there's a problem now, there's a possibility it will recur, and if the problem isn't solved it becomes an element in a toxic relationship that develops between the person and the agency.

He says the problem areas do not involve abuse of power, bad faith, or evil-minded bureaucrats. 'The real problems are complexity and huge agencies and rules that are changing all the time'. He says the legislative process moves so quickly that 'you don't get time to road-test the rules and see how they can be administered on the front line'.

There are critics of the Ombudsman's office, but not of the work it does. A former deputy Ombudsman, John Wood, says the Ombudsman must be described as an agency of the executive government. He says:[23]

> Unlike many of its international cousins – and indeed some of its state counterparts – the Ombudsman is not an officer of the Parliament. The Ombudsman is nominated by the Prime Minster, generally following some form of selection process, by the head of the Prime Minister's Department (itself subject to the Ombudsman's jurisdiction and thus having a theoretical conflict of interest) who recommends the person to the Governor-General for appointment. Parliament has no say in the process, not even the right to veto.

He says more worrying is the mechanism for funding the office. Under three Ombudsmen, says Wood, the office was starved for resources. In 1996 22 per cent of its annual budget was cut, at a time when the number of complaints to the Ombudsman was increasing by about 20 per cent a year.

Freedom of Information (FOI) is an accountability mechanism that may not be delivering the integrity that it should. Andrew Podger, in his parting remarks when he ceased to be Public Service Commissioner said there was widespread concern in government and the senior echelons of the public service that freedom of information had so widened access to information that counter-measures were needed:[24]

> Fewer file notes, diaries regularly destroyed, documents given security classifications at higher levels than are strictly required and handled to minimise the chances of FOI access. Most senior public servants recognise that these counter-measures must not hide the decision-making trail, but the trail that is left is often now just a skeleton without any sign of the flesh and blood of the real process, and even the skeleton is only visible to those with a need to know.
>
> Now what is being protected here? The public interest, or the partisan interest of the government of the day? Maybe the liberal interpretation of FOI legislation by the courts has undervalued the public interest in allowing the Government to deliberate on issues without constant public glare that tends to help special interests. But there must be strong suspicion that partisan interests are often the main consideration, and public servants desiring to be responsive may be encouraged to give more weight to the concerns of ministers than to the public interest and the implicit and explicit requirements of administrative law.

Limited responses

In 1996 the Australian Law Reform Commission published, jointly with the Administrative Review Council, a report *Open Government – A review of the federal Freedom of Information Act 1982*. Its recommendations for the government to have a lesser ability to prevent material being released to the public were not taken up by the government. A decision by the High Court in 2006 narrowly (3-2) supported the government's ability to restrict access to information through the use of conclusive, effectively unreviewable, ministerial certificates, based on a minister's conclusion that it was not in the public interest for material to be made public.[25]

One integrity measure not mentioned by Dr Shergold, no doubt because of its long absence at the federal level, is the existence of anti-corruption bodies such as the Independent Commission

Against Corruption, in NSW, the Crime and Misconduct Commission in Queensland and the Corruption and Crime Commission in Western Australia. A research project conducted under the auspices of Griffith University and Transparency International Australia says there 'is a clear case for a general purpose Commonwealth anti-corruption agency which includes educative, research and policy functions'. It notes that the Australian Law Reform Commission recommended such a body with limited jurisdiction in 1996, but it was never actioned.[26] In 2006 the Howard Government introduced legislation to establish the Australian Commission for Law Enforcement Integrity (ACLEI), headed by a Commissioner with Royal Commission-like powers, to investigate corruption within the Australian Federal Police, the Australian Crime Commission and prescribed law enforcement agencies, but not the public service generally as is the case with related bodies in most of the States.

Another integrity measure – though one not generally recognised as such – is the increasing willingness of insiders to 'blow the whistle' on malpractices within the public service. There is some very limited protection for whistleblowers at the Commonwealth level, though far more in some States. But the existence of s reasonable system does not guarantee its effectiveness. In 2005 Queensland discovered that its Health Department had ignored complaints by a nurse about the disastrous surgical exploits of a doctor in the Bundaberg Hospital, a doctor who became known to medical staff as 'Dr Death'. A subsequent Commission of Inquiry conducted by a retired Court of Appeal judge, Geoff Davies QC, recommended changes to the whistleblower legislation to ensure that complaints were properly investigated. He proposed that the Ombudsman should be able to carry out or oversight all whistleblower complaints, and if they are not adequately dealt with within specified time limits, disclosure can be made to a Member of Parliament and then the media.

Re-establishing control

In 20 years, federal governments went from disestablishing 'monolithic multifunctional departments and a greater reliance on third parties for the provision of services'[27] to 'a reassertion of the centre and the ministerial department'.[28] Throughout this period, and indeed for at least 30 years (as noted earlier in this chapter) governments have tried to reassert ministerial control over the public service, to make it more 'responsive' to what its political masters want. By 2005, according to Professors Halligan and Horrigan, the emerging model had four dimensions:

- Resurrection of the central agency as a major actor and of control over departments
- Whole of government as the current expression of a range of forms of coordination
- Central monitoring of agency implementation and delivery
- Departmentalisation through absorbing statutory authorities and reclaiming control of agencies with hybrid boards to accord with corporate governance prescriptions.[29]

They say:

> Underlying each of the four dimensions of change is a political control dimension: these include improved financial information on a program basis for ministers; strategic coordination under cabinet; control of major policy agendas; organisational integration through abolition of bodies and features of autonomy; and monitoring the implementation of government policy down to the delivery level. The overall result is unprecedented potential for policy and program control and integration using the conventional machinery of cabinet, central agencies, and departments'.[30]

A new element has been the gradual implementation of some of the reforms recommended by John Uhrig in 2003, in his report on corporate governance of statutory authorities and statutory office holders. He proposed to bring many of them under more direct control by government, reducing the number of independent boards and the independence of these authorities. The government responded favourably to the general tenor of the report, but began to implement it slowly and carefully. Eventually this led to the review of the governance of at least 150 separate bodies. Subsequently, and prompted in part by the scandal that began to emerge several years later of the Australian Wheat Board's involvement in paying several hundred million dollars worth of kickbacks to the regime of Saddam Hussein in Iraq in defiance of United Nations sanctions, the government began implementing a policy of bringing many bodies that were previously governed by boards back under ministerial control and departmental supervision.

These changes in the early 21st century may use different managerial techniques, but all are intended to make the public service more responsive to what ministers want government to deliver.

Notes

1 Kryger 2006.
2 Australian Public Service Commission 2005.
3 Podger 2005b.
4 Hawke 2005.
5 Fraser 2005.
6 Costello, M 2004.
7 *Barratt v Howard* [2000] FCA 190 (10 March 2000).
8 *Barratt v Howard*, at para 73.
9 Shergold, P (2006).
10 Podger 2005a.
11 Podger 2005a.
12 Davis 2005b.
13 Keating 2005.
14 Weller 2003: 85. Emphasis in original text.
15 Australian Public Service Commission 2005: 34.
16 Barratt 2006.
17 Evans, H. 2002.
18 Evans, H. 2005a: 48-49.
19 Podger 2004.
20 Metcalfe 2006.
21 Shergold 2006.
22 McMillan 2005.
23 Wood 2005.
24 Podger 2005b.
25 *McKinnon v Secretary, Department of Treasury* [2006] HCA 45.
26 Brown 2005: 35.
27 Halligan and Horrigan 2005: 1.
28 Halligan and Horrigan 2005: 2.
29 Halligan and Horrigan 2005: 2.
30 Halligan and Horrigan 2005: 3.

5

Courts and the law

It is only since 1986 that Australia could justly claim to have a completely independent legal and judicial system. That was when the *Australia Acts*, passed by the United Kingdom, Commonwealth and State Parliaments, finally abolished all appeals from Australia's courts to the Privy Council in Britain. Until then, Australian courts had to follow the precedents laid down by the Privy Council in dealing with Australian law (including its Constitution) and also had to follow decisions of the House of Lords and the English Court of Appeal on relevant common law issues where those decisions were not in conflict with judgments of the High Court. Even the High Court tended to pay deference to decisions of the highest British courts in areas where it was not required by direct precedent to follow Privy Council decisions.

Cutting the ties with Britain's top courts was a protracted business. Through the 1960s, 1970s and 1980s the High Court slowly established its ascendancy in the Australian judicial hierarchy, first declaring that it was not bound to follow decisions of the House of Lords, then that it was not bound to follow the Privy Council and finally that State courts, when faced with conflicting decisions of the Privy Council and the High Court must follow the decisions of the High Court.[1] The rejection of English authority was not easy: the English legal system was generally venerated by Australian lawyers and judges. Leading members of the profession regarded trips to London to argue appeals in the Privy Council as among the highlights of their careers. However several Privy Council decisions that displayed ignorance of Australian law made the break inevitable. In 1976, for example, the Privy Council stated that the legislative power of the Commonwealth did not extend to criminal law as that lay within the competence of the States. As High Court Justice Lionel Murphy pointed out, that statement was completely wrong as thousands of people were convicted every year of offences against the Commonwealth *Crimes Act*. He also pointed out that under the Constitution the Privy Council had no authority to make any judgment on the respective powers of the Commonwealth and the States.

The Commonwealth Parliament and the States slowly implemented legislative changes that cut the range of matters that could be appealed from the High Court and State courts to the Privy Council culminating in the ultimate blockage of all such appeals in the *Australia Acts*. Two years later, in 1988, the Federal Parliament passed legislation that specifically recognised that the common law of England no longer necessarily applied in Australia. Since then the courts, led by the High Court, have been developing what is referred to in federal legislation as the common law of Australia.

These changes coincided with enormous changes in the court system, particularly at the federal level. Through the 1960s and 1970s, successive federal governments of all political persuasions struggled with proposals to establish a federal court below the level of the High Court and equivalent in status to the State Supreme Courts. At that time, other than the High Court with its seven Justices, there was a single federal judge who dealt with bankruptcy and a number of judges of the Australian Industrial Court (later called the Australian Conciliation and Arbitration Commission). But governments were in no hurry to create a federal superior court as had been advocated by Liberal Attorney-General (and later High Court Chief Justice) Sir Garfield Barwick. One reason for hesitating, according to Chief Justice Murray Gleeson, was that the Constitution at that time required all federal judges to have lifetime appointments.[2] This remained the case until 1977 when a referendum changed the Constitution to impose an age limit of 70 on (new) federal judges. Before that occurred, however, the Commonwealth created first the Family Court, with jurisdiction under the *Family Law Act 1975*, and then the Federal Court, initially with responsibility for the *Trade Practices Act 1974*.

The creation of new federal courts and major changes in the States meant that the legal-judicial landscape is radically different at the beginning of the 21st century from what it was a generation earlier. As Chief Justice Gleeson has pointed out, while in the 20 years to 2003 Australia's population increased by one-third, the size of the NSW District Court increased by 63 per cent and that of the Queensland District Court by 71 per cent.[3] All told, the number of judges of State and Territory Supreme Courts and the main federal courts increased during this period by 184 to 248. The judiciary, including magistrates totalled just under 1000. Chief Justice Gleeson says, 'The judiciary, as an institution, is rapidly becoming larger and more diverse'.

Figure 5.1: Major Australian courts: appeals progress up the various links

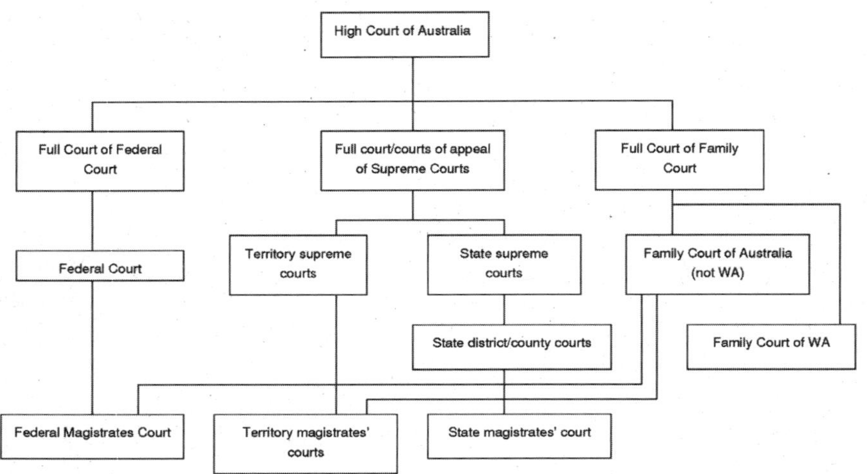

Source: Adapted from Steering Committee for the Review of Government Service Provision 2005.

One recent change is the creation by the Federal Government of a new court, of federal magistrates, that does 40 per cent of the family law work, most bankruptcy cases and also deals with hundreds of immigration cases each year. The Federal Magistrates Court began operating in 2000, with 16 magistrates. By 2006 there were 35 magistrates and in 2004-2005 they dealt with more than 77,000 cases. Chief Justice Gleeson says he expects that within 20 years it will become the largest court in Australia and he questions how much longer federal criminal offences will be tried in State courts rather than in the federal court system. He expects that will change in his lifetime.[4]

The standing of the courts

In 1994 a senior Queensland barrister, Ian Callinan QC, described the High Court as 'an over-mighty Court'.[5] In 2002 Dyson Heydon QC, a judge of the NSW Court of Appeal, described some High Court Justices as 'our new philosopher-kings and enlightened despots' and accused the High Court, under its former Chief Justice Sir Anthony Mason, as 'tending to treat itself as another legislature even though it was not chosen by the people'.[6] Callinan and Heydon were each rewarded for their attacks on judicial activism: the Howard Government appointed both of them to the High Court, Callinan in 1998, Heydon in February 2003. They were two of five Justices appointed by the Howard Government (to 2006) all of whom satisfied the promise made by Deputy Prime Minister Tim Fischer that the Coalition Government would appoint three 'capital C conservatives' to the High Court. (He was not to know the Howard Government would be able to make appointments to replace five of the seven members of the High Court.)

One of the main reasons the Howard Government wanted to change the 'political' composition of the court was its disapproval of the decision in the *Mabo* case in 1992,[7] when the High Court recognised (for the first time in Australia) the existence of native title under the common law. Conservative lawyers had long been critical of the approach of the 'liberal' High Court under Chief Justice Sir Anthony Mason (1987-1995) and Sir Gerard Brennan (1995-1998) complaining of their willingness to deliberately alter the law in areas such as the law of negligence, criminal law and defamation (by recognising an implied constitutional freedom of communication).[8] Heydon put together in his *Quadrant* article the fundamental criticisms of these critics, namely that the High Court had strayed from the doctrine of 'strict and complete legalism' enunciated by a former Chief Justice, Sir Owen Dixon. He described Mason as 'amongst the greatest innovators' on the High Court, a term he clearly did not mean to be flattering. He said judicial activism badly impaired two qualities required by judges – a firm grip on the applicable law and total probity, and said this tended to be destructive of the rule of law. In contrast to activism, Justice Heydon praised the doctrine of precedent as 'a safeguard against arbitrary, whimsical, capricious, unpredictable and autocratic decision-making'. He said the more courts freely changed the law, the more the public would come to view their function as political, and the more they would be open to vigorous and direct public attack on political grounds, and the greater would be demand for public hearings into the politics of judicial candidates.

Sir Anthony Mason responded to some of his critics, including Heydon, in a speech about the approaching centenary of the High Court.[9] He said the form of legalism being advocated by critics was 'not an approach considered acceptable by other common law jurisdictions'. He quoted Lord Bingham, then England's senior Law Lord, as saying that legalism had little support today because judges knew from experience that the cases that came before them could not always be decided by what had been decided previously and that the higher the court, the more the decisions they had to make involving issues of policy. Sir Anthony said law, whether made by judges or legislators, had to be adapted to the needs of society and that must be the ultimate criterion by which good law was differentiated from bad law.

Despite this formidable debate, it appeared the change in the conservative composition of the High Court made relatively little difference to the outcome of many cases, or even to the court's general approach. Michael McHugh, who was first appointed to the High Court when Sir Anthony Mason became Chief Justice, and who retired after serving on the Mason, Brennan and (for another seven years) Gleeson courts, believes it is correct to say, as Professor Leslie Zines has written, that there has been no discernible break in the judicial method applied by the majority in the Gleeson, Brennan and Mason courts.[10] He says what made the Mason court different from its predecessors was 'an attitude of mind'. This attitude:

> was the belief that Australia was now an independent nation whose political, legal and economic underpinnings had recently and essentially changed. These developments … required a different approach to the interpretation of the Constitution and a different approach to judging, generally. Strict legalism was no longer an efficient tool for interpreting a Constitution or deciding private or public law cases – assuming strict legalism ever really applied in practice and was not simply a piece of judicial rhetoric.[11]

In another speech McHugh explained:

> The reality is that the High Court is regularly required to determine private law issues that the legislature has not explicitly or directly regulated, whether by choice, practical inability or neglect. When the court does so, it frequently engages in a well-established function of making or developing the law, within principled constraints. In doing so, the High Court exercises a widely recognised and accepted authority to depart from long-standing precedent, whether its own or the previously applied authorities of overseas jurisdictions. Indeed, even those who take a conservative view of the court's function recognise that, as 'the keystone of the federal arch' it is entirely legitimate for the High Court to change the law from time to time.[12]

McHugh said:

> From time to time, individual judges and judgments are criticised – sometimes trenchantly – but overall the public has confidence in the judiciary as an institution. That must be so. Otherwise, chaos would long ago have overwhelmed the societies that make up the common law world. Because this public confidence exists, legislatures and executive officials cannot ignore the binding judgments of the judiciary. If they wish to overrule those judgments, they must do so by engaging the democratic process and enacting public legislation that is within the constitutional powers of the relevant legislature.[13]

In recent years the Federal Government has occasionally indulged in a process of court bashing and has also tried to change the law to silence, or at least sideline, some of the courts it has criticised.

Former Immigration Minister Philip Ruddock was a severe critic of the role of the Federal Court in immigration and refugee cases. He persuaded the Parliament to change the law to remove the Federal Court's power to deal with most of these cases, and to reduce the power of the High Court. However decisions of the High Court, relying on its constitutional power to review all decisions of the executive government and determine whether they are lawful, effectively reduced the impact of Mr Ruddock's proposals on that court's role.

While Justice McHugh thought continued criticism of judges by the executive government was likely to diminish the authority of the courts and public confidence in the integrity and impartiality of judges, Chief Justice Murray Gleeson is less concerned. 'Confidence is not maintained by stifling legitimate criticism of courts or of their decisions'. He says there has never been a golden age of media respect for the judiciary and we live in an age when the attitude of the general community towards authority and institutions, is more questioning and even challenging than in the past:

> Those who are alarmed by what appears to them to be an increase in criticism of, and complaints about, judges may have a somewhat romantic idea about what occurred in former times. They may also be missing a fairly obvious explanation. It may not be that the public is more cantankerous, or that judges are less disciplined. It may simply be that there are now many more judges.[14]

Former Federal Attorney-General Michael Lavarch, who became Dean of Law at the Queensland University of Technology, says he believes the standing of both political and judicial institutions has been diminished in recent years. He says:[15]

> What is new compared to a few decades ago is the same feature that is impacting on all institutions – the immediacy of communications and news reporting. In my view there is a greater emphasis on sensational reporting of the way courts operate and a blurring of the distinction between the political, judicial and governmental arms. Politicians feel less constrained in their criticism of the courts than may have been the case in the past. Governments and individual politicians have been prepared to belt judges when there's a political advantage in doing so, and I think there has been a drop in respect for the institution. Mind you, you'd be struggling to find an institution that hasn't suffered in the public view – legal institutions, churches, trade unions, business, the banks and politics and government.

Former Chief Justice Sir Anthony Mason claims that the public takes with a grain of salt what politicians say about judges.[16] But he says 'there is always a risk that what a politician says adverse to the judiciary reinforces some prejudice that some members of the public may have against the judges or the court system or the legal system generally'. His impression is that there is less respect for the courts now than there was a generation ago:

> One of the criticisms I would make of politicians is that in their desire to make political electoral points they have damaged the standing of the institutions of this country – and I don't confine this to the judiciary – in the eyes of the public. The consequences of that for any community are extremely damaging because the strength and the spirit of any community depend very much on the contribution that its institutions are making and the respect in which they are held by the community.

Appointing judges

In Australia, Federal Government and State Governments, usually on the recommendations of their Attorneys-General, have sole responsibility for the appointment of judges and magistrates in their respective courts. The Federal Attorney-General is required by law to 'consult' with the States when appointments to the High Court are being considered, but this invariably takes the form of the Commonwealth merely asking the States whether they have anyone they wish to be considered when the Federal Government is making the appointment. All appointments normally involve the relevant Attorney-General consulting the judicial head of the court where the appointment is to be made, together with the leaders of the Bar Association and Law Society, though if an appointment of an academic or government lawyer is planned, this practice may not be followed.

In the United States federal judges are selected by the President, but have to be confirmed by a vote of the Senate. Confirmation is by no means an automatic process and is sometimes withheld. The process leading to a Senate vote is often exhausting and embarrassing for nominees who are questioned in extraordinary detail about their past record and future intentions. Many of the American

States have equivalent procedures, though others require judges to be elected by the people.

Britain changed its system of choosing judges in 2006-2007. Before the passing of the *Constitutional Reform Act 2005*, judges were selected by the Lord Chancellor, who was both a member of the Cabinet and head of the judiciary. Under the new system the Lord Chancellor ceased to be a judge and a new Judicial Appointments Committee became responsible for all judicial appointments after a brief phase-in period. The Commission comprises an independent chair, four judges, one tribunal member, one lay justice, a barrister and a solicitor, and five lay members.

In 1993 a proposal by Australian Attorney-General Michael Lavarch to introduce a far less radical scheme – a commission that would simply act as a consultative body with the appointment power remaining with the government – was overwhelmingly rejected by his cabinet colleagues:

> The proposal was never that the decision would be taken from the executive government' he says. 'It was about institutionalising the consultation process and removing the perception that the executive might simply be appointing only on the basis of relationship of favourites from a party-political point of view. It was just to ensure there always were candidates of obvious merit who were being chosen between. I don't have any issue at all with the executive making the choice for a court, if all the standards you require in a judge are met. There's always a pool of people who on any objective criteria are considered appropriate for appointment – it might be five or six, or it might be smaller for the High Court. If you've got the pool, then it is perfectly appropriate for the executive to say, 'we think the court is deficient in a particular field' or 'I'm a centralist not a federalist' or 'I want a capital C conservative'.[17]

A dozen and more years later Australian judges, through their national body, the Judicial Conference of Australia, began considering adopting a policy on appointments, possibly prompted by and similar to the new English system. But most senior judges appear to support something like the present Australian method of appointment provided there is some form of independent commission that could provide advice on candidates to the government. However Chief Justice Murray Gleeson has expressed scepticism about the possibility of the government giving any real power to anyone else:

> You would have to ask to whom would they give the power? Who would be appointed to this body? It is one thing to say the executive, the Attorney-General, the Prime Minister ought to consult with different people, including people such as myself, different state governments and so forth. It is another thing to say that they ought to hand over the power to somebody else'.[18]

NSW Chief Justice Jim Spigelman says he would not be in favour of a judicial commission dominated by judges. 'There is no reason to believe anywhere in Australia we have a problem with this'.[19]

The question of judicial diversity

How appointments should be made is one issue. A separate but associated issue concerns who should be appointed. In Australia then Attorney-General Michael Lavarch sparked a major debate in legal circles when he questioned in 1993 whether judges should be more 'representative' of society. That was a shorthand way of suggesting there should be more women and people from minority groups appointed as judges. At the time he raised the issue there were only four women on the Supreme Courts of all of the States and Territories, with none in Victoria, Western Australia, Tasmania or the ACT. Including federal courts, almost 90 per cent of Australian judges were Anglo-Saxon or Celtic men who had been educated at private schools, practised as barristers, were former leaders of the Bar, and had been appointed to the bench in their early 50s. Lavarch suggested this indicated some bias in the selection process, or at least a failure to identify suitable women and people of different ethnic backgrounds as candidates for judicial office. Lavarch proposed there should be a new appointments system that would have three aims:

- ensure all appointees were of the highest possible calibre;
- identify a broader field of candidates so that women, Aboriginal and Torres Strait Islanders and members of other groups that were underrepresented in the judiciary would not be overlooked; and

- making the appointment process visible and comprehensive and by so doing increase public confidence in the judiciary.

At the time, the legal establishment was near-unanimous in its rejection of what the Attorney-General was proposing. John Mansfield QC, then president of the Law Council of Australia, described the concept of a representative judiciary as 'fundamentally dangerous' and said it should be rejected as inconsistent with judicial independence. Former Chief Justice of the High Court Sir Harry Gibbs described the proposals as nonsense and a 'heresy'. One of the few to express any support was High Court Chief Justice, Sir Anthony Mason, who told the Australian Legal Convention that it would be desirable for the judiciary to reflect the composition of the community to a greater extent.

Attorney-General Lavarch's proposals were rejected by the Keating Cabinet. However their spirit was accepted and put in place over the next decade by all State and Territory governments, and slowly also by the Commonwealth. It became common through the late 1990s for women to be appointed to senior judicial positions. By 2006 around half the appointments being made to the bench in most States were women, and slowly the character of the courts was changing. Queensland embraced the policy more quickly than the other States and as a result by 2005 around 30 per cent of the members of the Supreme Court were women. In other States in 2005 about one in six judges were women and the same proportion applies on the Federal Court. However by 2006 one in three judges on the Family Court was a woman and one in every four of the federal magistrates was female.

Most appointments to the bench still come from the ranks of barristers but it became far more common at the beginning of the 21st century for appointments to be made from other branches of the legal profession, including solicitors, government advisors and academic lawyers.

Many of these changes were resisted by the senior ranks of the profession, particularly at the Bar, but also by the judiciary. Former Queensland Attorney-General Matt Foley, who appointed 20 women and 15 men to the judiciary in a three-year period, says the 'old boys club' at the Bar 'could cope with one or two female appointments – token appointments – but when it became apparent that this was more than just a token effort, then the gloves came off and we had to have a skirmish'.[20] He says there was also resistance from the bench.

The positive discrimination in favour of women judges in this period is to be contrasted with the direct discrimination against women in the legal profession in earlier times. Before his retirement in 2004, High Court Justice Michael McHugh said discrimination against women lawyers had been 'rife throughout the 43 years I have been a member of the legal profession. In my early days at the Bar, discrimination was mainly direct and overt. Today I suspect it is mainly indirect'.[21] He said he first encountered the discrimination when he sold his chambers to move from one floor of barristers to another. The chambers were bought by Mary Gaudron:

> She had won the University Medal for Law, had worked for a middle-sized firm of solicitors and was on her way to becoming the greatest female lawyer that the legal profession of this country has yet produced. Unbelievably, the Floor I was leaving refused to accept her as a member.

He said the discriminatory, systemic and structural practices in the legal profession that prevented female advocates from getting the same opportunities as men had been well-documented in recent years. He pointed out that for many years women constituted about 50 per cent of graduates from Australian law schools and their academic results showed, if anything, that they were superior to male graduates. The discrimination against women meant that they were at a disadvantage in competing on merit for judicial positions.

His call for a woman to be appointed to the High Court when he retired was answered when the Howard Government appointed Susan Crennan in 2005. The only other woman to have served on the High Court was Mary Gaudron, from 1987 to 2003.

The idea of encouraging judicial diversity has also taken hold in Britain where the Lord Chancellor, the Lord Chief Justice and the Chair of the new Judicial appointments Commission have adopted a formal policy strategy to encourage a wider range of applicants for judicial positions and to promote diversity through fair and open processes for selection. As is customary, the policy insists that appointment is on merit.

Juries

The criminal justice system in Australia is downgrading and marginalising the role of juries. In all States the number of criminal cases dealt with by magistrates and intermediate courts sitting alone without a jury is increasing. In some States defendants can elect to be tried by a Supreme Court judge without a jury and juries in some States can deliver majority verdicts though not where federal charges are involved (for example, drug offences under the Commonwealth *Crimes Act*). Supreme Courts normally hear only the most serious charges, such as murder.

In 2004-2005 criminal courts throughout Australia dealt with almost three-quarters of a million charges. Only 4782 came before Supreme Courts, while 24,515 were determined in District or County Courts. The remainder – about 96 per cent of all criminal charges – were heard in magistrates or children's courts where juries are never used.[22] One reason for dealing with criminal charges in the lower courts is cost. The price of justice is smaller, the lower the court in the hierarchical system. In Queensland, which has one of the lowest cost structures, the net expenditure by the State in finalising a criminal charge in the magistrates court averages about $294, in the District Court about $4270 and in the Supreme Court about $5158. Nationally, the average cost in the magistrates court is $365, in the District or County Court $5892 and in the Supreme Court $12,946.

Incentives are provided for offenders to opt for trial before magistrates rather than juries. In most States, magistrates can only send an offender to prison for a maximum of two or three years though the crime might carry a 10 or 15 year maximum sentence if tried by a judge and jury. Normally the prosecution rather than the defendant decides whether the matter should be dealt with summarily (that is, by a magistrate). However there are some situations where the choice is given to the person being charged.

Juries are also used far less in civil matters. The new uniform defamation laws, for example, reduce the role juries normally play and gives to the judge alone the power to determine damages.

Technology has forced the authorities to adopt new rules to try to prevent jurors from using the Internet to discover, for example, whether a person has prior convictions and to discourage them from conducting other investigations. Judges are also concerned to ensure that jurors have not been exposed to prejudicial publicity in the media, or not affected by it.

The trend away from jury trials has not been universally welcomed. NSW Chief Justice Jim Spigelman says it is a problem for the standing of the courts when fewer members of the community participate in the justice system through their service on a jury. He says juries used to be a very important part of the interface between the community and the courts. 'Virtually everyone had the experience, often more than once, of detailed exposure to the administration of justice. That is no longer the case'.[23]

Self-represented litigants

The greatest contemporary challenge for Australian courts is a huge increase in unrepresented litigants over the past 20 or so years. According to the Queensland Chief Justice, Paul de Jersey, unrepresented litigants are having a significant impact on all courts, but particularly on appellate courts in the States.[24] In the High Court around one-third of all cases involve unrepresented litigants but the problem is being contained as a result of changes in court procedures. In 2006, partly in response to the disruptive effect of unrepresented litigants, the High Court introduced a new system of dealing with applications for special leave to appeal. These can now be rejected after an examination of the relevant papers by a panel of two judges once the Chief Justice has ruled that the application has insufficient merit. If an oral hearing is approved, unrepresented litigants – as with all others – are limited to just 20 minutes to present their case.

In 2001 the Australian Institute of Judicial Administration conducted a major study of litigants in person. It found that in the Family Court litigants in person were:

- more likely than the population as a whole to have a limited formal education, limited income and assets and have no paid employment; and
- that a significant number of them were dysfunctional serial litigants.[25]

It found that many litigants in person chose to be self-represented. Their reasons included suspicion and resentment towards the legal profession, the opportunity to use the court as a soap box to air grievances, the belief that they did not need a lawyer to present their case and the perception that there may be an advantage in being self-represented.

Chief Justice de Jersey says all these positions 'are completely misguided'.[26] He says self-represented litigants 'are often blinded by an intractable commitment to the rightness of their cause and display an obsessional attention to peripheral detail. They lack an objective view of legal and factual reality'.[27] He says that while the right to represent oneself in court proceedings is fundamental to accessible justice, in many instances exercising that right will inevitably reduce the chance of obtaining justice:

> Without legal training you will struggle to identify the issue and lack the capacity to present it. You will depend largely on the judge for help. But the judge will have to be circumspect to avoid a charge of unequal treatment.

Justice de Jersey says the percentage of unrepresented litigants in the Queensland Court of Appeal between 2001-2004 had been approximately 30 to 35 per cent. In the Supreme Court about one in six litigants was self-represented while in the District Court the figure was one in 14.

He says unrepresented litigants pose unique challenges:

> How far does one go to accommodate them without disadvantaging the represented party, for example. How far does one give them advice without compromising one's independence as the adjudicator? It is a very difficult situation. Of course the judge must be patient but that patience is sorely tried, frequently in these situations and a betrayal of irritation very often will feed a contention that the judge is biased. Even more important than that, the litigant in person will leave the court with a felling that he or she has not been given a fair hearing and that is always the ultimate judicial challenge,

> to have the losing party leave the court saying, 'at least I was given a fair hearing'.[28]

High Court Chief Justice Murray Gleeson says in his court the pressure on judges from self-represented litigants is not so great because oral arguments on special leave applications are limited to 20 minutes. However there is a greater burden on registry staff who have to give substantial assistance to many unrepresented litigants and monitor the progress of their cases.[29]

Administrative justice

Since 1975 the Commonwealth and States have established a series of tribunals that along with the courts review administrative decisions by governments. The first of these, the Commonwealth's Administrative Appeals Tribunal, has jurisdiction to review decisions made by public servants under more than 400 Acts of Parliament, covering such areas as social security and veterans entitlements, bankruptcy and broadcasting licences.[30] At the Commonwealth level these tribunals review the merits of particular decisions while courts such as the Federal Court and the High Court may review their legality.

The States also have networks of tribunals, in some cases with specialised jurisdictions reviewing decisions of a particular department. In South Australia and Tasmania administrative review is undertaken by a special division of the existing courts. However three States have established generalist tribunals with both original and review jurisdictions, and can adjudicate disputes in such areas as consumer affairs, trading and tenancy. In Victoria this tribunal is called the Victorian Civil and Administrative Tribunal, in New South Wales it is the Administrative Decisions Tribunal and in Western Australia the State Administrative Tribunal. These State tribunals operate in some areas which at the Commonwealth level can only be exercised by the courts, because of the strict separation of judicial power required under the Constitution. At the State level, there has been some criticism of the encroachment by tribunals of judicial power. Victorian Chief Justice Marilyn Warren has questioned whether it is desirable for matters historically decided by a judge now to be determined by a member of a tribunal who may lack legal qualifications or experience:

> Doubtless the tribunal approach represents speed, efficiency, economy and expertise … it may even provide 'feel-good justice', but does it offer full independence from the executive government of the day? Does it offer legal certainty? Does it offer that oft-quoted principle – the rule of law?[31]

Pressure on the system

The law – criminal, civil and administrative – is becoming increasingly complex. Every year the Commonwealth and State Parliament add many thousands of pages to the statute books, and executive governments proclaim a similar volume of regulations. Courts and tribunals are being expanded at a rapid rate, to cope with a vast increase in the volume of work thrust on them. The judicial system is becoming more 'representative' – but not democratic – as an increasing number of women are appointed as judges and magistrates. Cost pressures are resulting in justice being delivered at lower and lower levels in the judicial system, in both criminal and civil matters, and that trend seems certain to continue. The challenge for the system is to prevent the quality of justice being eroded.

Notes

1 Solomon 1999: 171-174.
2 Gleeson 2005.
3 Gleeson 2004.
4 Gleeson 2005.
5 Callinan 1994.
6 Heydon 2003: 9-22.
7 *Mabo v Queensland (No 2)* (1992) 175 CLR 1.
8 Heydon 2003: 16.
9 Mason 2003.
10 McHugh 2004a: 2; Zines 2000: 231.
11 McHugh 2004a: 13-14.
12 McHugh 2004b: 4. The conservative judges he referred to are Justices Heydon and Hayne.
13 McHugh 2004b: 6.
14 Gleeson 2005.
15 Lavarch 2005.
16 Mason 2005.

17 Lavarch 2005.
18 Gleeson 2006: 61.
19 Spigelman 2005.
20 Foley 2005.
21 McHugh 2004c.
22 Productivity Commission 2006b.
23 Spigelman 2005.
24 de Jersey 2005.
25 AIJA 2001.
26 de Jersey 2003: 7.
27 de Jersey 2003: 1.
28 de Jersey 2005.
29 Gleeson 2005.
30 Downs 2006. Also, see *Reform* Issue 84 – 'Tribunals', 2004, Australian Law Reform Commission.
31 Warren 2004: 6-7.

6

Defence and security

Launching the Coalition Government's formal national counter-terrorism policy in 2004, Prime Minister John Howard said, 'The attacks on the World Trade Center and the Pentagon on September 11, 2001 introduced a new and confronting dimension to the international security environment'.[1] The document acknowledged that terrorism as a weapon is not new – 'It is a tactic of the militarily weak in which terrorist groups deliberately target non-combatants'.

Terrorism as a mode of attacking and attempting to undermine, destabilise and even overthrow the established order has a history of several thousand years. It has been practised unrelentingly in modern times – until recently in Britain by the Irish Republican Army, in Spain by the Basque independence movement ETA, in Sri Lanka by the Tamil Tigers, in the Philippines by Muslim separatists and in a number of countries in Africa and South America. But '9/11', as it is known in the United States, was different in many ways, but not least in the responses that it produced in the US, which unleashed a real war against the Taliban in Afghanistan (which was closely associated with Al Qaeda) and then against the Government of Saddam Hussein in Iraq (that in part justified by Iraq's alleged links with Al Qaeda and international terrorism). Australia was directly affected by the actions of the US, joining in both those military actions. Prime

Minister Howard was in Washington at the time of the 9/11 attacks, and immediately signalled Australia's commitment to be an ally in the 'war on terror' by invoking the ANZUS pact (see Chapter 12).

The decision to participate in the 'war on terror' had significant consequences for Australia's defence and security forces. Initially, the government committed itself to substantially increasing the strength of its domestic and international security services and the Australian Federal Police. It also decided over a period of several years on changes to the Australian Defence Force (ADF), affecting both the equipment that would be made available to it and the composition of the forces, particularly of the army. These came with the adoption by the government of a new strategic assessment: that 'for the foreseeable future, the major threats to Australia are more likely to come from terrorists and international criminals than from conventional military attack'.[2] The nature of the changes can be seen in the formal policy documents, the *Defence White Paper* of 2000 that preceded the terrorist attacks on the US on 11 September 2001 and on Bali on 12 October 2002, and the two subsequent *Updates* on the *White Paper* that the government issued, the first in 2003, the second in 2005, and in some of the subsequent decisions affecting the composition of the ADF, particularly the 2006 proposal to expand the army.

In the 2000 *White Paper* Defence Minister John Moore said:

> Australia's most important long-term strategic objective is to ensure the defence of Australia and its direct approaches. Our second strategic objective is to foster the security of our immediate neighbourhood ... Our third strategic objective is to work with others to promote stability and cooperation in Southeast Asia ... Our fourth strategic objective is to contribute in appropriate ways to maintaining strategic stability in the wider Asia Pacific region ... Our fifth strategic objective is to contribute to the efforts of the international community, especially the United Nations, to uphold global security. We will continue to support the United States in the major role it plays in maintaining and strengthening the global security order.[3]

The *Defence Update 2003* said 'Compared with 2000, the significance of the global strategic and security environment for Australia's defence and security has become much more evident'. In releasing the 2005 *Defence Update*, the then Defence Minister Robert Hill said it 'highlights the longer-term trends associated with the impacts of globalisation and changing relationships between the major powers of our region'.[4] One striking statement in the 2005 *Defence Update* is its opening statement, 'The first duty of the Australian Government is to provide for the security and defence of Australia and Australian interests'. As Mark Thomson, Program Director, budget and management, at the Australian Strategic Policy Institute observed, there is a striking difference between this statement and what was said almost 30 years earlier at the beginning of the Fraser Government's *1976 Defence White Paper*, 'The first responsibility of government is to provide the nation with security from armed attack and from the constraints on independent national decisions imposed by the threat of such attack'.[5] Thomson says the differences between these two statements say a lot about how things have changed over the years and where policy sits today. He says three things stand out:

> First, armed attack no longer warrants an explicit mention. This is not simply a matter of wording. The main body of *Defence Update 2005* only briefly talks about the territorial defence of Australia in its introduction and conclusion, and nowhere in between. In fact, the *Update* reassures us that for the foreseeable future it remains unlikely that Australians will face "conventional threats". What used to be the overriding focus of Australia's strategic policy has – in the view of the *Update* – been relegated to little more than a perfunctory aside. In its place is a pair of competing priorities: Australia's role in the immediate region and its interests further afield on the global stage.
>
> Second, security and defence rate separate and equal mention in the opening to the *Update*. In the sense they are used, they imply the equal importance of defending against traditional military threats and securing against non-traditional threats like terrorism, trans-national crime, drug smuggling and unauthorised border crossing. Of course, one of the key features in recent years has been the melding between these two areas. This has seen an increasing whole-of-government response to many security problems and the involvement of the Australian Defence Force (ADF) in humanitarian assistance, domestic security and offshore Federal Police operations.
>
> Third, in today's world it's not just Australia that needs to be defended (and secured) but also Australia's *interests*. Indeed, if the *Update* has a theme it's 'Australian interests' – a forgivingly malleable term that can and does mean many things. At the very least it includes the safety of Australians abroad and, to some extent, our

> various overseas economic, political, trade and financial relationships. More generally, the *Update* argues that our security interests are global and says that 'Australia's vital interests are inextricably linked to the achievement of peace and security in the Middle East'.
>
> Whatever Australia's interests might be, two clearly stand out in understanding our recent military endeavours: the alliance with the US and the security of our local region.[6]

He says that what has changed in the past 30 years is that both the US and the immediate region are more demanding than at any time since the 1960s:

> In response, Australia is undertaking the most comprehensive and expensive military build-up since the mid-1960s. This has two threads: first, the force structure is being modernised and expanded; and second, the preparedness of the ADF for rapid deployment is being steadily improved along with its capacity for strategic mobility. What's more, the ADF is being used more often and in more diverse theatres than at any time over the past five decades.[7]

When the Howard Government was elected in 1996, it engaged in a major cost-cutting exercise from which only one major expenditure area was spared – defence. In its 2000 *White Paper* the government delivered to defence a promise for a 3 per cent annual increase in real spending for the next 10 years. The 2005 *Defence Update* extended that commitment for a further 5 years. The government agreed to several significant equipment purchases for the ADF that were additional to the agreed Budget including, for example, a decision in 2006 to buy four C-17 Globemaster III transport aircraft (each with four times the capacity of existing Hercules aircraft, and considerably faster) at a cost of $2.2 billion. The aircraft and an earlier commitment to developing a 'hardened and networked Army' (HNA) at a cost of $1.5 billion were taken with a view to the ADF working on a global scale in support of its US ally.

Defence spending

Australia's spending on defence this century has hovered around 1.9 per cent of Gross Domestic Product (GDP). To put this in context: the United States and Russia spend (respectively) 4.2 and 4.4 per cent of GDP on defence, Israel, Singapore and North Korea more than 8 per cent, while China, India, Pakistan and Indonesia all spend over 3 per cent of GDP. In absolute terms and measured in US dollars, Australia's defence budget is considerably greater than that of Indonesia and other Asian neighbours: Australia spends $US11.4 million, Singapore $US8.6 million, Indonesia $US7.6 million, Malaysia $US2.3 million and Thailand $US1.9 million. However Australia's armed forces, at just over 50,000, are dwarfed by those of many of its neighbours: Indonesia, 302,000, Malaysia, the Philippines and Singapore, each in excess of 100,000.[8] But as Thomson points out, Australia 'as a country with no land borders and no prospective adversaries with an amphibious capacity' does not need to develop a large, manpower-intensive land force.[9]

The state of the ADF

The changed strategic circumstances since 9/11 made little impact on the size of the Australian Defence Forces but greatly affected the way it was organised and deployed. In conventional terms as at mid-2006 the ADF included just over 50,000 full-time military personnel, of whom just under half were in the Army, with the remainder divided almost equally between the Air Force and the Navy. A further 19,000 people were in the reserve forces and in addition the Defence Department employed more than 17,000 civilians.[10] The number of full-time servicemen and women fell during the 1990s from around 70,000 while the number of civilians also fell, by about 8000. Numbers in the ADF also fell slightly in the years after 2003, with all services having shortages in specific skill categories.

The Army included three infantry battalions, a mechanised infantry battalion, two field artillery regiments, two cavalry regiments and an armoured regiment together with special operations groups including an SAS regiment and a commando regiment. It also had an air defence regiment and three regional surveillance units based in northern Australia manned mainly by reservists. The Army also had two aviation regiments with 35 Black Hawk helicopters, 42 Kiowa light observation helicopters and six Chinook medium lift helicopters.

Three months after the 2006 Budget was delivered the government announced that a further $10 billion would be spent over an 11-year period establishing two new battalions, involving the recruitment of an additional 2600 soldiers. The first would be manned by 2008 and be ready for overseas deployment two years later.[11]

The Navy had five guided missile frigates, and six ANZAC Class frigates (with two further ANZAC Class frigates due for delivery by 2007. It had 16 Seahawk helicopters capable of operating from these ships, together with six Sea King helicopters and other helicopters used for training. It had six Collins Class submarines, two sea-going tankers, nine landing ships, mine-sweepers, more than a dozen patrol boats and several hydrographic ships.

The Air Force had 22 operational F-111 strike aircraft and four reconnaissance versions of the F-111, all due to be retired by 2010. It had 71 F/A-18 Hornet fighters and 33 jet trainers. It operated 19 Orion maritime patrol aircraft and more than 30 transport aircraft, together with four Boeing 707 aircraft used for air-to-air refuelling.

In mid-2006 around 4200 ADF personnel were engaged in overseas operations with another 300 involved in security operations in the Australian maritime protection zone.[12] Around 1400 were in Iraq, 310 in Afghanistan (to increase to around 500 later in 2006), 2200 in East Timor (of whom about 1000 were scheduled for withdrawal in August 2006 and 140 in the Solomons (supporting the Australian-led Regional Assistance Mission to the Solomon Islands – RAMSI). The ADF also sent 120 personnel to the Lebanon in July-August 2006 to help evacuate Australian nationals. There were smaller numbers of ADF personnel in such places as the Middle East, supporting UN missions, Sinai and the Sudan.

The missions covering Iraq and Afghanistan were a major part of the government's response to what it called the threat of terrorism and countering the proliferation of weapons of mass destruction. The total cost of the Australian commitment to Iraq, from 2003 to the middle of 2007 was officially estimated at $1.6 billion, and of the Afghanistan action which began in 2002, $840 million.[13] Decisions by the government on new equipment such as the acquisition of the fleet of Globemaster aircraft were intended to enhance this global strategic role for the ADF as well as providing support for regional operations. Other major re-equipment decisions included a commitment to a new strike aircraft, the yet-to-be built F-35 Joint Strike Fighter. The government decided in 2002 it was prepared to spend at least $15 billion to replace the RAAF's F-111s and F/A-18 Hornets with up to 100 F-35s. The RAAF was to acquire in 2006-2007 six Wedgetail airborne early warning and control aircraft and was due to buy five A330 air refueller tanker/transport aircraft to replace its Boeing 707s. The Navy is also to get three Air Warfare Destroyers at a cost of at least $6 billion. The government was due to decide on the design of the destroyers in 2007, intending for them to commence service in 2013. The Navy will also get two large amphibious ships, the first in 2012. The government decided to buy 59 (second-hand) Abrams tanks – the standard tank used by the US Army – for $550 million. The first of these tanks were due in service in 2007. The Army will also get replacements for its ageing Black Hawk helicopters, in a $5 billion project that will include at least 28 Eurocopter MRH90s, the first by the end of 2007.

Thomson describes this as:

> [Australia's] most comprehensive and expensive military build-up since the mid-1960s. This has two threads: first, the force structure is being modernised and expanded, and second, the preparedness of the ADF for rapid deployment is being steadily improved along with its capacity for strategic mobility. What's more, the ADF is now being used more often and in more diverse theatres than at any time over the past five decades.[14]

The re-equipment of the ADF has not gone smoothly in recent years – if it ever did. Controversy raged over the Hawke Government's decision to build the Oberon Class submarines in Australia, and that did not abate until all were in operation. It was the same story with the Menzies Government's decision in the 1960s to buy and have modified for Australian requirements the then untested F-111. Indeed controversy seems to be ignited every time a government decides not to buy off-the-shelf defence equipment, and sometimes when it does (as occurred when the Howard Government decided to buy reconditioned and updated Abrams tanks for the Army). One of the major equipment failures of the Howard Government was its decision to buy 11 Seasprite helicopters to operate from the Anzac frigates. The aircraft were old technology and needed to be fitted with modern technology to be operationally useful, at a total cost of $1 billion. However the contractors had problems delivering the product specified, and after 10 years the Minister for Defence was weighing up whether to abandon the whole project (despite its cost) or pay even more money to get helicopters that did not fully meet operational requirements. The Defence Department also had problems with upgrading its AP-3C maritime reconnaissance Orion aircraft. The job was completed, but four years late. It was a similar story with the upgrade of technology for the guided missile frigates – that took more than two years longer than scheduled – and a half a billion dollar upgrade of most of the Army's M113 armoured personnel carriers – also running about two years late. And once equipment is obtained, its not always properly maintained. In 2006 the Auditor-General reported that of the $2 billion worth of bombs, missiles and ammunition held by the ADF, $1.04 billion worth of that ordnance was not 'serviceable', and at least $300 million worth was unfixable.

The intelligence build-up

Australia's major security and intelligence organisations were the major beneficiaries of the Government's response to 9/11. While spending on the ADF increased at the three per cent rate determined by the *2000 Defence White Paper*, spending on the major intelligence organisations increased quite dramatically. The Australian Security and Intelligence Organisation (ASIO), responsible for domestic intelligence, had its budget boosted by almost 400 per cent over five years. The Office of National Assessments (ONA) had a 300 per cent budget increase, while Australia's overseas spy organisation, the Australian Secret Intelligence Service (ASIS) had its budget increase by 143 per cent in that period. The Australian Federal Police (AFP), which previously had only a relatively small intelligence role, had a 70 per cent boost to its funding over the five years.[15] From 2000 to 2005 the overall spending on intelligence organisations rose from $332 million to $659 million, while staff numbers jumped by 44 per cent from 2301 to 3324.[16] Another 900 ADF personnel were also involved in intelligence work.

ASIO had been in decline for many years before being revived as part of the 9/11 response. Its staff had peaked at 790 in 1983 when it was dominated by cold war concerns but by the turn of the century its numbers had fallen by about a third to about 530. Following the reaction of the government to the US and Bali terrorism attacks of 2001-2002, by 2005 it had expanded significantly, to 930 staff, and that number was scheduled to double by 2010-2011. Dennis Richardson, who as ASIO Director-General oversaw the first four years of this expansion, says 9/11 resulted in a significant change in ASIO's role. Before that date it was 'predominantly' concerned with counter-espionage. That, he rightly explains, was its *raison d'être*. 'But while we are still involved in counter-espionage, since 9/11 the overwhelming issues engaging ASIO concern peoples' safety – counter-terrorism. That gets priority'.[17] ASIO's staff are overwhelmingly deployed within Australia. Richardson says only about three per cent is now based overseas, considerably less than during the height of the cold war in the 1970s and 1980s. ASIO at that time was involved in checking would-be migrants. These days it only conducts security clearances when specifically requested by the Department of Immigration, and in a far more selective and targeted way. Now its foreign-based staff are mainly involved in liaison work with other intelligence agencies.[18]

The overseas intelligence function is the primary responsibility of ASIS. It too is undergoing a major expansion program. In the 10 years from 11 September 2001 its staff will treble in size. The expansion of both ASIO and ASIS has had its problems for both organisations and resulted in both conducting extensive public advertising campaigns to recruit suitable staff. One problem, according to Richardson, is a lack of cultural diversity within the organisations. There is a reticence on the part of many people from migrant families to join the organisations because of family experiences with police or security back in their former countries. Language skills are another problem area. 'It is easy enough to get people who speak another language, but more difficult to get those who speak it well enough to satisfy our criteria', Richardson says.

Another two organisations to benefit from higher spending are the Office of National Assessments (ONA) and the Defence Intelligence Organisation (DIO). Both were expanded following a review of their performance in providing incorrect advice over whether Iraq had extensive weapons of mass destruction (WMD). It was Iraq's refusal to hand over its WMD that was the main reason cited by the Australian Government for joining the US in the so-called coalition of the willing in attacking Iraq. The review of the WMD advice given to the Australian Government was conducted by Philip Flood, a former head of ONA and former Secretary of the Department of Foreign Affairs. Flood found that ONA had not produced a comprehensive 'national assessment' on Iraq before the decision to commit to war, while the DIO did not produce an intelligence estimate to support the deployment of the ADF. ONA had only allocated three analysts to work on the Iraq sector before the war. 'Intelligence', Flood reported, 'was thin, ambiguous and incomplete'.[19]

The other members of the intelligence community also expanded following 9/11. The Defence Signals Directorate (DSD) collects and disseminates foreign signals intelligence to the ADF and various government agencies while the Defence Imagery and Geospatial Organisation (DIGO) collects and analyses photographic and other imagery and geospatial information, though about 70 per cent of its output is specifically devoted to supporting the ADF. Both received additional funding though the government did not disclose the extent of this.[20]

Australian Federal Police

Another major beneficiary of the government's preparedness to expand its security and intelligence resources was the Australian Federal Police (the AFP). The AFP was not previously regarded as in any way part of Australia's defence establishment. But according to the Police Federation of Australia, police are absorbing more and more of what were previously identified as military roles. Increasingly, it says, the government is aiming to address regional military concerns by taking the fight off-shore. Whereas 10 years ago government policy was based on meeting security concerns with troops and military hardware, these days police are being sent to off-shore hotspots to undertake preventative peacekeeping and peace-building activities like restoring law and order, and rebuilding governance infrastructures.[21] The AFP was created after the Hilton bomb blasts in Sydney in 1978 that occurred during a meeting of the regional leaders of the Commonwealth Heads of Government. However it did not have an anti-terrorism role until after 9/11 when following a Commonwealth-State meeting in March 2002, the AFP was given a task of investigating terrorist offences. That led to the creation of joint task forces between the AFP and State police and also close liaison between the AFP and ASIO. Following the Bali bombing in October 2002, the AFP significantly expanded its overseas work. As well as developing considerable forensic expertise, the AFP reached a close working relationship with the Indonesian police. At one stage it had 120 police working in Bali. In 2004 it established the Jakarta Centre for Law Enforcement Cooperation to provide a forum for academics and other experts to look at the situation in the region and also to allow practitioners to keep up to date with the latest developments in terrorism and other forms of trans-national crime. Federal Police Commissioner Mick Keelty says the centre also has an operational focus, allowing for the exchange on the latest technology in forensics, in bomb blast analysis and about techniques for investigating terrorist activities. At the end of 2005 the AFP had a presence in 26 countries, liaising with local police in such countries as China, Vietnam, India, Bangladesh and Sri Lanka, and South Africa.[22] Keelty says counter-terrorism only represents about 20 per cent of the work of the AFP, but that task meant the recruitment of an additional 660 staff after 9/11. 'We are still doing a lot of work on high-tech crime, on people-smuggling, on major frauds against the Commonwealth and in the narcotics area'. It is also involved in 'capacity building' in the Solomon Islands, East Timor and Papua New Guinea, to help local police maintain law and order. To equip the AFP to undertake this role in 2005 it opened north of Canberra what Keelty describes as a third-world village, equipped with modern technology, to train about 500 police a year for deployment in the region.

As part of its anti-terrorism role, the AFP within Australia regained control of the Australian Protective Service and became responsible for air security, through the provision of Sky Marshals, as well as for anti-terrorism at all major airports and the creation of rapid deployment teams to ensure regional airports maintained their security arrangements at the required level. Its expanded role was formalised in a ministerial directive in 2004.

Keelty says his aim has been to use intelligence to support the criminal justice system:

> The delineation between law enforcement and intelligence needs to be maintained to preserve the criminal justice system … There's a lot we achieve at the international level that wouldn't be achieved if we were an intelligence agency rather than a police agency. It's all done on a police to police basis.

In August 2006 the government announced a further, major expansion of the AFP to allow it to deploy more police in the region. Its International Deployment Group (IDG) would be expanded by half, from 800 to 1200, the largest single increase in its staff since the creation of the AFP. This would cost $493 over five years. One aim of the boost of the IDG was to allow it to establish a 150-strong operational response group ready to respond at short notice to emerging law and order issues and undertake stabilisation operations, according to the official announcement.[23]

New security powers

The Australian Parliament passed a series of laws extending criminal sanctions for offences associated with terrorism following 9/11. As well as creating a specific crime of terrorism, the laws criminalise preparatory offences such as training, financing or assisting in terrorism, they ban specified (by regulation) terrorist groups and make membership of them or association with them criminal offences, they allow for preventative detention and control orders for people who have not been charged with any criminal offences, recreate the old crime of sedition in the widest possible terms, and allow ASIO to detain and question people who are not suspected of terrorism offences but may know something about them. Regular procedures for the issue of search and other warrants have been abrogated. The intelligence agencies have been given extraordinarily wide powers to intercept phone and other communications, even of people who are not suspects. For most of the new offences there is no requirement that a terrorist act has occurred nor is it necessary for the prosecution to prove that the activity was being carried out for 'a specific terrorist act'. A threat to commit a terrorist act qualifies itself as a terrorist act.[24] The laws also make it an offence to disclose or make public operational information, with a penalty of five years imprisonment. This would prevent the media publicising any actions of ASIO or the Federal Police, even if an abuse of power were involved.

Many of the laws have been passed on the basis that they would be reviewed at a later stage, having been rushed through Parliament with little inquiry or debate. However, as Dr Andrew Lynch complains, this 'pass now-review later' approach confounds full and informed debate over the measures being introduced to combat terrorism:

> No one doubts that strong and effective national security depends in part upon a sound legislative base, but it is important that government powers are kept in proportion to the threat and that safeguards for the essential liberties of individuals are not simply steamrolled ... Too often in recent months we have seen 'urgency' used to justify laws being enacted after brief and inconclusive debate as to their merits. Holding out the prospect of a future review is a strategy which lets some steam out of the process and is clearly designed to string out and obfuscate the debate.[25]

And when review does occur, it does not necessarily result in the law being changed. For example, the government established the Security Legislation Review Committee, under the chair of former New South Wales Supreme Court judge Simon Sheller QC, to review the laws passed in 2002 and 2003. The committee recommended significant amendments. However the government showed no interest in introducing the changes proposed. The government also agreed to allow the Australian Law Reform Commission (ALRC) to conduct a review of its new sedition laws. It proposed the term 'sedition' should be dropped altogether, and that the laws be significantly modified, particularly to preserve free speech, so long as it was not used to urge the use of violence. Attorney-General Philip Ruddock indicated that most of the ALRC proposals would not be accepted.[26]

Nor has it been demonstrated that there is an objective need for laws of the kind that have been passed. As Dr Ben Saul told a conference conducted by the International Society for the Reform of the Criminal Law in Brisbane in 2006, Australians have been told officially there is a 'medium' risk of terrorist attack – not 'high' or 'extreme' risk – meaning that a terrorist attack 'could occur'. The government, he says, has also not demonstrated that the previous counter-terrorism laws were insufficient to meet the terrorist threat, so as to justify radical new laws.[27]

Australia has experienced minor terrorism previously. During the late 1960s and early 1970s there were 102 serious acts of terrorism reported by ASIO to federal Cabinet through the Attorney-General, Senator Ivor Greenwood.[28] They mostly involved attacks originated by Yugoslav extremists against supporters of the then communist Yugoslav Government, or attacks against Israeli or Jewish establishments or people. They included bombings that resulted in some people being seriously injured, and property damage. Because a federal election was due within months, the government decided in late 1972 against establishing a public inquiry into terrorism and the Attorney-General did not put forward changes to the law though he had suggested to cabinet he was considering them. The following year the Labor Attorney-General, Senator Lionel Murphy, also considered possible changes to the law to better deal with terrorism but the government decided to take no action.

There is an earlier precedent, however, for extremely tough legislation designed to outlaw a body that allegedly poses a direct threat to the nation. In 1950 the Menzies Government believed Australia faced the possibility of another world war within three years, a war against the Soviet Union and other communist powers. It sought to ban the Community Party within Australia, and other bodies affiliated with it. Any person associated with such organisations would be banned from holding a public service position, or a job in an industry vital to the security and defence of the country. This legislation, far less repressive than the laws introduced since 9/11, was claimed by the government to fall within the Commonwealth's power to make laws for defence. The High Court, with just one dissenting voice, ruled the law was unconstitutional. Undeterred, Prime Minister Robert Menzies held a referendum to change the Constitution to allow the law to take effect. The referendum to approve the constitutional change was narrowly rejected by the Australian people.

The Labor Party's deputy leader, Dr HV Evatt, led the High Court challenge against the legislation and subsequently, as Leader, persuaded the party to oppose the referendum. His successes came at a considerable political cost. He was portrayed as a friend of communism and lost a federal election shortly after his success in the referendum. That lesson may still have been in the consciousness of the Labor Party in the 21st century, as it studiously avoided opposing the Howard Government's anti-terrorism legislation for fear of being branded soft on terrorism.

Unlike Sir Robert Menzies, the Howard Government did not have any constitutional difficulties with its various anti-terrorist laws because it was able to persuade all six Labor-governed States to refer to the Commonwealth the relevant powers that they possessed under their State constitutions. There was only one hitch, and it was of no consequence, when the ACT Government decided to limit the power of security authorities to hold juveniles in preventative detention. The Commonwealth has the constitutional authority to override the laws of any of the Territories.

One other significant expansion of the defence powers occurred as a result of 9/11. In 2005 the government introduced amendments to the *Defence Act* that would make it easy for it to call out the ADF to protect Commonwealth and other interests in the States and elsewhere, and to allow the use of reasonable and necessary force by the ADF in protecting critical infrastructure. The call-out can, in an emergency, be authorised by the Prime Minister or by two other senior ministers, by-passing the need for the Governor-General to be consulted. The law would also ensure that only Commonwealth laws would be involved if any alleged criminal conduct was committed by ADF members.

Terrorism and defence

Many commentators have complained that the notion of the 'war' on terrorism that emerged after 9/11 was ill-defined. One problem is to know what constitutes victory, and when it might be achieved.

Another problem is that it appears to justify 'an open-ended global conflict to be waged on a global scale'.[29] Those who advise the Australian Government have no doubt, however, that terrorism is 'a danger to Australian and allied nationals, a challenge to the authority of many governments, and a disruption to the patterns of trust and openness globalised economies need'.[30] Mr Peter Varghese, Director-General of the Office of National Assessments, says Islamist terrorism has:

> in-built limits as a strategic threat to Australia. It has no scope to endanger the existence of, or take territory from, the Australian state. Nor will terrorism threaten Australia's fundamental freedom of action to the extent that might, for example, coercion by an economically or militarily powerful state.[31]

But those concerned about the war on terrorism cannot expect an early end. According to Mr Varghese, 'Terrorism will stay a destabilising force globally for at least a decade, and possibly a generation'. That is certainly the premise on which the Howard Government in 2006 was structuring the defence and security forces.

Notes

1 Howard, J 2004b: v.
2 Howard, J 2004a: 2.
3 Moore 2000: 3.
4 The *2000 White Paper* and *Updates*, including speeches by Ministers, are available on the Defence Department website, <www.defence.gov.au>.
5 Thomson 2006b: 7. These quotations, and the analysis that follows, are taken from ASPI's publication, prepared by Thomson, *Your Defence Dollar: The 2006-07 Defence Budget*.
6 Thomson, M 2006b: 7-8.
7 Thomson, M 2006b: 8.
8 Thomson 2006a: 113, 116. This analysis is from Thomson, Section 5 – Australian Defence Economics in *The Cost of Defence: ASPI Defence Budget Brief 2006-07*.
9 Thomson 2006a: 117.
10 Thomson 2006b: 33-34. The make-up of the forces and its recent history are set out in chapter 4 of Thomson, *The Cost of Defence: ASPI Defence Budget Brief 2006-07*.
11 Howard, J 2006b.
12 Defence Department website, <www.defence.gov.au>.
13 2006 Budget papers.
14 Thomson 2006a: 2.
15 2006 Budget papers.

16 Veit 2005: 35.

17 Richardson 2005.

18 Richardson 2005.

19 Flood 2004: 177.

20 See, *Protecting Australia against Terrorism* and the *Flood Report*. <www.dpmc.gov.au>, and *The Australian Intelligence Community*, Australian Government, Canberra, 2006.

21 Police Federation of Australia 2006: 2.

22 Keelty 2005.

23 Howard, J 2006a.

24 Lynch 2006b.

25 Lynch 2006a.

26 ALRC 2006; *New Matilda*, 20 September 2006: 15.

27 Saul 2006.

28 1972 Federal Cabinet papers, National Archives of Australia.

29 Bacevich 2006: 26.

30 Varghese 2006: 3.

31 Varghese 2006: 4.

7

Economic regulators

'Competition delivers the best outcomes in "free" markets. Yet to achieve the reforms of National Competition Policy independent regulation in the Australian economy has been increased'.[1] Graeme Samuel, chair of the Australian Competition and Consumer Commission (ACCC), calls this a paradox. 'For some markets', he explains, 'increased competition can only be achieved with increased regulation'. Samuel was concerned in this address with infrastructure development, and was anxious to demonstrate that his organisation's involvement in the regulatory framework that had been created under the National Competition Policy had made a positive contribution towards the much acclaimed 2.5 per cent annual boost in productivity that occurred in the decade after the reforms were introduced. This productivity boost paused after June 2004, falling by more than half. (See Figure 7.1 over page.)

However paradoxical it might seem that increased regulation can improve competition and then deliver the benefits flowing from increased competition, what emerges from recent Australian history is the importance and influence of the institutions that superintend the regulatory framework along with the economic reforms that accompanied the establishment of that framework. The nature of those economic reforms has been summarised by Gary Banks, chairman of the Productivity Commission. (See Box 7.1 over page.) [2]

Figure 7.1: Australia's productivity turnaround

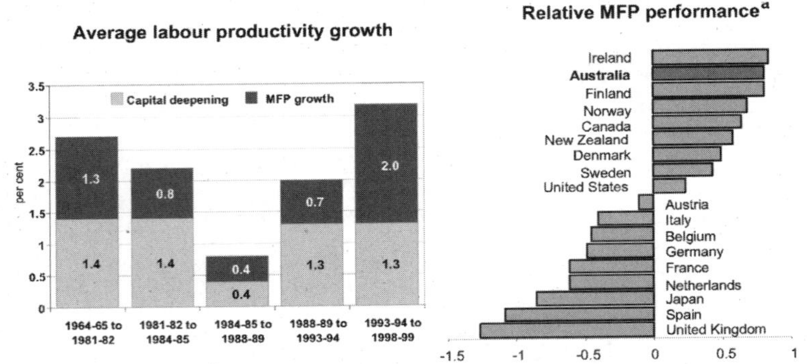

a Percentage points change to average annual MFP growth 1980-1990 to 1990-2000

Source: Productivity Commission.

Box 7.1: Two decades of economic reform

Trade liberalisation – reductions in tariff assistance (that began in 1973) and the abolition of quantitative import controls (mainly in the automotive, whitegoods and textile, clothing and footwear industries) – gathered pace from the mid 1980s. The effective rate of assistance to manufacturing fell from around 35% in the early 1970s to 5% by 2000.

Capital markets – the Australian dollar was floated in March 1983, foreign exchange controls and capital rationing (through interest rate controls) were removed progressively from the early 1980s and foreign-owned banks were allowed to compete – initially for corporate customers and then, in the 1990s, to act as deposit-taking institutions.

Infrastructure – partial deregulation and restructuring of airlines, coastal shipping, telecommunications and the waterfront occurred from the late 1980s. Across-the-board commercialisation, corporatisation and privatisation initiatives for government business enterprises were progressively implemented from around the same time.

Labour markets – the Prices and Incomes Accord operated from 1983 to 1996. Award restructuring and simplification, and the shift from centralised wage fixing to enterprise bargaining, began in the late 1980s. Reform accelerated in the mid-1990s with the introduction of the *Workplace Relations Act 1996*, further award simplification (through limiting prescribed employment conditions in enterprise bargaining agreements) and the introduction of individual employment contracts (Australian Workplace Agreements).

Human services – competitive tendering and contracting out, performance-based funding and user charges were introduced in the late 1980s and extended in scope during the 1990s; administrative reforms (for example, financial management and program budgeting) were introduced in health, education and community services in the early 1990s.

'National Competition policy' reforms – In 1995, further broad-ranging reforms to essential service industries (including energy and road transport), government businesses and anti-competitive regulation was commenced by all Australian governments through a coordinated national program.

Macroeconomic policy – inflation targeting was introduced in 1993. From the mid 1980s, fiscal policy targeted higher national saving (and a lower current account deficit) and, from the mid 1990s, concentrated on reducing government debt, primarily financed through asset sales (privatisation).

Taxation reform – capital gains tax and the dividend imputation system were introduced in 1985 and 1987, respectively. The company tax rate was lowered progressively from the late 1980s. A broad-based consumption tax (GST) was implemented in 2000, replacing the narrow wholesale sales tax system and a range of inefficient State-based duties. And income tax rates were lowered at the same time.

The individual contributions of each of these reforms may be difficult to assess: what is not in doubt is that Australia's economic performance during the period was – by world standards – outstanding. Banks says during the 1990s Australia experienced a surge in multi-factor productivity (MFP) that averaged almost 2 per cent, more than double its previous rate:

Figure 7.2: Fall and rise of Australia's economic ranking

Sources: Productivity Commission.

> Australia's MFP performance was also among the best in the OECD and its labour productivity growth exceeded even that of the USA. Accompanied by rising labour utilisation, this translated into annual growth in per capita incomes of around 2 1/2 [2.5] per cent in that decade, well above the previous average and that for the OECD as a whole (1.7 per cent). As a consequence, Australia saw its position on the international per capita GDP scale rise again from 15th to 8th over the past decade or so.[3]

Banks claims the institution most identified with the microeconomic reforms during this period is the Productivity Commission, which had its origins as the Tariff Board in 1922, became the Industry Assistance Commission under the Whitlam Government in the 1970s, then the Industry Commission from 1990 to 1998.[4] However as he acknowledges, the Commission's role ultimately is 'informational and advisory'.[5] The Commission cannot implement its recommendation: decisions ultimately are taken by government. In the case of National Competition Policy, decisions have to go through the processes of the Council of Australian Government (COAG), and may require separate decisions then by State and Territory governments (encouraged by competition payments from the Federal Government). Banks says:

> Political leadership is critical to structural reform, but its influence on policy in the longer term can be ephemeral. Its most enduring legacy may well come from more fundamental actions to entrench institutions and processes that can facilitate ongoing reform beyond the life of any one government.[6]

The four independent regulators that have played a crucial role during this process, and seem likely to continue to do so, are the Reserve Bank, the Australian Competition and Consumer Commission, the Australian Securities and Investment Commission and the Australian Prudential Regulation Authority.

The Reserve Bank

The Reserve Bank was created in 1959 to take over the central banking functions previously exercised by the Commonwealth Bank.[7] It became responsible for administering banking and monetary policy and for exchange control, though that last function came to an end with the floating of the dollar in 1983. The Reserve's direct controls over banks gradually eased around the same time as the financial system was deregulated in accordance with decisions by the Hawke Government. In its place the Reserve Bank then created a specialised banking supervisory function. But that was removed and given to the newly created Australian Prudential Regulation Authority in 1998. At the same time the Reserve Bank took full responsibility for the national payments system and it subsequently used that power to supervise and control credit card and other interchange fees. It manages Australia's holdings of gold and foreign exchange and other assets of in excess of $70 billion. The Reserve Bank's most well-known function is to set interest rates, but it has only done so independently of the government since the early 1990s, and in formal terms, only since the mid-1990s. Under the *Reserve Bank Act*, the Bank's board is required 'to ensure that the monetary and banking policy of the Bank is directed to the greatest advantage of the people of Australia' and in a way that will best contribute to:

(a) the stability of the currency of Australia;
(b) the maintenance of full employment in Australia; and
(c) the economic prosperity and welfare of the people of Australia'.[8]

In 1993 Governor of the Bank, Bernie Fraser, said the objective of price stability involved holding the rate of inflation at an average of 2-3 per cent over a period of years. After the election of the Howard Government in 1996 the Governor-Designate, Ian Macfarlane, and Treasurer Peter Costello issued a 'Statement on the Conduct of Monetary Policy' reiterating and clarifying the respective roles and responsibilities of the Bank and the government in relation to monetary policy and providing formal government approval of the inflation objective. It also explained the need for the Reserve Bank to pay attention to economic activity and employment as well as to inflation. The bank itself believes that having these several goals are a counter to the preoccupation of many central banks with low inflation.

Later, as Governor, Ian Macfarlane made it clear the Reserve Bank paid much more attention to world economic trends than to the various monthly domestic statistics that measure the local economy and that tend to excite the interest of politicians and economic commentators in the media and the market trying to second-guess the Bank's next interest rate adjustment:

> You could be forgiven for thinking that the formulation of monetary policy was simply a matter of collecting the latest month's statistics, weighing them up to see whether they were strong or weak on balance, and then adjusting interest rates accordingly. But monetary policy is a much more slowly evolving process than this, and there are elements in the process that are more important than the evaluation of the latest statistics. The first of these is to have a clearly enunciated framework of what monetary policy is seeking to do, and the second is to have a view of how the world economy is evolving and how this will affect Australia.[9]

Macfarlane said the current consensus (in 2005) on what monetary policy can achieve, based on the experience of the post-war period is:

> [T]he principal contribution it can make to economic well-being is to maintain low and stable inflation. As a result a number of countries, including Australia, have adopted a monetary policy regime based on inflation-targeting. Ours is designed to ensure that the average rate of increase in consumer prices is between 2 and 3 percent. The centrality of inflation in the monetary policy regime is not because inflation is all we care about. It is there because we believe that low inflation is a necessary condition for sustainable economic growth and good monetary policy is essential to its achievement. The results over the past 14 years provide evidence in support of this assessment. It is important to have a framework because there has historically been a temptation to use monetary policy for too many purposes. We still hear calls from time to time to raise interest rates to improve the balance of payments or to stop rising house prices, or, on the other hand, to lower rates because the economy has slowed. In the past, these and other motives often lay behind monetary policy changes, but now it is easier to resist such temptations because they have to be viewed within a more general framework based on their likely implication for future inflation.[10]

Macfarlane said an important second element was to have a view about how the world economy was evolving and how this would affect Australia:

> It is fair to say that the major macro-economic events that have affected Australia have to a large extent been imported rather than

> home-grown. In Australia, the two major economic events of the last century, the Depression of the thirties and the Inflation of the seventies – the world's only peacetime inflation – were both part of world-wide developments. More recently, the international business cycle has been the main determinant of our own; the three most recent recessions of 1974, 1982 and 1990 were part of global recessions. Over this period we have not had an entirely self-induced recession. Our one significant deviation from the international business cycle is that we did avoid the (admittedly mild) 2001 recession that affected most G7 countries. Similarly, our inflation experience shadowed that of the OECD area, though we were later than most in bringing it down after the initial surge in the seventies; our good inflation record only dates from the early 1990s. I think it is true to say that if you wished to forecast the path of the Australian economy, and you were able to have foreknowledge of only one economic variable, the one you would choose would be the path of the world economy. That is not to say that we have no influence over our own destiny – we can make the situation better or worse than it would otherwise be – but we cannot escape the influence of the world business cycle and the other factors that feed off it.[11]

Nevertheless, governments still try to influence the decisions that the Reserve Bank makes on interest rates, or claim during election campaigns that they are able to do so better than their opponents. There is no evidence to suggest that in recent years the Reserve Bank's decisions on rates have been influenced by politicians – certainly in 2005 and 2006 it ignored suggestions from senior ministers that it would be wrong for it to notch up the basic interest rate. However Macfarlane waited until his retirement before he (indirectly) criticised the claims made by the Howard Government during the 2004 election campaign that it would keep interest rates low. He was concerned at the suggestion that the Reserve Bank was not independent when it set rates. However he did not speak out at the time because that would have politicised the Bank even more than the claims about interest rates.[12]

It is perhaps a measure of the Reserve Bank's independence that it is prepared occasionally to voice unpalatable (in political terms) views about economic events. In 2005 Macfarlane defended the 1990 recession (the recession famously characterised by then Treasurer Paul Keating as 'the recession we had to have'). Macfarlane said it had paved the way for the low inflation and strong growth Australia had since enjoyed. He said the recession has been greatly misunderstood, particularly by politicians:

> I think that some of the economic interpretations are completely wrong and, even more importantly, the political interpretations are completely wrong. The episode in Australia which returned us to a low-inflation, stable-growth economy was regarded as a policy error, whereas in America, it is regarded as a policy triumph.[13]

Prime Minister John Howard expressed his disagreement with this assessment during a book launch some six months later. He said it was a myth that the recession had set the economy on the path of low inflation. 'I do not accept that. I think the recession and certainly the severity of the recession in the early 1990s was a product of their policy failure'.[14] International opinion, however, appears to support Macfarlane. The International Monetary Fund survey of Australia in 2005 suggested that the depth and duration of the recession could be blamed on weakness in banking and corporate balance sheets associated with high credit growth, and that the recession 'provided an opportunity to establish medium-term macroeconomic policy frameworks' followed by other structural reforms and 'uninterrupted economic expansion since 1992'.[15]

Australian Prudential Regulation Authority[16]

A strong economy does not guarantee that there will not be financial hiccups or even corporate failures. The Australian Prudential Regulation Authority (APRA) was established by legislation in 1998 following the Wallis Committee inquiry in 1997 into the financial system. The legislation was meant to ensure that prudentially regulated financial entities maintained a minimum level of financial soundness. APRA inherited the responsibilities of the former Insurance and Superannuation Commission plus the Reserve Bank's role as supervisor of the banking industry, together with some functions that had been exercised by some State regulators. APRA is required to oversee deposit takers such as banks, building societies and credit unions, insurance companies, friendly societies and much of the superannuation industry. In 2006 the institutions it supervised held assets in excess of $2.2 trillion for 20 million Australian depositors, policy holders and superannuation fund members. APRA sees its primary task as supervising the bodies for which it has oversight, rather than enforcement. Its aim is to ensure the financial health of those entities in the interests of depositors and policy holders.

But several major corporate failures occurred within a few years of APRA's creation – HIH, FAI, One.Tel and Ansett. The HIH Insurance collapse was Australia's worst corporate failure, costing around $5.3 billion. According to Justice Neville Owen, who conducted the Royal Commission to investigate what happened, the company failed because of ineptitude, mismanagement and incompetence. He reported the company's management failed dismally in the business of being an insurer. His report led to a number of prosecutions and the jailing of two of the principals, Ray Williams and Rodney Adler.

APRA had some excuses for its failure to anticipate the HIH debacle. Justice Owen found that APRA had taken about three years to get into its full regulatory stride. It was required by the government to establish itself in Sydney rather than Canberra where its predecessor, the Insurance and Superannuation Commission had been based. The move resulted in a loss of staff and experience. Justice Owen nevertheless concluded:

> APRA's performance in supervising HIH was not good. It missed many warning signs, was slow to act, and made misjudgments about some vital matters. But two things need to be said.
>
> First, APRA did not cause or contribute to the collapse of HIH; nor could it have taken steps to prevent the failure of the company. A regulator cannot be expected to provide a guarantee that no company under its supervision will ever fail. Second APRA faced several handicaps in its supervision of the HIH group as a direct result of the implementation of the new regime.[17]

But despite this he found that APRA did comparatively little in response to mounting evidence of HIH's problems and it lacked commitment in enforcing its requests for information.[18]

As a result of the Royal Commission and several other inquiries APRA was given additional investigative responsibilities and power. In 2002 it was provided with greater flexibility to intervene early in response to warning signals in general insurance.[19] In 2004 it was given additional powers to take preventative action in the superannuation area.[20] In 2003 its board was replaced by a three-person executive group that was required to keep the Minister informed of its policies.[21]

Another wake-up call for APRA came in 2004 when the National Australia Bank discovered that so-called 'rogue' traders had lost the bank $360 million through unauthorised foreign currency trading. APRA had warned the bank six months before the bank began to incur losses about its risk management systems but senior executives took no notice of the warning and did not pass it on to the bank's board, despite informing APRA it would remedy its systems.[22] Following the disclosure of the extent of the losses actually incurred by the bank, APRA imposed new standards on the bank.

APRA does not have the public profile of the other major regulators, not least because secrecy provisions in its legislation and its need to retain the confidence of those it is supervising impose severe limits on what it might say. However it retains the government's support, winning a significant increase in its budget in 2006 (up by about 15 per cent to $97.6 million for 2006-2007).

Australian Securities and Investments Commission

The Australian Securities and Investments Commission (ASIC) is the largest of the regulators, with an annual budget (for 2005-2006) of $312.3 million. It was originally established as the Australian Securities Commission in 1991 as the national regulator of companies. It in turn had replaced the National Companies and Securities Commission and the Corporate Affairs offices of the States and Territories. ASIC was recreated in 1998 after the Wallis Inquiry into the Financial System. It is responsible for the general administration of the federal *Corporations Act 2001* and has specific responsibility for investor and consumer protection for all financial entities including the licensing of products and services offered by financial entities. ASIC regulates more than 1.3 million companies, over 6500 company auditors, almost 3900 financial services businesses and a similar number of managed investment schemes. It also supervises eight financial markets including the stock exchange and the futures exchange. Its workload increased considerably after the Howard

Government began implementing its Corporate Law Economic Reform Program (*CLERP*), which was intended to ensure that regulation kept pace with a rapidly changing business environment. Those reforms were subsequently extended (particularly in *CLERP9*) to deal with recommendations arising out of the HIH collapse as well as to implement much of the Wallis report.[23]

In its strategy plan for 2005 to 2010, ASIC noted that following significant international and domestic corporate failures, new and more demanding standards of financial reporting, audit, disclosure, and corporate conduct had been introduced. 'As a result, more will be expected of ASIC to forestall failures in financial reporting, to promote a vigorous, independent audit profession and to enforce the law on continuous disclosure'.[24] Its emphasis on enforcement is carried through all its annual reports. Under the heading *Upholding the law uniformly, effectively and quickly* the report for 2004-2005 begins by listing:

- Criminals jailed: 2
- Civil orders against people or companies: 121
- % litigation successful: 94%
- Additional disclosures achieved through ASIC intervention: 161.

It then reports that ASIC required additional disclosure from directors in company fundraisings involving more than $6 billion and that financial penalties, cost recoveries and assets frozen totalled $123 million.[25] Among those it successfully prosecuted were former HIH directors, Ray Williams and Rodney Adler.

Australian Competition and Consumer Commission

The Australian Competition and Consumer Commission (ACCC) was established in 1995 through the merger of the Trade Practices Commission and the Prices Surveillance Authority. Its primary role is the enforcement through the *Trade Practices Act 1974* (TPA) of general competition law and consumer protection. Its concerns under the TPA include mergers and acquisitions that substantially lessen competition, boycotts, misuse of market power, price agreements, exclusive dealing and retail price maintenance. It also has to ensure the competitiveness of key network industries such as electricity, gas, telecommunications and transport. Both civil and criminal penalties are available under the TPA where breaches are found, and the ACCC uses prosecutions – and the threat of them – to try to force compliance with the provisions of the law. Under the chairmanship of Gordon Samuel it adopted a leniency policy in the form of an offer of immunity for the exposure of illegal cartels. Under the previous chairman Allan Fels it played a vital role during the introduction of the Goods and Services Tax (GST) through its prices surveillance role and its threats to prosecute anyone who took advantage of the introduction of the new tax to ramp up prices. It was allocated $105.6 million for its running costs in the 2006 federal budget.

The ACCC has a much more public (and better publicised) role than the Trade Practices Commission enjoyed. The ACCC's jurisdiction is much wider than that of its predecessor, as it was given additional powers to implement the national competition policy. Codes regulating access to essential facilities were formulated, penalties under the Act increased and consumer protection provisions more vigorously enforced. The TPA was also extended through complementary legislation passed by the States. The Commonwealth's constitutional power was limited to making laws concerning foreign, trading and financial corporations. But the addition of powers granted by the States meant the TPA could also cover unincorporated bodies and government business enterprises. Merger law was strengthened to allow the ACCC to play a crucial role in mergers and acquisitions.[26] The ACCC in 2004-2005 refused permission for the merger/takeover of Qantas and Air New Zealand. In 2005-2006 it delayed the takeover by Toll of the Patrick Corporation until Toll Holdings agreed to sell half of the Australian National rail operation it previously owned jointly with Patrick and required Toll Holdings to give various other undertakings to meet the ACCC's concerns about competition issues. In 2006 the ACCC approved the merger of the Australian Stock Exchange and the Sydney Futures Exchange, a proposal it had rejected in 1999, after it changed its mind and decided the two were separate monopolies that did not substantially compete.

Through the 1970s and 1980s the Trade Practices Commission adopted a relatively low-key approach to its tasks and it was a reluctant litigator and enforcer.[27] Allan Fels brought a different, more confrontational approach when he took over the Trade Practices Commission in 1991 which he carried through into the newly created ACCC in 1995. He used prosecutions and the media aggressively to enforce the law and to warn business the ACCC was in business – naming and shaming was part of his technique.[28] His successor, Graeme Samuel, adopted a less confrontational approach. The number of cases commenced by the ACCC in Samuel's first year, 2003-2004, was 22, compared with 60, two years earlier. The number of press releases issued also declined, though to a lesser extent, from 339 in 2002 to 310 in 2004.[29]

An international survey of competition regulators in 2006 rated the ACCC as the fifth most admired in the world, with the European Union's regulator ranked first, followed by those in Britain, Germany and the US. The survey suggested that under Samuel the ACCC had improved in mergers and transparency, but lost ground for abuse of dominance and willingness to litigate or conclude anti-trust cases. It said it lagged in the area of abuse of market power.[30]

Governments and regulators

According to Dr Michael Keating, government during this period had been 'marketised'.[31] Keating, who served as head of the Department of Prime Minister and Cabinet under Paul Keating and then John Howard, says the key features of marketisation are:

> [F]irst, substantial changes in the regulatory environment affecting the financial, product and labour markets, ostensibly in favour of deregulation. Secondly, the role of the state in the provision of government services has been affected by contracting out, privatisation, corporatisation, user charging, competition policy and other changes in public administration that borrow, to some extent, from private business practice.

However his thesis is that:

> [M]arkets can most often be *managed* to assist in the achievement of many of the state's policy directions and goals.

> [The] shift to marketisation largely represents an attempt by governments to enhance or restore their power to achieve their economic and social objectives, while minimising any loss of efficiency. In effect, governments aim to construct and manage markets so that their characteristic patterns of positive and negative incentives turn the apparently independent activities of free agents into instruments of government.[32]

Management during this period, essentially fell to the regulators, the ACCC, ASIC and APRA. It was possibly all the more effective because those being regulated and managed – individually as corporations and businesses, and collectively as the 'markets' – did not feel as though the government was directing their ordinary activities. The regulators are, through the legislation that creates them, independent of government and of those whose conduct they are required to monitor. But the regulators are not beyond the reach of government. Indirectly they can be *managed*, though not always instantly. This happens through changes to legislation – for example, changing the tests that the regulators or the courts have to apply in assessing what is happening in the marketplace – and changes in the administration of the regulators – for example, by starving them of resources, and carefully selecting those who will run them. The former Trade Practices Commission (TPC), for example, hit the wrong note with the Hawke Government's Attorney-General Michael Duffy who complained that its then chairman, Bob Baxt, was always criticising the government for not giving it sufficient resources and speaking out against it. Its request to quadruple fines to $10 million was not granted until after Baxt ceased to be chairman. Earlier, during the Fraser Government, the Commission was required by Ministers to drop investigations or prosecutions of businesses with which it had sympathetic ties.[33]

Managing the ACCC

Fels' rigour in prosecuting alleged breaches and his use of the media to damn those who might have fallen foul of the *Trade Practices Act* resulted in concerted action by business lobby groups to quell his powers. When it came time for his five-year appointment to be reviewed in 2000, Treasurer Peter Costello offered him not another full term, but three years and eight months. Costello expressed concern to Fels that he had become 'very, very powerful'.[34] And to moderate that power the Howard Government announced before the 2001 election that it would appoint an inquiry headed by former High Court judge Sir Daryl Dawson to review the *Trade Practices Act* and the ACCC's administration of it. One (successful) aim of the campaign undertaken by business interests that persuaded the government to appoint this inquiry was to force the ACCC to moderate its use of the media to denounce misconduct before the conduct had been proved in the courts to be contrary to the law.

Fels' successor, Samuel, was very much aware of the need to take account of the desires of the various governments he was required to serve. His appointment, on the nomination of Liberal Treasurer Peter Costello, required the approval of State Labor Governments if it was to take effect. Initially, a majority said no, because of his previous ties with big business – he had been president of the Australian Chamber of Commerce and Industry (ACCI) – and then his role as president of the National Competition Council (NCC). Eventually Costello was able to persuade South Australia to change its vote. Samuel said after his appointment was confirmed that he had learned a fundamental lesson from his experience at the ACCI and NCC:

> You don't lecture governments in public about what they should do in setting policy ... What we try to do is to provide an honest view about what we think policy setting should be. It will be an independent view. It will be provided in private. We respect the fact that ultimately government is going to set policy and it is elected to do it. It is not for agencies or regulators to set policy – we are there to administer.[35]

The way Samuel administered the ACCC was very different from the way Fels approached the task. The most significant change was in the enforcement area. He says that under Fels the ACCC had been putting a lot of things into court, many of which did not need to go there – 'but they were notches in the belt. They created publicity in the media and the media was particularly interested in small consumer protection matters'. Samuel's policy was to go to court only where serious harm had been done and the ACCC had been unable to get the business concerned to respond positively to compliance with the law and dealing with the harm and providing restitution to those who might have been affected. He sent smaller consumer protection matters back to the States to be dealt with by their consumer protection bodies. As a result the work of the ACCC was more evenly balanced between consumer protection and competition, whereas previously it had been more heavily weighted towards consumer protection.

However like his predecessor Samuel believes in bringing criminal prosecutions to try to get jail sentences for those involved in serious offences against the law, including in the consumer protection area, though he was particularly concerned to target breaches of competition law. 'We need to understand that anti-competitive activity is criminal activity and is very serious'.

The government has provided the legislative changes that make significant jail sentences and heavy financial penalties real possibilities for breaches of the TPA and business groups appear to accept this. The government warmed to this approach during the introduction of the GST. It was Treasurer Costello who proposed that the ACCC should handle the implementation of the new tax, because of its enforcement reputation.[36] And he proposed a $10 million maximum fine for price exploitation as the big stick the ACCC could wield, though he wanted as few prosecutions as possible.[37] The threat, and the launch of a major prosecution (later dropped) helped the government achieve its aim of a relatively trouble-free introduction of the tax.

Regulating the economy

The economic regulators have had many more success than failures in the past two decades. They have largely helped governments expand the size and health of the economy. As Dr Keating argues (see above, pages 139-140) they provide governments with a way of trying to manage the economy that is more acceptable to markets than direct government controls would be, and more effective.

As a result, reliance on regulators is likely to increase. And governments will continue to use their control of the appointment of those who head the various regulators, and their ability to make changes to the laws the regulators administer, to ensure government policies are pursued and implemented by the regulators.

Notes

1 Samuel 2006a.
2 Banks 2005: 6.
3 Banks 2005: 8-9.
4 Banks 2005: 16-17.
5 Banks 2005: 22.
6 Banks 2005: 29.
7 A brief history of the bank and an outline of its activities can be found at <www.rba.gov.au>, along with speeches by its Governors and other senior officials.
8 *Reserve Bank Act 1959*, s 10(2).
9 Macfarlane 2005a: 1.
10 Macfarlane 2005a: 1.
11 Macfarlane 2005a: 1-2.
12 Macfarlane 2006.
13 Macfarlane 2005b.
14 Howard 2006c.
15 IMF 2005: 324-325.
16 For a detailed, extended analysis of APRA, the ACCC and ASIC, see the Parliamentary Library Research Brief of 14 June 2005 on Australia's Corporate Regulators.
17 Owen 2003: 34.
18 Owen 2003: 34.
19 *General Insurance Reform Act 2001*. Laker 2003.
20 *Superannuation Safety Amendment Act 2004*.
21 *APRA Amendment Act 2003*.
22 Laker 2004.
23 Parliamentary Library 2005a: 14-17.
24 ASIC 2005b: 5.
25 ASIC 2005a: 8.
26 Samuel, G 2006b.
27 Brenchley 2003: 4-6.
28 Brenchley 2003: 20-22.
29 Parliamentary Library 2005a: 23, 29.
30 Brenchley 2006.
31 Keating 2004: 2.
32 Keating 2004: 5. Emphasis in original text.
33 Brenchley 2003: 39.
34 Brenchley 2003: 214-215.
35 Samuel 2005a.
36 Brenchley 2003: 98.
37 Brenchley 2003: 100.

8

Unions

The first 10 years of the Howard Government fundamentally changed the nature of Australia's industrial relations system. A series of laws effectively ended at the national level the conciliation and arbitration system that was envisaged in the Constitution and brought into being in 1904. The changes were strongly resisted by the trade union movement which recognised that they would seriously diminish the role of the unions and undermine their power in the workplace and the political system. The government acted at a time when the nature of the workforce was also undergoing significant changes, some of which were also impacting detrimentally on trade unions.

The notion that the Commonwealth should have any involvement in industrial relations was initially rejected in the conventions during the 1890s when the Constitution was drafted, and only finally accepted when the most conservative delegates to the final Convention in 1898 decided that the power being proposed either would not be used, or would be used more moderately by the Commonwealth than by the States.[1] The power granted to the Commonwealth was quite limited, and deliberately so. Parliament was given power to pass laws with respect to 'conciliation and arbitration for the prevention and settlement of industrial disputes extending beyond the limits of any one State'.[2] Neither the Parliament nor the government, using this power, would be able to determine the outcome of any dispute, nor could they set wages. The Parliament could merely establish procedures for conciliation and arbitration, and then only for interstate, 'industrial' disputes.

The first few attempts to introduce laws putting this power into effect were aborted. Opposition amendments resulted first in the proposed law being dropped, then in two successive governments resigning. When the new industrial court was eventually established, various rulings by the High Court limiting its scope prompted a number of governments to try to change the constitution to strengthen the arbitration power, but all the referendums failed to gain a sufficient majority. One such attempt, by Prime Minister Stanley Melbourne Bruce, sought power to allow the government to directly settle industrial disputes. Its rejection, and a series of political battles over other arbitration issues including the control of waterside workers, led Bruce in 1929 to propose that the Commonwealth should almost completely abandon its role in the arbitration system. Legislation to put this policy into effect was held up by rebels within his own party. Bruce called an election, and was defeated. From that time Conservative governments supported the extension of the Commonwealth's powers in the area.

Changes in the way the High Court interpreted the constitutional power helped increase the reach of the Commonwealth's industrial tribunals so that by the 1980s they could potentially cover about 40 per cent of the workforce. These changes helped the development of national trade unions and of the peak national body, the Australian Council of Trade Unions (ACTU). This body had a significant political presence, even under Coalition governments, because of the media attention it could generate, because it could threaten to extend strikes and because it could also play a decisive role in helping to settle national strikes.

The Howard revolution

The Howard Government's first legislative initiative was the *Workplace Relations Act 1996*. This introduced a system of individual contracts (Australian Workplace Agreements, or AWAs), it reduced the role and powers of the Australian Industrial Relations Commission, it restricted the scope of awards that could be negotiated by unions to 20 allowable matters, it curbed union access to workplaces and reduced their power to interfere in workplace matters and it encouraged collective bargaining between employers and employees, or their unions. It also created a number of federal bureaucratic based organisations to implement its policies, rather than handing this function to the independent Commission.

The AWAs were a rapid success with employers. At the end of 1997, 5000 had been registered with the Office of Employment Advocate (OEA) while by mid-2005 there were over 709,000 and they were increasing at a rate of almost 40 per cent a year.[3] Initially the AWAs had to meet the 'no disadvantage test' – they could only be approved if they did not reduce overall terms and conditions of employees under a relevant award or law. Under the 2005 Work Choices laws the test was replaced by a requirement that just six minimum standards had to be met, the minimum award wage, four leave entitlements and ordinary working hours. However even these minimal requirements could be averaged out (the 38 hour week could be averaged over 12 months and a worker would not be entitled to special overtime rates simply because he or she was required to work excessive hours in a particularly week or month) or paid out (two weeks holiday could be cashed out).

While squeezing unions out of the wage negotiating process for AWAs and most collective agreements, the Howard Government also made changes to the industrial relations system designed to make it easier for employers to prevent their employees from striking or taking any other form of industrial action. It banned 'pattern bargaining', (preventing unions from taking industrial action to achieve common outcomes across a range of workplaces), it prohibited strikes during the life of a certified agreement and strictly limited the time when industrial action could be taken legally, and it introduced secret ballot requirements. Another of the government's policies, not finally achieved till it took control of the Senate in 2005, was to exclude most employees from State and federal laws and awards protecting employees against unfair dismissal.

The changes in the laws meant the Australian Industrial Relations Commission lost much of its ability to intervene in disputes to provide what it considers a fair outcome: rather its role became to police the rules set by the government for terminating industrial action. It would be involved in administering secret ballots. Minimum award standards, previously set by the Commission, would in future be determined by the government (subject to disallowance by the Senate). It would no longer have the role of vetting certified agreements (this taken over fully by the OEA) or hearing unfair dismissal claims (except for employers of more than 100 people). Its role of setting minimum award wages was abolished and a newly created Australian Fair Pay Commission would set minimum wages instead.

Trade unions

Even before Work Choices, the trade union movement was facing a battle to establish its continuing relevance, a battle it shares with trade unions in most western countries. All have had to adjust to the fact that their membership, as a proportion of the total workforce, has been steadily falling. In Australia the decline of trade union power has also been associated with legislative efforts by conservative governments to make strikes – their most effective weapon – either illegal or extremely difficult to employ. According to Breen Creighton and Andrew Stewart (authors of *Labour Law*), a 'combination of common law and statute presently make it virtually impossible for any union or group of workers in Australia lawfully to take any form of effective industrial action'.[4] This, the authors say, is unjust and contrary to internationally accepted norms. But the threat that governments or employers may take court action has never been able to stop all strikes, even some that were plainly illegal. Employers generally hesitate to use the ordinary courts to penalise individual strikers or their unions. Nevertheless, since the outlawing of strike action for secondary boycotts under the Fraser Government in the late 1970s, the number of strikes and their duration has fallen away. And the latest Work Choices changes by the Howard Government introduced a new element into the anti-strike equation: they made it possible for the government (or one of its agencies) to take responsibility for the prosecution of strikers and unions.

Through the 1970s days lost through strikes averaged about 4 million a year, while through the 1980s the average was about 2 million a year. But in 2002 only 259,000 days were lost. The picture is remarkably similar in Britain. In 1979 13.2 million workers were union members compared to only 7.5 million in 2005. In the 1970s strikes accounted for 12.9 million lost working days, in the 1980s 7.2 million while in 2005 the figure was 158,000 (see Figure 8.1).[5]

There are many factors contributing to this fall in industrial conflict, but one of the most important is a change in the strategy of the union movement as it faces a serious decline in membership. From 1983 the unions, through its peak body, the ACTU, joined forces with the new Labor Government headed by former ACTU president Bob Hawke, to implement many of the government's economic reforms, using various accords that limited wage rises in return for social wage improvements in health, education, transport and superannuation. Partly as a consequence of the accords union demands were modified and the need for strike action reduced.

Figure 8.1: Industrial Disputes

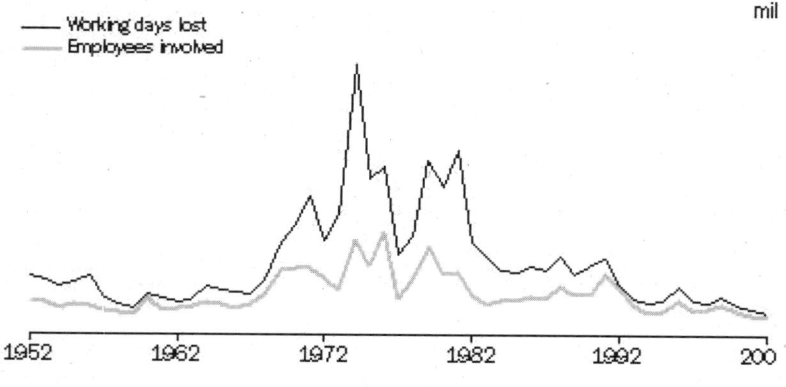

Source: ABS.

By the time John Howard became Prime Minister in 1996 leading the Coalition back into power, the union movement was far less capable of mounting any sizeable resistance to renewed efforts by him to reduce union power. According to Bob Hawke, the unions are being challenged because they represent a decreasing proportion of the workforce as a consequence of changes in the nature of economic activity and the structure of the workforce:[6]

> You now have a decline in the numbers in manufacturing industry, more in the services industry, much more part-time work, and a lot of work being done from home ... With all those fundamental changes, it is inevitable that the natural recruiting base for trade unions would diminish, contracting not just in Australia but in the US and elsewhere.

Over the past generation the number of people in the workforce has increased from about 6.3 million to just over 10 million, but the number belonging to unions has fallen, from 2.5 million to 1.8 million. Fewer than one in four employees are now members of a trade union. Trade union membership remains relatively high in the various public services, State and federal – just under 50 per cent – but relatively small among employees of private firms – only about 17 per cent, and the proportion is falling (see Figure 8.2).

Figure 8.2: Trade Union Membership, proportion of employees

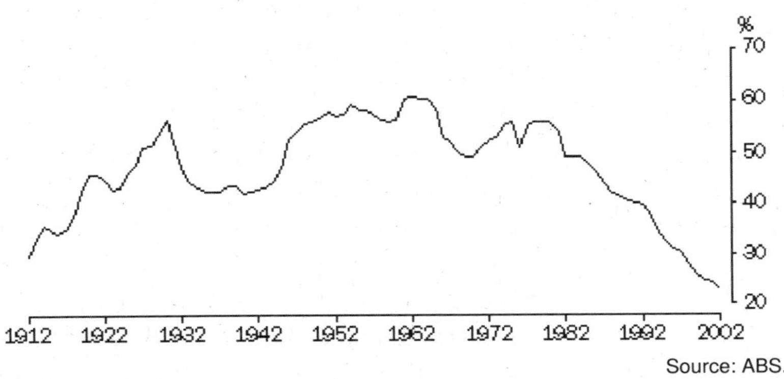

Source: ABS.

The least unionised industries are forestry and fishing (five per cent), property and business services (seven per cent) and wholesale trade (seven per cent).[7] In finance and insurance the proportion of people belonging to trade unions fell between 1997 and 2002 from 36 per cent to 18 per cent. Over the same period the number of people in mining (once a hotbed of union militancy) who belonged to a union fell from 44 per cent to 29 per cent.

One of the problems for the union movement is that huge changes in the way people work make it difficult for unions to recruit them. ACTU President Sharan Burrow says that, since 1996, 54 per cent of new full-time jobs have been filled on a casual basis, while 80 per cent of the part-time jobs are casual. Almost two-thirds of all the jobs created pay less than $600 a week.[8]

However the main challenge facing the union movement is not structural but political. Burrow says that in 1996 the Howard Government made it clear it didn't see a role for trade unions. She admits that the Work Choices changes will mean there will be areas where trade unions will have little power or influence. 'But there will be a union movement here in three years time, in six years, in 10 years. But governments come and go'.

Governments, however, can pass laws that help determine whether workers are more or less likely to join a union. Through the early 1990s most State governments, when controlled by Liberal, National or Coalition parties, passed laws that prohibited compulsory unionisation, and encouraged individual bargaining. In 1996 the Howard Government abolished compulsory unionism on a national scale.

The Work Choices law means for the first time that most Australian workers will have their employment conditions governed by the national industrial relations system rather than by a State law. Before 2005, only about 40 per cent of the workforce came under the federal system. That proportion was expected by the Federal Government to more than double to 85 per cent within a few years of the new law coming into effect. This expansion of the coverage of the national system was achieved by the Howard Government's use of the Commonwealth's constitutional power to make laws about corporations to assume control of the regulation of the workplaces of all relevant corporations.

Under the previous industrial relations regime, the Commonwealth's power was limited: it could only make laws for the conciliation and arbitration of industrial disputes extending beyond the boundaries of any State. In the early years of the 20th century only a few disputes met the criteria suggested by this limited constitutional power. However the High Court decided that a dispute could be created simply by a written demand by a union for wages or conditions, that demand having been rejected by an employer. 'Interstateness' could similarly be satisfied by ensuring that the demand was made of employers in more than one State. And finally the High Court decided that the word 'industrial' did not mean the dispute had to be in an 'industry': it could mean a dispute involving school teachers, nurses or firemen (the last group had been excluded by an earlier High Court decision).

The final limitation of this power was that it could only be used to establish a system of conciliation and arbitration. It could not be used by Parliament or the government to set wages or working conditions.

None of these restrictions apply when the Commonwealth makes laws under the 'Corporations Power'. The Commonwealth Government can dictate the minimum wages that corporations must pay their employees, and the minimum terms and conditions they must offer their workers. And it can deal with businesses that are established solely within a State, as well as those that extend beyond the State. The only large groups of workers not covered by the corporations power are those employed directly by State governments, though many of those employed by government owned corporations will be covered.

This massive change in the reach of national regulation of industrial relations and in the nature of that regulatory control directly by the Federal Government, will impact on the States as well as many trade unions. Membership of State-based unions will tumble as they cease to be able to win award coverage for members under State industrial laws. Cuts in the membership of State-based unions will impact on their ability to directly influence Labor Party policies. Under changes to the Labor Party's constitution introduced through the efforts of former leader Simon Crean, the representation of affiliated unions at Labor's Federal Conference was reduced from 60 per cent to 50 per cent in 2003. However the influence of the unions at the State level depends mostly on the size of the union membership and when that begins to fall, so will the ability of the unions to determine policies and choose Labor's candidates for political office.

The States will be left with responsibility over industrial relations only of their direct employees and a relatively small number of workers employed by unincorporated enterprises. This will have a significant impact on the State arbitral bodies. In recent years much of their work has involved cases where workers were seeking reinstatement for unfair dismissal. These cases will largely disappear as a result of the new federal law. They will have relatively few awards to administer, just those involving a handful of unions representing State public servants. These awards tend to be settled by direct negotiation between unions and the relevant government.

The workforce

The nature of Australia's workforce changed considerably in the last two decades of the 20th century and at the beginning of the 21st. The main changes were in the increased participation of women in the workforce, increased casualisation, a higher proportion of part-time workers, a significant proportion of workers establishing themselves as independent contractors and the use of labour hire firms.

The number of women in the workforce increased steadily from the early 1970s. In 1970 about 40 per cent of women between the ages of 15 and 65 were in the workforce. This reached 50 per cent in 1980, 57 per cent by 1990 and in 2003 stood at 62 per cent. This was well above the OECD average of 55.3 per cent but 3 or 4 per cent below the rate in the US and Britain.[9]

Casual employment jumped at an even faster rate. In the 15 years to 2003, the percentage of casual workers in Australia increased from 19 per cent to almost 28 per cent, and since 1988 more than half all newly created jobs were for casual workers. In 2003 more than 10 per cent of all people in work were self-employed contractors while more than 3 per cent of workers were employed by labour hire firms.

OECD statistics show Australia is one of only four countries in the (developed) world where part-time employment exceeds 25 per cent of those in employment. The average for the OECD is 15 per cent.

Self-employed workers, contractors and labour hire firms are the subject of special legislation introduced by Kevin Andrews, the Minister for Employment and Workplace Relations. As with workers in the general workforce the government's aim is to remove them from the jurisdiction of the State industrial relations systems. In a discussion paper Andrews released while the legislation was being prepared he says various estimates agreed that about 10 per cent of workers were self-employed contractors and about a quarter of these were involved in the construction industry, mainly in housing, while a fifth were in computer services.

According to research by the Parliamentary Library, casual workers are younger, less well educated and more likely to be in a job with inferior conditions of employment compared with ongoing employees. It says statistics tend to support the argument that casual employment (like unemployment) is mainly involuntary in nature and that many casual workers would prefer to be in an ongoing job. It says that while there are about an equal number of males and females in casual work, the incidence of casual work is higher among females in the workforce (32 per cent) than males (24 per cent).[10] The Productivity Commission says that among casual employees, those with fixed-term employment, plus students and mothers mostly declare themselves to be satisfied with their employment circumstances. Prime working age males are often recorded as less satisfied but these are a small proportion of all casual employees.[11]

Destruction of the AIRC

As noted earlier, the AIRC (Australian Industrial Relations Commission), for a little over a century, was the central institution in the Australian industrial relations world, a world characterised by its critics (mainly ultra-conservatives) as a club. It was certainly a fairly cosy environment. For much of its history, the members of the Commission and its predecessors were chosen from among those who appeared before it or were close associates of it – unions, employer organisations, academics and public servants from the relevant (industrial relations) disciplines. Appointments through most of the second half of the 20th century followed a predictable pattern, with one from the union side, one from the employer side and one 'neutral'. It meant that none of the principals involved complained about bias, even when decisions went against them.

That changed under the Howard Government: the unions were out of favour and frozen out of any chance of appointment to the Commission. But this was not enough for the opponents of the club. Former senior Treasury official Des Moore, for example, in speeches to the HR Nichols Society (a forum for those who disapproved of the arbitration system) continued to argue that the Commission should be abolished, or if retained, converted to a mediatory body with no legal powers of arbitration or intervention. He claims that when viewed from a broad economic and social perspective, the record of the Commission was extremely poor.[12]

One of the main public defenders of the Commission has been High Court Justice Michael Kirby, who was a presidential member of the Commission in the 1970s. In a speech in 2004 marking the centenary of the passage of the law establishing the Commission's original predecessor, the Arbitration Court, Justice Kirby said:

> There are those who see no future whatsoever in the Australian Industrial Relations Commission. For them it should be closed down, lock stock and barrel … Persons of such views tend to live in a remote world of fantasy, inflaming themselves by their rhetoric into more and more unreal passions, usually engaging in serious dialogue only with persons of like persuasion. For the rest of us, who live in the real world, and know our country and institutions better, time will not be wasted over such fairytales. Australia is not a land of extremes. Irritatingly enough to those of extreme persuasions, Australia's basic institutions and laws tend to adapt slowly over time: adjusting to changing economic and social forces only as such adjustment is truly needed. So it has been with the national conciliation and arbitration tribunal. So it will be in the future. Those who want more dramatic change, as distinct from constant adjustment, need to look for another country.[13]

Within two years, the implementation of the legislation demonstrated that the prospect of destroying the Australian Industrial

Relations Commission was neither fantasy nor unreal. The extreme changes that Justice Kirby predicted would not eventuate were put into law and into effect, and were endorsed by a High Court decision that Justice Kirby said 'effectively discards a century of constitutional doctrine'.[14]

The Australian Industrial Relations Commission by 2006 had become an institution in name only, an empty shell. And in April 2007 Labor undertook that if it was elected to government it would establish a new body, Fair Work Australia, to absorb the AIRC and three agencies created by the Howard Government, the Fair Pay Commission, the Office of Workplace Services and the Office of the Employment Advocate.

And the unions, too?

In the 12 months to August 2006, trade union membership declined steeply, from 22.4 per cent of the workforce a year earlier, to 20.3 per cent. The number of trade union members fell by almost 126,000, to 1.79 million.[15] One commentator, Gerard Henderson, wrote that the message of the figures was clear: 'no matter how draconian the Work Choices legislation is deemed to be, it is unlikely to lead to a surge in union membership'.[16] This misses the point of the government's Work Choices exercise. As noted above (page 150) of this chapter) one of the principal aims of the Work Choices law was to reduce the role of trade unions, and to make them less likely to retain or attract membership. By largely excluding unions from the wage negotiation process and reducing their ability to access workplaces and bargain for better and healthier working conditions, the law was intended to make them largely irrelevant. The unions, recognising this threat to their very existence, decided to spend about $12 million in a television campaign opposing the introduction of the law, and then up to $20 million trying to defeat the Howard government at the 2007 elections. As Henderson correctly noted, the election was crucial for the ACTU. A Labor loss would mean:

> [U]nion privileges would not be restored in legislation until at least 2010. By then, judged by the rate of present membership decline, the union movement would be a shell of its former self with membership in the private sector all but non-existent.[17]

Notes

1 Solomon 1999: 131.
2 Constitution, s 51 (xxxv).
3 Submission by the OEA to a Senate Committee of Inquiry into workplace agreements, 25 August 2005.
4 Creighton and Stewart 2005: 582.
5 *The Economist*, 10 June 2006: 57.
6 Hawke 2005.
7 ABS *Year Book of Australia 2006*
8 Burrows 2005.
9 OECD 2005.
10 Kryger 2004.
11 Productivity Commission 2006c.
12 Moore 2001: 3.
13 Kirby 2004: 24-25.
14 *New South Wales v The Commonwealth* [2006] HCA 52 (14 November 2006) at para 608.
15 ABS 2007.
16 Henderson 2007.
17 Henderson 2007.

9

Universities

At the beginning of the 20th century, university education in Australia was a rarity. There were just four universities – Sydney, Melbourne, Adelaide and Tasmania. Australia had a population then of 3.8 million, but just 2652 university students. At the beginning of the Second World War, almost 40 years later, a university education was still out of the reach of ordinary Australians. There were then six universities serving the needs of 7 million Australians, but just 10,354 studying for a degree, including 81 studying for a higher degree. But after the war there began a series of important developments that began to transform the educational outlook for Australians. By 1960 12 per cent of young Australians were expected to attend university at some stage in their lives; 40 years later that figure had quadrupled. The Australian Vice-Chancellors Committee (AVCC) estimated that by 2020, 60 per cent of all Australians would complete higher education.[1]

World War II provided the impetus for the Commonwealth Government to become seriously involved in the provision of higher education. The Curtin Government initiated the Commonwealth Reconstruction Training Scheme (CRTS) providing university scholarships to thousands of returned servicemen. It also prompted the government to found the Australian National University in Canberra as a research university concentrating on nationally important areas such as nuclear physics, medicine and Asian and Pacific studies. The Commonwealth had begun providing some research funding for the universities during the Depression. This was stepped up in 1943 and continued after the war to help the universities cope with the huge increase in enrolments flowing from the CRTS scheme and later its Commonwealth Scholarship scheme for the best secondary school students. In 1948 there were 32,000 students – a figure that declined after the ex-servicemen completed their studies. While most funding was provided by the States (which had established all the universities other than the ANU) the Commonwealth had made itself responsible for about a quarter of the income for the university sector by the early-1950s.

In 1954 Prime Minister Sir Robert Menzies established an inquiry headed by Sir Keith Murray, chair of the UK University Grants Committee, to examine the needs of the universities in Australia. At that stage Australia had eight universities and three small university colleges – outposts of three of the major universities. The Murray Committee found the universities generally were in a parlous financial position leading to under-staffing, poor infrastructure, high failure rates and weak honours and postgraduate schools. It recommended a massive increase in federal funding, virtually doubling the Commonwealth's contribution (then around $30 million) to meet a huge increase in student numbers. While there were about 31,000 students in 1956, the Murray Committee estimated there would be a further 120 increase over 10 years. In fact growth exceeded these expectations. For example, between 1958 and 1960 enrolments increased by 13 per cent each year. By 1960 there were 10 universities in Australia with 53,000 students, 15 years later there were 19 universities with 148,000 students.

In 1974 the Whitlam Government decided the Commonwealth would accept full responsibility for funding the universities and colleges of advanced education, subject to student fees being abolished.

By 1985 Australia had 19 universities with 175,000 students and 46 colleges of advanced education many of which were involved in teacher education and were issuing degrees. During 1987-1988 the system was revolutionised. Education Minister John Dawkins introduced reforms that replaced the so-called binary system by effectively abolishing the distinction between universities and colleges of advanced education, and forcing the amalgamation of many institutions. The Commonwealth took a more active role in determining university activities to ensure they conformed with its national economic model. Increases in student numbers were encouraged, but from 1989 a user-pays element was reintroduced through the creation of a Higher Education Contribution Scheme (HECS), effectively a tax on the future earnings of students. (HECS fees were set at 25 per cent of the nominal cost.) International students were also encouraged, but they had to pay the full cost of their courses.

By 1997 Australia had 37 universities with 650,000 students. In the first few years of the Howard Government financial support from the Commonwealth was sharply reduced. The government also decided to allow universities to accept full-fee paying domestic students up to 25 per cent above the quotas set by the Commonwealth, and increased HECS by providing for three (later increased to four) different fee bands, depending on the course or faculty in which a student was enrolled.[2]

The Dawkins revolution

The changes effected by Education Minister John Dawkins in the late 1980s transformed the tertiary education sector, creating many new universities, amalgamating many institutions and ending the life of scores of smaller education providers. Institutions with fewer than 2000 students were amalgamated with others as they were considered too small, some colleges of advanced education were taken over by universities, while about two score were promoted to full university status. Opinions remain strongly divided as to whether the changes were beneficial or took Australia down the wrong educational road, while most probably agree with the former head of the Australian-Vice-Chancellors Committee, Professor Di Yerbury, who says some of the changes were very good, while some just didn't work.[3]

One of the senior advisors to Dawkins in designing and implementing the creation of what Dawkins called the 'unified national system' was Professor Don Aitkin, then head of the Australian

Research Grants Committee and subsequently (for 12 years) Vice-Chancellor of the University of Canberra. He thought that by and large the changes worked 'pretty well', though he says the way the University of New England was expanded was wrong and the merger that Dawkins proposed for the Australian National University and the Canberra College of Advanced Education (CCAE) was also wrong.[4] As it happened the latter proposal was dropped when the Council of the ANU responded to the concerns of staff and others and pulled out of what had been largely completed negotiations. The CCAE was transformed into the University of Canberra.

Aitkin says the former 'binary' system that Dawkins overturned was 'preposterous'. He says in retrospect he cannot understand how anyone had agreed to its creation, on the recommendations of the Murray committee in 1963. The reason for its development was that Sir Robert Menzies at the time thought he couldn't afford to have a proliferation of universities of the Oxford kind, and his cabinet didn't want them. They thought Australia needed more skilled people, but that could be achieved without lecturers doing research. Hence the decision to create colleges of advanced education that were not funded for research activities.

Aitkin says he would give the Dawkins reforms 'a nine out of 10 mark. It's now 15 years since it was done, and it's pretty robust. It put everyone on a competitive basis, as opposed to a status basis'.

However most Vice-Chancellors are highly critical of what was done and the outcome. Glyn Davis, Vice-Chancellor of Melbourne University and formerly of Griffith University believes:

> people will look back and say we made a mistake as a nation.[5] They'll say, on the one hand what Dawkins did was very good for equity, he provided opportunities for hundreds of thousands of kids to go to universities over the next decade who would otherwise have missed out. That's of course a good thing. On the other hand what he imposed was a uniformity on the system that actually drove out innovation and produced a grey flatness to higher education that we didn't need to have. And that was a mistake. Now everyone understands that something went wrong. Why have we got 38 versions of the same thing and so little difference between (the universities)?

Professor John Hay, Vice-Chancellor of the University of Queensland is even more scathing. 'The Dawkins revolution was and is a failure'.[6] He says the idea that all post-secondary education would be provided by universities was a big mistake. 'I think differentiated post-secondary education on the American model had always been the model to follow. That possibility wasn't entertained, as far as I can recall'. The model he favours, where people would do a general degree before doing a professional or higher degree, was not followed because of a reluctance by the government and the opposition to fund it. He says it was a catastrophe that the differentiation of institutions did not take place:

> But this is a fraud. No-one believes that all institutions are of the same standing. This is not just a snobbish remark. It is simply saying to students, as Americans do, that if you go to this kind of institution you can do well, that you will have a more substantial qualification than going to an institution that doesn't attract the best students and the best staff. I think that's just saying to students that merit will be rewarded. It's a kind of meritocracy, but not an elitist or snobbish one.

Funding

The Whitlam Government assumed effective control of Australia's universities and other tertiary institutions in 1973-1974, when the Commonwealth made a financial offer to the States they could not refuse. Whitlam promised to provide the funding the States had previously supplied, for the universities they had established. The Commonwealth, which had provided one-fifth of the income universities received in 1951 and 43 per cent in 1961 (the increase the result of the implementation of the policies adopted by the Menzies Government) would now contribute around 98 per cent of their income.[7]

In financial terms, the early 1970s were the golden age for universities. Later Commonwealth governments were not as committed to providing them with the money they needed for adequate staffing or capital expenditure on buildings and equipment. With the introduction of the HECS scheme students, domestic as well as international, were required to contribute an increasing proportion of university budgets. Early in the 21st century the Commonwealth's contribution had dropped to around 40 per cent of the income for the university sector.

Melbourne University Vice-Chancellor Dr Glyn Davis points out that the funding cuts happened much earlier than most people realised.[8] 'The slide began in 1983 if you measure dollars provided per student. From 1983 it is a slow, gentle but consistent fall'. He says the Dawkins reforms, which were about providing opportunities for more people to attend universities, accelerated the process because it meant the available dollars per student fell more dramatically. But while this pattern persisted for almost 20 years, most people identified the Vanstone cuts (Amanda Vanstone, former Minister for Education) in 1996 as the time when you saw a sharp deterioration in what was happening in universities.

Funding declined from around $13,000 per student in 1984 to $7340 in 2003. As a proportion of overall funding, the Commonwealth Government's contribution fell over a 14-year period from 82 per cent in 1989 to 41 per cent in 2003 (see Figure 9.1).

The University of Queensland's Vice-Chancellor, John Hay, is equally concerned about the steep decline in federal funding.[9] He points out that the Commonwealth now provides more financial assistance for private secondary schools than it does for public universities. The universities now have to rely increasingly on the money they obtain from both international students (who pay full fees) and local students through the HECS scheme or who can pay their full tuition fees upfront.

Not every university has been able to find the money it needs from non-government sources to support its budget. Professor Peter Coaldrake, Vice-Chancellor of the Queensland University of Technology, points out that the reports by various State Auditors-General show that around 10 universities throughout Australia had operating deficits in 2005.[10] This was not a situation that could continue, though it was not practical to consider closing any universities. He believes there needs to be more collaboration between metropolitan and regional universities. In Perth two or three universities in 2005 began exploring the possibility of amalgamation.

Don Aitkin believes the universities generally have coped well with the relative reduction in Commonwealth funding, in finding alternative sources of income. 'It forced them to become quasi-private institutions', he says.[11] 'Institutionally it has been a very good

Figure 9.1: Changing Funding Sources (%) 1989-2005

Source: Adapted from DEST Finance Statistics 1989-2005.

thing. But for the people of Australia a very bad thing. Lots and lots of kids are not going to university who might have and should have'.

Economist Dr John Quiggin describes the Howard Government's post-secondary education policy as 'a disaster area, with a succession of ministers pursuing ideological hobby horses at the expense of any coherent attempt at addressing Australia's needs'.[12] Writing after the 2006 budget was delivered, Dr Quiggin specified three particular hobby horses:

- voluntary student unionism (see below);
- pushing the government's industrial relations agenda; and
- establishing its rival TAFE network.

He says the central idea in the agenda was to replace subsidised university places with a system based entirely on upfront fees, supposedly to produce a system more accessible, competitive, diverse and market responsive than the existing system which it regarded as a socialised enterprise. Dr Quiggin says:

> The freeze on subsidised places, and the cutbacks in funding have certainly forced universities to pay more attention to market (or,

since the whole process is so heavily managed, pseudo-market) forces. But the results of the policy have gone nowhere near satisfying the projections put forward by advocates. Far from diversifying, universities have become more homogenous in their offerings, differing primarily in the status and wealth they inherited from the fully public system. High-cost academic disciplines have been squeezed, while business courses and (often misleadingly named) vocational degrees have proliferated.

Responsiveness to student demand has been reflected in 'cappuccino courses' on subjects such as surfing. This and other predictable but apparently unforeseen developments have produced a reaction in the form of tighter centralised control, with the result that universities face the worst of all worlds, with declining funding, ever more bureaucratic controls and inconsistent mandates. Even if these policies eventually produce benefits, and there is no reason to believe this, such benefits will be greatly outweighed costs of a decade of continuous and pointless reorganisation, frozen domestic enrolments and strained resources.

Policy control

It was inevitable that as the Commonwealth Government increasingly involved itself in funding the university system, it would want to influence or determine how the system should evolve and what the universities would do with the money it was providing to them.

Former Liberal Prime Minister Malcolm Fraser says Sir Robert Menzies was very conscious of the power the Commonwealth would acquire if it became the greatest funder of the universities. He was adamant that there should be an independent, high-level body created to stand between the universities and the government, that would make its own recommendations about the development of universities.[13] So he says Menzies created the Australian Universities Commission as a means of ensuring there would be no diminution in the intellectual integrity and freedom of the universities. The expert intermediary body was abolished as part of the Dawkins revolution. Fraser says this was a totally retrograde step by Labor, and:

> our mob [the Liberals] seized on that with alacrity and threw principle out of the window. Dawkins wanted to be able to tell universities what to do, and our people grabbed at that because they also want to be able to tell universities what to do.
>
> I don't want any politician telling universities what to do. I really do want academic freedom and intellectual integrity to be

> maintained at the highest level. That sometimes means things might operate a little less efficiently. It will be a small price to pay. I know people now in universities who don't want to say what I know is in their minds because they are frightened their funding will be cut.

Commonwealth control

What is most surprising about the Commonwealth's control of the universities is how it has increased despite the relative fall in the value of the Commonwealth's financial contribution to the universities. The disappearance of an expert advisory body like the Universities Commission is just one aspect of this. That aside, the Commonwealth has become increasingly involved in determining not only how many students the universities should each have, but what courses universities may offer, what student facilities they may charge for, even what contractual method should be adopted by universities for their staffing.

Professor Glyn Davis says it is a very odd phenomenon:

> On the one hand universities have been required to raise more of their income. But almost in parallel Commonwealth controls have increased. You would expect as the Commonwealth contribution declined so would the Commonwealth's desire to control, but it works the other way.[14]

He says there was a dramatic increase in Commonwealth control under Education Minister Brendan Nelson (2001-2005).

As Dr Michael Keating, former Secretary of the Prime Minister's Department, writes:

> The universities have found that they cannot rely solely on governments for their funding, while the government has responded to the increasing demands on its budget by tightening its control over what were once self-governing institutions. This bureaucratic control has come at a cost to university independence and diversity. Moreover the emphasis on uniformity of funding means that excellence is bound to suffer as Australia – like other countries – really does not have the resources for more than a few universities to be numbered among the world's best.[15]

Professor Peter Coaldrake, Vice Chancellor of the Queensland University of Technology, makes the point that former Labor Education Minister Simon Crean, in the early 1990s, was the first who tried to limit wage rises in universities by bribing universities to resist them, but that became encouragement money, then inducement money and then became punishment money under the Howard Government.[16] The extent of the punishment is sometimes directly measurable. ANU Vice Chancellor Ian Chubb calculates that if he was not to put into effect the Commonwealth's requirement that he introduce Australian Workplace Agreements (AWAs) for every member of staff it would cost the ANU $4.5 million.[17] 'I can't say no. They know we need it. But I am constantly reminded it is voluntary'. Chubb points out that even without AWAs the ANU was paying 110 different rates to its 160 professors.

Don Aitkin says the government does not want universities to be free and independent institutions. He complains that within university administrations the section that has to report to the government about its compliance with government requirements is now one of the largest. Such a section did not exist a quarter of a century ago. 'Compliance has got us by the short hairs'.[18]

Professor Greg Craven, executive director of the John Curtin Institute of Public Policy at Curtin University, describes the Commonwealth's relationship with the universities as 'intrusive micro-management'. He suggests its approach is failing to deliver what he considers is needed – true diversity. To attain this goal it would have to 'kick its expensive habit for excessive regulation'.[19] As a constitutional lawyer Craven's fear is that the Commonwealth will be able to use its success in the industrial relations field using the corporations power to directly threaten the independence of the universities and that this is 'deeply, deeply troubling'.[20] He says there is a world of difference between:

> being able to bribe someone and being able to command them. Direct Commonwealth power over the operations of universities will ground a thicket of prescriptive legislation and regulation in areas such as teaching and research that will make the Department of Education, Science and Training's present strictures seem positively negligent.

A related point is made by Dr Michael Keating:

> Equity does not demand that all universities are the same and equal. Rather, equity demands that entrance to a university is based on merit and not on wealth. The parameters of HECS can be adjusted and scholarships introduced to ensure equity of access, while allow-

> ing universities more freedom to determine their fees. The real flaw in the Coalition Government's new arrangements is that they do not allow universities to compete for students. Freedom to set fees is next to useless if there is no incentive to use fees to increase student intakes; either by increasing the quality of the university or by reducing its price.[21]

Professor Davis believes there should be an independent regulatory body to oversee higher education standards.[22] He says this was overlooked in Education Minister Brendan Nelson's push for greater diversity in the higher education market:

> In other major industries that have been reformed – electricity, gas, financial services – the reform process has included the establishment of transparent regulatory processes. Separating the source of subsidies from the regulation of players has been a standard marker of successful macro-economic reform. The main risk for the public sector is not the capacity of public universities but consistency of regulation.

International students

Australia's universities have become increasingly reliant – some of them to an extraordinary and possibly dangerous extent – on their success in attracting international full-fee paying students. To attract those foreign students, some universities have adopted practices that are ethically and educationally questionable and in a few cases verge on misrepresentation. Some have been accused of massaging exam results in order to retain or attract overseas students.

Australia is not unique in its use of international students to provide funding its universities can no longer obtain from governments. A survey by *The Economist* magazine in 2005 found:

> Foreign students keep British universities from crumbling. Some 9 per cent of students come from outside the European Union. Their numbers rose by a quarter last year. There are good academic reasons for wanting foreign students, but the main motivation is mercenary. Foreign students subsidise the loss-making teaching of home students (and the EU ones who pay domestic rates).[23]

Australia was twice as dependent on foreign students as Britain in 2002, the last year for which comparable figures are available. But the number of foreign students in Australia was continuing to increase at a rate that in 2005 was greater than most other countries with which it was competing for those students. Whether that increase was sustainable was beginning to worry university administrators and others. By 2005 the number of international students at Australian universities as a proportion of the total student population was the highest in the world – almost one in five. In absolute terms Australia was the third biggest destination for international students, after the United States and Britain. But foreign students constituted only 4 per cent of students in the US and about 10 per cent of students in Britain.[24]

Figure 9.2: Growth in international students 1993-2005

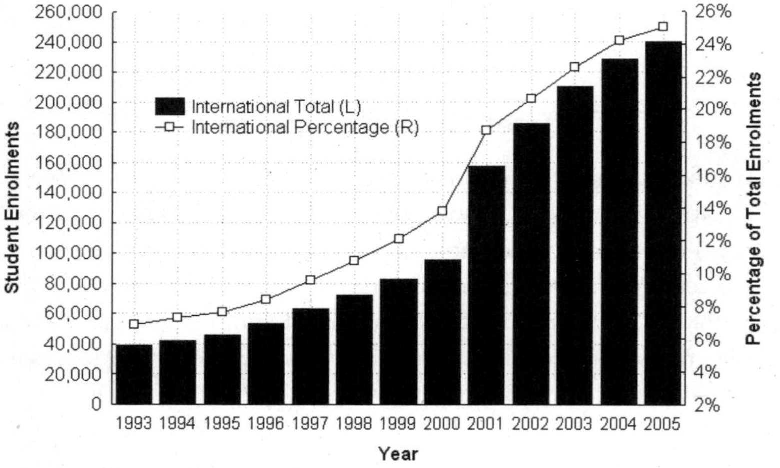

Source: Adapted from DEST Students Selected Higher Education Statistics 1993-2005.

The main sources of foreign students at Australian universities are Singapore, Hong Kong, Malaysia and China, each country providing between 27,000 and 30,000 students in 2003.[25] China was the most rapidly growing, with a 38 per cent increase over 2002, while India increased its student numbers in Australia by one third over that year, to a total of more than 11,000. Most students are enrolled in bachelor degrees (about 55 per cent) with about 30 per cent in masters degree courses. About 2.6 per cent were enrolled courses leading to a doctorate by research. The most popular subject areas were management and commerce (over 40 per cent) and information technology (15 per cent).

The students paid a total of $1.3 billion in fees to the universities in 2003, about half the amount the universities received in grants from the Commonwealth Government. But the contribution of the students to the national economy was far greater.[26] The Department of Education, Science and Technology estimated that in 2003 the total expenditure by students in Australia was $5.1 billion, including fees. The AVCC says the export value of educational services in 2003-2004 was $5.6 billion, about the same Australia earns from the export of cars or aluminium and slightly higher than it earns from wheat or beef exports.

Government policies, through the reduction in proportionate terms of the financial support it provides to universities and by directly encouraging them to take on full fee-paying international students (who are also encouraged through the grant of special visas) have made a huge impact on the internationalisation of the student body in Australian universities. In 1991 there were just 31,408 foreign students at Australian universities. This more than doubled by 1998 (72,183) increased to 112,342 in 2001 and soared to 185,058 in the following year. Between 2002 and 2003 the increase was a more moderate 14 per cent.

Another feature of the export trade in student services was that much of it was provided in the home countries of the students. Offshore students made up about a quarter of the total enrolled (112,258) in 2001, about 30 per cent of the 185,058 in 2002 and a similar proportion of the 210,397 in 2003.[27]

Many universities are concerned that the benefits from the boom in international students may begin to evaporate. ANU Vice Chancellor Ian Chubb says Australia was a beneficiary of the '9/11' attacks on the US in 2001, which resulted in an immediate tightening of the United States' screening of international students. He believes most students would prefer to go to Britain or the US rather than Australia, and when the US begins to open its doors again, Australia will suffer. Professor Chubb is also concerned with the standard of education being provided by some universities in Australia. He says in some areas some of them have more international students than

Australian students, and many are being taught in high-rise buildings far from the main campuses and away from other students.[28]

Queensland University Vice-Chancellor John Hay is also concerned about how many students universities can physically accommodate on their campuses. He considers a lot of Australia's traditional and new markets will become problematic because the market is becoming more competitive as Malaysia and China expand their own tertiary institutions.[29]

The reliance of universities on international students is raising concerns elsewhere. NSW Auditor-General Bob Sendt considers universities have become too reliant on overseas students and need to find other sources of revenue. He says they are risking their academic reputations by rushing into dubious offshore ventures and leaving themselves financially exposed as the boom in overseas students tapers off.[30] Former Prime Minister Malcolm Fraser says the idea that higher education can pay its way in a commercial sense is ridiculous:[31]

> Our universities have become too financially dependent on international students. They are in a very vulnerable position. We are third on the list for most international students behind the US and Canada. You wouldn't need a big change in policy in those countries to have more students going there.

University of Melbourne Vice-Chancellor Glyn Davis raises another fundamental problem. He points out that one effect of the growth of international student load is the way it has distorted the whole university system. He says the Vanstone cuts forced all universities to go out and recruit international students to fill the gaps in their funding income:[32]

> The perverse effect of that was to turn every university into a growth machine. As the dollars fell the only way to maintain what you had, was by ever-increasing the student body so you got more international fee-paying students. Australian universities are right out of whack with the rest of the world. They are much bigger than in any other system in the world. You don't find a small university in Australia unless it is regional and new and desperately trying to grow. The notion that you might cap a university as 20,000 students and say this is the right size to have, is not open to Australian universities because you can't make it work financially. This is a distinctly Australian pattern. If you look at a market system like America you see they work out their own optimum size and settle down to it. We can't afford to do that because our Commonwealth-

based funding continues to slowly decline, forcing us ever more into the search for new students.

Voluntary Student Unionism

Of all the changes wrought by the Howard Government to the university sector the one most dictated by ideology, passion and history was the abolition of the requirement that all enrolled students should be members of (and pay fees to) student organisations such as student political, social and sporting unions. There had been an attempt by the Fraser Government to abolish these fees for student organisations and student facilities including the provision of cheap meals and sporting facilities on campus. That was dropped because all the universities made representations about the impact the measure would have on their ability to provide support for students. The Howard Government renewed the move to abolish the compulsory fees and introduce what it described as Voluntary Student Unionism (VSU). Its first two attempts were rejected in the Senate: the third passed after it won full control of the Senate. Its legislation was opposed by every Vice-Chancellor.

The Australian Vice-Chancellors Committee pointed out to the government that student organisations played an important role in providing child care facilities or subsidising its cost and also providing health and welfare services for student members and study aids. It claimed less than 15 per cent of fees collected for student organisations went to student unions clubs and societies. The remaining 85 per cent – or $146 million – provided sporting facilities, health and welfare services, computing and other study aids, including photocopying and library services.

AVCC analysis of student services and amenities charges for 2004 shows that the activity targeted by the government leading to the abolition of student fees – advocacy, representation and political activity – was financed by just 17 per cent of the fees raised. More than 19 per cent went on sporting facilities.

The AVCC

The Australian Vice-Chancellors Committee (AVCC) was created in 1920 as the principal national representative of the university system, when there were just six universities. It has acted as a consultative and advisory body, making submissions to public inquiries of interest to the university sector, lobbying politicians and opinion leaders. However its ability to reach unanimity or achieve consensus on vital issues such as how funding for the university sector was increasingly compromised by the increasingly diverse interests of the universities its members represent. Since 1994 groups of Vice-Chancellors began informally developing policy agendas that were more directly relevant to their own universities rather than the sector as a whole. In 1999 eight of the Vice-Chancellors announced they had formally established the Group of Eight (Go8), describing itself as representing Australia's leading universities – the Australian National University, the Universities of Adelaide, Melbourne, New South Wales, Queensland, Sydney and Western Australia, and Monash University. The eight receive more than 70 per cent of national competitive research grants and conduct more than 60 per cent of all university research in Australia. The Go8 established their own secretariat in Canberra in 2000 to advance their own interests. Like the AVCC they regularly issue position papers and respond to government policy announcements, and try to influence those policies.

Two other groups subsequently emerged within the AVCC. The Innovative Research Universities (IRU) comprises Griffith, Flinders, La Trobe, Macquarie and Murdoch Universities and the University of Newcastle. The Australian Technology Network of Universities (ATNU) is made up of Queensland University of Technology, the University of South Australia, the University of Technology in Sydney, Curtin University of Technology and the RMIT University.

According to Professor Simon Marginson, Director of the Monash Centre for Research in International Education, the Go8 has a coherent agenda, focussing on its special role in research, but the interests of the other groupings are less clear. He says the ATN universities have a common identity summed up by the Queensland

University of Technology slogan, 'A university for the real world' but says that without the research credibility of the Go8 their global competitiveness is in question. 'The Innovative Research Universities are individualistic and more focussed on becoming Go8 than being with each other. In the present environment the IRU is essentially a defensive grouping'.[33]

In October 2005 the Go8 gave the AVCC formal notice that it wanted the AVCC to identify a narrower range of issues on which a genuine 'AVCC view' that represented the interests of the whole sector could be developed.[34] Professor Glyn Davis, chair of the Go8, wrote that:

> The range of issues on which the AVCC could lay claim to be 'the peak national representative body of Australia's university sector' is narrower than ever – and getting narrower. This is no fault of the AVCC, just the inevitable consequence of a more diverse sector.

These pressures finally led to the AVCC agreeing, in effect, to restructure, re-badging itself as Universities Australia. This was to come into effect in mid-2007.

A new diversity

The main players in the university sector have set their sights on increasing diversity. As Education Minister, Dr Nelson floated the idea of 'teaching only' universities. In the context of redesigning the Research Quality Framework, his successor, Julie Bishop, accepted that the Dawkins changes of the late 1980s that created the unified national system might need to be reversed, at least in part.[35]

In March 2005 Dr Nelson released two issues papers that indicated possible changes in the sector.[36] One, *Building University Diversity* was concerned with the way approval and accreditation processes for higher education might be changed in the future. It raised issues about the specific combinations of teaching, scholarship and research which should define universities and other types of higher education institutions, whether there should be provision for specialist institutions covering a narrow field of study in-depth, rather than a wide range of disciplines and the role of private and for profit institutions in the future. The other paper discussed the roles of the Commonwealth and the States in achieving a diverse but nationally consistent 'brand' of universities. It pointed to three areas where it said the 'current arrangements' impeded efficiency and innovation. All were regulated by the States and Territories. Dr Nelson said he was happy to consider proposals for the States to hand over their powers and was particularly interested in exploring and improving ways 'in which the Australian government can work strategically with States and Territories to promote greater national consistency and a more level playing field for universities'.

Melbourne University Vice-Chancellor Glyn Davis welcomed the debate generated by the option papers and used it to explain some of the changes that were already occurring in the system and the way it might develop in the future.[37] He pointed out that public universities had already found ways to circumvent the ban on teaching-only operations, creating inner city or offshore campuses that offer a narrow range of popular programs without the usual infrastructure of a university setting, while private providers had found ways to fill specialist interest in education, offering courses outside the academic mainstream.

He proposed a different way of regulating the tertiary system, based on that operating in California for half a century. This involved three broad tiers:

- the first would be colleges (and would include TAFE) offering diplomas and associate degrees and would cover vocational fields;
- the second would have teaching-focussed universities, public and private; and
- the third would be a smaller number of research universities, public and private, that would also have to meet national teaching standards and maintain standards of excellence and performance.

Only universities in the third tier would be able to award research higher degrees. He predicted this could eventuate within a decade.

In the meantime he is introducing changes within his own university that could affect the way others (particularly in the Go8) develop the system. Students will be offered up to five generalist strands of undergraduate programs including arts, science and the humanities. A good academic performance would be necessary before the student could progress to graduate school, where students could specialise in a particular field, such as medicine.[38] Professor Davis is introducing changes to meet new challenges to the public universities. He says a rapidly growing private sector is challenging their domination.

> A burgeoning number of private colleges, institutes, church organizations and companies have won the right to offer degree programs, supported by government-guaranteed student loans. Some are religious in orientation but most are vocational. The successful players are highly specialised, offering courses only in business administration, hospitality, sound engineering or natural medicine ... Australia's 37 public universities already compete in the international market. Now public universities face competition at home as well from established American brands and nimble private providers that avoid the costs of traditional campus settings, expensive libraries, playing fields, subsidised student facilities and deliberative, collegial governance.[39]

Professor Don Aitkin, who helped design the Dawkins model, warns against returning to a system where there were teaching-only universities:

> We've actually done this before and it didn't work ... In today's Australian university system, teaching-only is a no-no. There is no promotion that way, no peer respect, and indeed, little intellectual refreshment ... Yes, I can imagine a high-quality teaching-only undergraduate system. But it will need special staff and there aren't many of them.[40]

Major challenges

Increasing diversity is likely among Australia's universities as they compete for students and in some cases battle to survive as independent institutions. Their increasing reliance on full-fee paying overseas students makes them vulnerable to many factors outside their control – for example, a reduction in demand if the value of the Australian dollar increases, causing prospective students to go elsewhere. The universities, collectively, have provided an ever-increasing proportion of the Australian population with a tertiary education. But they are finding it increasingly more frustrating to have the way they function dictated to them by the federal government, a government that is requiring them to become increasingly more self-reliant by reducing their per capita funding. And some of them are finding it difficult to cope with the challenges they face.

Notes

1 AVCC 2004: 18-19 and Keating 2004: 106-107.
2 AVCC 2006: 7-11.
3 Yerbury 2005.
4 Aitkin 2005.
5 Davis 2005b.
6 Hay 2005.
7 Macintyre and Marginson 2000: 61.
8 Davis 2005b.
9 Hay 2005.
10 Coaldrake 2005.
11 Aitkin 2005.
12 Quiggin 2006.
13 Fraser 2005.
14 Davis 2005b.
15 Keating 2004: 107.
16 Coaldrake 2005.
17 Chubb 2005.
18 Aitkin 2005.
19 Craven 2006a.
20 Craven 2006b.
21 Keating 2004: 107.
22 Davis 2005a.
23 *The Economist* 15 January 2005: 49.
24 OECD figures quoted by *The Economist* magazine, 25 September 2004.
25 AVCC 2005.
26 AVCC 2005.
27 AVCC 2005.
28 Chubb 2005.
29 Hay 2005.
30 The *Australian*, 18 May 2006: 7.
31 Fraser 2005.
32 Davis 2005b.
33 The *Australian*, 12 October 2005: 31.
34 The *Australian*, 12 October 2005: 31.
35 The *Australian*, 19 June 2006: 6.
36 See <www.dest.gov.au>.
37 Davis 2005c: 38-39.
38 'Melbourne opts for a new model', The *Australian*, 1 March 2006: 4.
39 'Competition takes a local approach' The *Australian*, 1 March 2006: 25.
40 Aitkin 2004: 16.

10

Media

A survey of the new media published by *The Economist* magazine on 22 April 2006 argued 'that society is in the early phases of what appears to be a media revolution on the scale of that launched by Gutenberg in 1448'[1] when he invented a technology for commercial use that became known as moveable type. It called the new era the 'age of personal' or 'participatory media' based not so much on the internet, which it pointed out was decades old, but on the increasingly available always-on broadband access to it. 'With participatory media, the boundaries between audiences and creators become blurred and often invisible'.[2] And it suggested that it needed to be understood not as a publishing phenomenon but as a social one.[3]

A year earlier News Limited founder and chief Rupert Murdoch said in an address to the American Society of Newspaper Editors:

> What is happening is, in short, a revolution in the way young people are accessing news. They don't want to rely on the morning newspaper for their up-to-date information. They don't want to rely on a God-like figure from above to tell them what's important. And to carry the religion analogy a bit further, they certainly don't want news presented as gospel. Instead they want their news on demand, when it works for them. They want control over their media. They want control over their media, instead of being controlled by it.[4]

Significant changes are occurring in the Australian media for a number of reasons directly associated with the new media revolution, including changes in the financial basics of the media, competition between the various mediums including the new ones, and regulatory changes (or the threat or possibility of such changes). In some of these areas, what is happening in Australia reflects developments overseas. But more slowly.

In 2006, the television industry in Australia celebrated its 50th anniversary. But while it was commercially healthy, it was facing unprecedented competition. The same was true of the other established media: newspapers, radio and magazines. All were threatened by the technological revolution that allowed people to change the way they accessed information and entertainment.

Television, which as a relatively new technology half a century ago seemed to threaten the much older broadcast medium, radio, and to devastate cinema-going (and did help kill off afternoon newspapers in Australia) is in turn under threat. For some time free-to-air television has been slipping in its competition for viewers against the non-commercial stations, the ABC and SBS. In recent years pay television has been increasing its share of the market, also at the expense of free-to-air television. In 1983 the commercial share of free-to-air television was 86.8 per cent. In 2004 the commercial share had fallen to 78.6 per cent. Despite population growth, audience reach also declined. Figures published by Roy Morgan Research showed the free-to-air commercial television audience fell by 1.6 per cent in the nine years to 2004. In the same period the commercial radio audience fell 11.3 per cent and magazine readership fell 7 per cent. But the number of people who read a newspaper at least once a week increased by 1.6 per cent, while the number who went to a cinema at least once every three months grew by 3.2 per cent.

These trends tend to be obscured by the ongoing public battle between the television networks as to who is number one, which programs reach the biggest audience and which stations can produce the particular audience for which an advertiser is searching. But advertisers are conscious of the fact, for example, that between 2003 and 2005, the average audience for free-to-air, commercial television declined by 3.7 per cent while the average audience for pay television increased by 24.5 per cent.[5] It was estimated, based on trends to 2006, that the profits of the free-to-air television industry would decline from $600 million in 2006 to about $250 million in 2014.[6]

Newspapers in Australia have become increasingly aggressive in promoting their virtues (ie increasing circulation and readership) against the decline in television audiences. In 2006 News Limited and John Fairfax, who jointly overwhelmingly dominate major city newspapers throughout Australia, launched a campaign trying to persuade advertisers that, as News Limited put it, 'adults are watching less commercial television than 12 months ago while newspaper sales have increased'. They established an organisation, 'The Newspaper Works' to promote the medium. A year earlier they pointed out that in the previous 6 months the circulation of all metropolitan and regional newspapers rose by 0.3 per cent while the average number of adults watching commercial, free-to-air television fell by 2.6 per cent in the five major capital cities. News Limited's Australian chief, John Hartigan, said it was about time the newspaper industry started to market itself against the competition of other media:[7]

> Newspapers have seen off television. They have seen off the internet. The truth is that in a world where we are increasingly competing for people's time, it is a mark of what newspapers mean to their communities that people continue to buy us in ever-increasing numbers.

While that argument could be advanced in Australia at that time, it was certainly untrue in the United States where News Corporation's chair Rupert Murdoch lamented that in the face of the Internet revolution 'we've been slow to react. We've sat by and watched while our newspapers have gradually lost circulation … Where four out of five Americans in 1964 read a newspaper every day, today only half do'. The problem was mainly with young people:

> Consumers between the ages of 18-34 are increasingly using the web as their medium of choice for news consumption. While local television news remained the most accessed source of news, the internet, and more specifically internet portals, are quickly becoming the favoured destination for news among young consumers.

Murdoch said a recent study showed that 44 per cent of those surveyed used an internet portal such as Yahoo, Google or MSN at least once a day for news compared to just 19 per cent who used a newspaper on a daily basis. 'More ominously, looking out over three years, the study found that 39 per cent expected to use the internet more to learn about the news, versus only eight per cent who expected to use traditional newspapers more'.[8]

In the US, media organisations have changed their commercial strategies to meet the new challenges, and profit from them. The Mitchell submission to the government's issues paper on media regulation noted that:

> Acquisitions made by the major media magnates recognise advertising revenues and audiences are shifting away from traditional media to the Internet and pay-TV. There are a countless number of examples of the convergence of the old media with the new.

It pointed out, for example, that in the US, CBS and NBC had made deals with cable and satellite providers to distribute prime-time shows ('Survivor', 'Law and Order') for 99 (US) cents an episode. (American) ABC struck a deal with Apple Computer for some of its leading programs ('Desperate Housewives', 'Lost') enabling the downloading to Apple video iPod for US$1.99 an episode. Warner Brothers was planning to put old episodes of some of its major series on the America Online web portal. Whilst Britain's BBC2 is being simultaneously transmitted on the Internet.

The issues paper itself noted that the traditional media services were being challenged by new digital technologies:

> resulting in the emergence of new players, content, services and platform delivery … Digital technologies blur the lines between the traditionally distinct telecommunications, broadcasting, print and IT sectors as they deliver an increasingly common range of services.
>
> The shift has substantially impacted not only upon entertainment services, but also on sources of news, public opinion and information. For instance, use of internet-based news media has been growing rapidly. While many popular news sites are provided by traditional media companies, the emergence of weblogging, news via mobile phones and independent online news services means news and current affairs reporting has become more interactive.[9]

The press

Newspapers may have held their own against other mainstream media in the first years of the new century, and may have done better than some of their counterparts overseas, particularly in the United States. But history shows they are under pressure. And the changes in which many are engaged demonstrate their awareness of the problems they face.

When Professor Henry Mayer published his landmark account *The Press in Australia* in 1964, there were 14 State capital city daily newspapers in Australia, with a combined circulation (in 1962) of almost 3.5 million copies. The newspapers included six afternoon papers, all of which had ceased publication by the mid-1990s. At the turn of the 21st century there were two national papers published from Sydney (the *Australian* and the *Financial Review*), two Sydney papers (the *Telegraph* and the *Sydney Morning Herald*), two Melbourne papers (the *Herald-Sun*, and *The Age*) and one paper in each of the other capitals – the *Courier-Mail* (Brisbane), the Adelaide *Advertiser*, the *West Australian* (Perth) and the Hobart *Mercury*. Their combined (weekday) circulations in 2004 totalled about 2,270,000. In 40 years the circulation of the major metropolitan newspapers had fallen by a third, while the population had more than doubled.

However those associated with the industry reject suggestions that newspapers have no future. The secretary of the Australian Press Council, Jack Herman, says within two years of him joining the organisation in 1991, 'we were being told that newspapers were going to die – because of the Internet'. He said their circulations had declined for 10 years or so, but picked up after 11 September 2001:

> My view is that the media don't die, they adapt. Radio faced with TV became a different medium, television faced with movies and DVDs became a different medium. Newspapers have adapted too. Newspapers are no longer – can no longer be – a medium of record. They don't present the facts – they are not the thing that people read to get their first information. They are becoming much more a medium for detailed analysis, providing depth that isn't available in the other media. If newspapers are going to die, its a long way off.[10]

Rupert Murdoch appears to be equally sanguine:

> What happens to print journalism in an age when consumers are increasingly being offered on-demand, interactive, news, entertainment, sport and classifieds via broadband on their computer screens, TV screens, mobile phones and handsets?

> The answer is that great journalism will always attract readers. The words, pictures and graphics that are the stuff of journalism have to be brilliantly packaged; they must feed the mind and move the heart. And crucially, newspapers must give readers a choice of accessing their journalism in the pages of the paper or on websites such as Times Online or – and this is important – on any platform that appeals to them, mobile phones, hand-held devices, ipods, whatever.
>
> [N]ewspapers may become news-sites. As long as news organisations create must-read, must-have content, and deliver it in the medium that suits the reader, they will endure. Great content always has been, and I think always will be, king of the media castle.
>
> Caxton's printing press marked a revolution that is with us 500 years later. But the history of that revolution is not one in which the new wipes out the old. Radio did not destroy newspapers, television did not destroy radio and neither eliminated the printing of books …
>
> Each wave of new technology in our industry forced an improvement in the old. Each new medium forced it predecessor to become more creative and more relevant to the consumer.[11]

According to the *State of the News Print Media in Australia*, published by the Australian Press Council (APC) in October 2006, newspaper companies are rapidly transforming themselves into multi-media companies, by which the report meant companies that provided an Internet version of their newspapers. However what was important was that journalists were increasingly filing for both mediums and news was being put into a newspaper's website as it happened. Initially the Internet merely recorded what had already been reported in the printed version of the newspaper. Another finding of the survey was that reading habits are changing in the Australian community. 'The data are threatening', it said. 'Some age groups are reading newspapers less. Circulation is threatened. Nearly half of those who read Australian newspapers are over fifty'.[12]

In 1964 Mayer recorded another important feature of the press – there were just six 'independent' owners of the 14 major newspapers. He noted that one economist had said of four major newspaper mergers that had occurred between 1946 and 1959 that their 'most disturbing feature' had been the concentration of Australia's mass communications media in the full control of one firm – The Herald and Weekly Times – which by 1960 controlled 43 per cent of daily newspaper circulation throughout Australia.

Since then the trend towards oligarchy has increased. In 2004 there were just three 'independent' publishers. The Herald and Weekly Times was taken over by News Limited in 1987. By 2004 News Limited was the publisher of the sole newspapers in Brisbane, Adelaide and Hobart, of one national daily (*The Australian*) and of the largest circulation paper in each of Sydney (*Daily Telegraph*) and Melbourne (*Herald Sun*). All told, it published newspapers with about 70 per cent of the total circulation of Australia's metropolitan daily newspapers. The John Fairfax group published the other national daily (*Financial Review*) and one paper in Sydney (*Sydney Morning Herald*) and in Melbourne (*The Age*). The only other major publisher was the Western Australian Newspapers Ltd, publisher of the Perth newspaper, the *West Australian.*

The major newspapers provide readers with any significant diversity of editorial opinion only when the Fairfax group takes a different line from the News Limited group. Over recent years there has been a greater spread of opinion inside the Fairfax group than within News Limited, but editorially each group evidences the same line on the most important political issues, such as participation in the war in Iraq. The editors of News Limited group papers appear to have some freedom to determine their approach to matters affecting their domestic markets, but on national issues they all tend to follow the same line. At election time they have to clear their final verdict editorial with head office in Sydney.

Media regulation

At the 2004 federal election, the Howard Government committed itself to a review of media laws. In the late 1990s it addressed the need to set a transitional policy and legal framework for the eventual transfer of the broadcasting media from analogue to digital. Its aim was to encourage the industry to invest in the new technology and consumers to adopt it. It set an indicative deadline for the change-over of television to digital and provided encouragement to the existing networks by announcing a temporary moratorium on the allocation of any new television licences. By 2006 the government recognised it had to make further decisions, as the deadlines set in its own legislation required it to act. It approached that task in conjunction with an undertaking to review media ownership laws, those limiting cross-media ownership as well as a law restricting foreign ownership.

The government released a discussion paper in March 2006 canvassing its options to meet what it referred to as the 'digital challenge'. These included:

- the development of a digital action plan to expedite conversion to digital television by 2010-2012;
- allocation in 2007 of spectrum for two channels for new digital services, including subscription TV services, narrowcasting or datacasting;
- new channels for the public broadcasters, ABC and SBS;
- an indication that the decision on whether there should be future commercial channels would be made by the government, not by the regulator, the Australian Communications and Media Authority; and
- an indication that no such licences would be issued before 2012.

The cross-media laws would be altered but there would be a requirement for a minimum number of commercial media groups in each market – four in regional markets, five in mainland State capitals.

The reaction of the existing media groups was predictable and far from uniform as each sought to advance its own commercial interests. The main thrust of the reforms was supported by Publishing and Broadcasting (Channel Nine) and the Ten Network. Channel Seven wanted major changes while News Limited opposed them because they favoured the existing television networks at the expense of pay television, particularly Foxtel, of which it owned 25 per cent. News Limited chair Rupert Murdoch said the proposals were 'anti-free market'. 'It protects an industry that … is not about to disappear but it is in decline in nearly every advanced economy'. He said:

> The nearest thing to a monopoly in media is the Australian tri-opoly in broadcasting. I don't think it matters whether you have five, six, seven or eight television stations. It wouldn't matter if one or two went broke. That's what capitalism's about.[13]

Fairfax (*Sydney Morning Herald* and *The Age*) also opposed the reforms.

The government did succeed in having most of its proposals pass through the Parliament, despite the opposition of some National Party Senators, though some amendments had to be accepted. On cross-media ownership, the law designed by Treasurer Paul Keating in 1987 to limit media companies to just one medium (print, radio or television) in a single market was changed to allow companies to own two media. Foreign ownership restrictions were essentially lifted. New rules were introduced requiring regional radio stations to air 4.5 hours of local content each day, including 12.5 minutes of news. The changes were not designed to increase media diversity.

The Federal Government's involvement in media regulation has several constitutional bases though it has no direct power to regulate the print medium. Under s 51(v) the Commonwealth Parliament may make laws with respect to 'postal, telegraphic, telephonic, and other like services'. Radio and television have been held by the High Court to fall within that broad description. And the need to regulate access to the relatively limited radio spectrum made it essential that there be government regulation of some kind. The Commonwealth Parliament made laws to provide for the ways in which radio and later television licences would be allocated, and incidentally set standards for who could hold those licences. It was mainly by this means that it became able to control the extent to which those who owned newspapers could hold controlling interests in radio and television licences. The cross-media laws flow from this, as do foreign ownership issues though these also arise under laws made under other constitutional provisions including trade and corporations.

The corporations power provides another way in which media issues arise. Under the *Trade Practices Act 1974* the Australian Competition and Consumer Commission (ACCC) has the ability to scrutinise media ownership changes, and if it sees fit, prevent takeovers or mergers. The ACCC's chair, Graeme Samuel, in a number of speeches while the new media laws were being developed, repeatedly stressed the role his commission would have to play in the future, and how this would depend on the view it took of the great changes he saw taking place in technology and the way the media was developing. In one speech he made the point that 'relative to most industries, the Australian media is highly regulated'.[14] Protection of the free-to-air television networks was the cornerstone of this regulation, its justification being the need to ensure diversity in the services available to Australians at large:

> There is an outright prohibition on new entry into free-to-air television markets. Existing free-to-air broadcasters also have first rights of refusal over most popular sporting content, with competition from pay-TV precluded by anti-siphoning legislation. Other potential competitors have spectrum available, but are defined as datacasters and subject to extensive limitations on the types of content they can offer. On the flip-side, there is a prohibition on free-to-air broadcasters using currently available technology and spectrum capacity to start multi-channelling: that is, offering additional channels and choices to consumers, either on a subscription or free-to-air basis. This lessens the competitive pressures faced by pay-TV providers. But these protective regulations are dependent not only on continuing government support, but on the maintenance of the existing top down structure of the Australian media, and its now clear the environment is ripe for change …

Samuel said the revolution seemed inevitable and the possibility was for not one but hundreds of new competitors to today's broadcasters. However a crucial factor for the success of any ventures using these new technologies would be content rights and control of sporting content such as AFL, rugby, rugby league, cricket and tennis 'could be pivotal'. This was where his organisation, the ACCC, would play a crucial and possibly decisive role.

He pointed out that the *Trade Practices Act* had always recognised the potential for exclusive contracts to be anti-competitive and that exclusive dealing that caused a substantial lessening of competition was illegal. He said the ACCC had a role also when there were mergers or changes in ownership resulting in a substantial lessening of competition.

One of the crucial issues in Trade Practices law was determining what was the relevant market. In future media markets might be defined by the ACCC not by the specific medium but by the content – for example – advertising, or a particular type of advertising such as for jobs.

Defamation law reform

Until 2005, eight separate laws in the States and Territories governed the liability of the media for defamation. All those with any interest in defamation – the media, politicians, judges and people who might want to bring an action in the courts – thought the system needed to be changed so that there was a single, national law or uniform State and Territory laws. The Australian Law Reform Commission recommended action and the Standing Committee of Attorneys-General (SCAG) began seriously investigating the possibility of reaching a consensus. The issue remained on the SCAG agenda for more than a quarter of a century, unresolved.

When Philip Ruddock was moved from the Immigration portfolio to become Federal Attorney-General in 2003 he decided to act. He issued an ultimatum to the other Attorneys, warning that unless they could come up with an agreed uniform law, he would use the Commonwealth's corporations power to impose a national law on the media and make the laws in the States and Territories largely irrelevant. Ruddock had his own ideas about what the content of the law should be, and some of his proposals met with the unanimous disapproval of the States (for example, he wanted the law to protect the reputations of the dead, a feature of defamation law long abolished in most States). That helped push the States to reach agreement on a new uniform law to replace their own codes while retaining some aspects of the common law. The Australian Press Council and the main media proprietors were not happy with all of the provisions of the legislation, but were prepared to support it for the benefits it would provide, which included a cap on damages ($250,000), the abolition of exemplary damages, restrictions on the ability of most corporations to sue for defamation, and a requirement that in most cases actions for defamation must be initiated within a year of the publication of the alleged tort.

While the new law provides a more convenient method of resolving defamation actions, it contributes little to media freedom. And this in a situation where Associate Professor Chris Nash, director of the Australian Centre for Independent Journalism at Sydney's University of Technology says 'the Australian constitutional framework for freedom of the press is weaker than in other liberal democracies'.[15] He says 'the terrain on which the contest for freedom of expression and then press occurs is hostile to the public compared to other liberal democracies'.[16] This is partly the result of Australia being 'one of literally a handful of States that does not have a legal instrument (either a constitutional or statutory bill of rights) asserting the range and scope of its citizens' freedoms, including freedom of speech'.[17] He points out that despite the High Court's decisions recognising an implied right to freedom of political communication, 'Australian parliaments have a much broader power to restrict freedom of expression and the press than the legislatures in other liberal democracies'.[18] The result is defamation laws more repressive than similar laws in most liberal democracies – a conclusion that would not need to be altered after the enactment of the latest uniform laws.

Certainly Australia's defamation regime is far more restrictive on freedom of expression than that in the United States, where there is constitutional protection for freedom of expression, in the first amendment. According to Chris Dent and Andrew Kenyon at the Centre for Media and Communications Law at the University of Melbourne the Australian media is 'chilled' in comparison to the US. They say the American law's greater protection for opinion appears to allow stronger commentary than is possible in Australia.[19]

The Commentariat

Newspapers, in their search for ways to counter the ability of the electronic and new media to produce 'instant' news, have increasingly come to rely on providing their readers with expert or opinionated commentary on the news. From the mid 1990s much and probably perhaps most of that commentary became aggressively right wing. That was certainly the case in the Murdoch press, which was responsible for more than two-thirds of all daily newspaper sales throughout Australia. The leading commentators in the largest selling newspapers in the group, the *Herald Sun* (Andrew Bolt) and the *Daily Telegraph* (Piers Akerman) have pushed a conservative, pro-Coalition government line in almost everything they write. Most of the regular commentators in *The Australian* are of the same character. In the course of their commentary these writers frequently maintain that a left-liberal elite dominated the Australian media. They depict themselves as the underdogs in a 'culture war' in which they are fighting everyone who does not conform to their own neo-conservative views.

Immediately after the 2004 federal election, for example, Piers Akerman wrote:

> The election may be over, but the culture war is never ending. The gulf between those few who claim to occupy the moral high ground and the vast number of ordinary Australians who are hectored by the odious commentariat given free rein on the ABC and through the pages of the Fairfax press and The Bulletin magazine – with scant benefit of any countervailing views – continues to widen …
>
> The culture war will continue until the current generation of sinecured, self-pronounced opinion leaders gives way to a generation of thinkers who can see beyond the dead ideologies of the last century.
>
> Like the international struggle against terrorism, it won't be over soon and it won't be easy, but the victory will be worthwhile if the public is to be informed without fear or favour.[20]

Following a study of three Murdoch newspapers (the *Australian*, the *Daily Telegraph* and the *Courier-Mail*) over a seven-year period, two Macquarie University academics make the point that the relationship between elites and non-elites over a wide range of discussion of elites in Australian politics (not just among journalists) is constructed as 'a most intense antagonism'. They say it could be argued that elites are constructed as enemies rather than adversaries:

> 'The differences between adversaries are tactical; those that separate enemies are moral. Enemies are characterised by inherent traits that make them a threat. They are evil. They possess no legitimacy. Unlike adversaries they cannot be tolerated, only destroyed. Indeed, the presence of an enemy presupposes combat rather than coexistence. To the extent that 'elites' are enemies, they are unworthy of a place in Australian politics or society.[21]

Their conclusions help explain the vitriolic nature of the Akerman quotation above, and of similar terms applied by many of the other neo-conservative commentators.

According to Guy Rundle to any reasonable observer of the Australian press:

> [T]he tale of left-liberal domination was pure fantasy, yet it was a necessary fantasy if the right were to maintain their image of being lonely, rugged outsiders, crying in the wilderness. It was also necessary to mask the control of two overwhelmingly interventionist proprietors, Rupert Murdoch and Kerry Packer. The forces that were transforming the lives of the mass of people living in suburban and regional Australia were those of neo-liberal globalisation, as ardently promoted by the above mentioned proprietors. To disguise that, it was necessary to find a fifth-column of cosmopolitans, who were Australian by citizenship, but 'un-Australian' by inclination.[22]

A study by David McKnight of the op-ed pages of the *Australian* between February and July 2004 showed that of 358 contributed articles, 43.2 per cent came from writers 'identifiably of the right' while the remainder were neutral or non-conservative. He points out that of the former, many came from writers associated with conservative think tanks in Australia such as the Centre for Independent Studies and the Institute for Public Affairs or from American neo-conservative writers from think-tanks or organisations with which Rupert Murdoch was associated.[23]

The commentariat includes four notables whose voices are heard on radio – Alan Jones, John Laws and Neil Mitchell on commercial radio, and Phillip Adams on the ABC. Commercial radio provides an extremely significant contribution to the dissemination of political information and opinion. According to Jon Faine, who runs a morning talk program on local ABC in Melbourne, 'Talk radio has overtaken all other forms of media – electronic or print – as a political medium in Australia'.[24] He points out that politicians now devote more time during election campaigns to talk and talkback radio than to any other public activity, not least because it allows them to get their message across to the public without the intervention of an editor[25] (or indeed, print journalist). Appearing on a morning talk-show allows the politician to set the day's political agenda. And for conservative politicians, commercial talk shows with

Jones, Mitchell or Laws are largely stress-free because their interviews are rarely hostile and frequently provide them with the opportunity to have a free kick against their political opponents. Commentary by Jones and Mitchell in particular, follows the same neo-conservative agenda of the main Murdoch newspaper columnists.

The ABC radio talk hosts tend to be less combative and, other than Adams, less inclined to express overtly their political views. Yet the ABC remains a major target of the Murdoch press commentators, continually attacked for its supposed left wing bias and agenda. These attacks persisted even after the Howard Government appointed three of the right wing commentators – Dr Ron Brunton, Janet Albrechtsen and Keith Windschuttle – to the eight-member ABC Board. The ABC remains an enemy of the neo-conservatives in the culture wars despite all the members of the Board being Howard Government appointees (other than the managing director, who is appointed by the Board itself). They complain about the Board's lack of power to change the ABC's culture. Yet in 2006 they used their strength on the Board to protect one of their 'fellow travellers' when the Board rejected a proposal by ABC enterprises to publish a book by ABC journalist Chris Masters, about radio announcer Alan Jones. The Board said it was concerned about 'unrecoverable post-publication legal expenses'. A commercial publisher signed a contract with Masters within a few days to publish the book.

The wars will nevertheless continue because the ABC's charter requires the ABC gather and present news and information that is accurate and impartial, according to recognised standards of journalism. Donald McDonald, a close friend of John Howard, who was one of the first appointments to the ABC by the Howard Government and who served for 10 and a half years as ABC chair, has frequently stressed the importance of the ABC's role in providing diversity to the Australian media. For example, in a speech to the National Press Club in 2005 and in the context of the government's consideration of changes in media policy, he said:

> Media ownership is a difficult, conflict-of-interest issue for any government. They don't need my advice. I would simply like to say this: keep the ABC at the front of your minds when these changes are being considered. If we are looking for a means to maintain

> diversity of voices – always a difficult proposition to guarantee when competition is so fierce – the ABC is part of the solution, a big part of the solution.[26]

Perhaps the possibility (or likelihood) that McDonald is correct, helps explain the continuing attacks on the ABC, even when its leadership was taken over by those aligned with the conservative commentators. In a highly competitive situation, where the print media was under some threat from the new media, diversity was not something they sought.

Journalism

Journalists have a very low reputation for 'honesty and ethical standards', as low as the politicians whose conduct they report: they were all rated about the 10 per cent mark in a 2004 poll asking respondents to rate various professions on these criteria.[27] Mirroring this is their credibility level: the survey found, in relation to newspaper journalists, that 86 per cent of respondents believed they were biased, 63 per cent thought they often got their facts wrong. The relevant marks for television reporters and talkback hosts were about 10 per cent less condemnatory in both categories. People were equally divided (at 22 per cent) as to whether newspaper journalists were too left wing leaning or right wing leaning. There were a slight inclination to believe television reporters leant too far to the left (20 per cent as against 17 per cent) but there was a strong view that talkback hosts went the other way (17 per cent too left, 26 per cent too right.)

The journalism program at the RMIT conducted a survey of 129 media workers to discover what they thought of their industry.[28] Asked which was the most politically partisan media organisation in Australia, 40 per cent said News Limited, 25 per cent the ABC and 12 per cent the *Australian* (which is published by News Limited). The journalists believed the community predominately thought of them as being 'left' – 64 per cent. Both 'centre' and 'small "l" liberal' rated around 10 per cent while rights and conservative totalled 16 per cent. Asked to describe their own political affiliations, one-third of the journalists said 'left', 58 per cent 'centre' or 'small "l" liberal' and nine per cent 'right' or 'conservative'. When asked how much of an influence the prominent journalists had on public opinion there was none who answered 'not at all'. 'Moderately' rated 39 per cent, 'very' 36 per cent and 'it depends on the journalist' 24 per cent.

The answers to the question about influence might help to explain why despite the low ranking journalism has as a trustworthy occupation, journalism courses at 26 universities throughout Australia are in high demand among students with good academic qualifications. Around 1000 people graduate from Australian universities with journalism degrees each year. (A generation ago it was uncommon for people with degrees of any sort to become journalists.) However only about 35 per cent of journalism graduates find jobs in the mainstream media while about 30 per cent move to non-mainstream media.[29] Most metropolitan newspapers take on fewer than half a dozen cadets each year, though many of these have journalism degrees. But according to the executive secretary of the Australian Press Council, Jack Herman, many senior journalists are concerned that these trainees are not 'news ready'.[30] 'They are over trained and overly alerted to issues that shouldn't impinge on them', he says. Herman says some of the public members of the Press Council are concerned about possible changes in the quality of journalism in Australia. While not necessarily agreeing there has been a decline, he says there have been important changes:

> One, is that the distinction between reporting and opinion is lessening and they are merging more and more. This is very worrying for the Press Council which is talking about ethical questions where fact and opinion should be clearly distinguished. It is more difficult to make that distinction now – if ever you could. To an extent that kind of blurring is what people see as a problem with the quality of journalism.

He says a second problem is the rise of the by-line. A generation ago the by-line was rare. A newspaper might say a story was 'by our political correspondent' but that correspondent would not be identified. 'Now every Tom, Dick or Harry gets their by-line on articles'. A third change was that there was no-one between the journalist and the newspaper production process – no reader or compositor – and material went directly from the computer to the layout page. 'That had occurred because of changes in the economics of the business but it resulted in mistakes appearing in newspapers'. The Press Council found that about 40 per cent of the complaints it received were about inaccuracy.

The Press Council's report on the *State of the News Print Media in Australia* identifies other problems. According to the Council's chair, Professor Ken McKinnon, the most worrying trend identified in the report is the erosion of press freedom through administrative and legal curbs. 'Recent federal anti-terrorism, ASIO, telecommunications interception and national security legislation have all expanded restrictions on the ability of the press to report matters of public interest', he says 'The courts … are restricting the right of the public to be informed, especially in the lower courts, through excessive use of suppression orders'.[31]

The report itself says:

> Retention of a civil society depends to a large extent on the openness of government and public confidence in the probity and intentions of its public institutions. The unmistakeable trend is towards inhibiting the capacity of newspapers to report openly and in detail, despite their responsibility to hold a mirror to society reflecting its workings, good and bad, including terrorism, corruption, hypocrisy and malfeasance.[32]

It claims:

> The use of 'media management' techniques may be the greatest threat to the press's ability properly to report matters of public interest and concern. The fact that other institutions, the courts, the police, business, universities and sporting bodies, among many others, have looked at and learned from government on these techniques means the situation will only worsen.[33]

Although the report was prepared before the government's new media laws were finalised, it had this warning: 'The potential in the proposals to concentrate media ownership gives rise to concerns about the ability of the media to present a plurality of viewpoints and about the ability of journalists to move between employers'.[34]

Notes

1 *The Economist*, 22 April 2006: 15.
2 *The Economist*, 22 April 2006: 4.

3 *The Economist*, 22 April 2006: 5.
4 Murdoch 2005.
5 Mitchell & Partners 2006: 15.
6 Mitchell & Partners 2006: 21.
7 Hartigan 2004.
8 Murdoch 2005.
9 Australian Government 2006b: 3.
10 Herman 2005.
11 Murdoch 2006a.
12 APC 2006: 1.
13 Murdoch 2006b: 13.
14 Samuel 2005b: 2.
15 Nash 2005: 7.
16 Nash 2005: 8.
17 Nash 2005: 1.
18 Nash 2005: 2.
19 Dent and Kenyon 2004.
20 Akerman 2004.
21 Scalmer and Goot 2004: 157-158.
22 Rundle 2005: 40.
23 McKnight 2005: 56-57.
24 Faine 2005: 169.
25 Faine 2005: 170.
26 McDonald 2005.
27 Roy Morgan Research 2005: 117-119.
28 RMIT Journalism Program 2005: 120-122.
29 APC 2006: 60.
30 Herman 2005.
31 McKinnon 2006: 15.
32 APC 2006: 9.
33 APC 2006: 70.
34 APC 2006: 74.

11

Sport

In the final quarter of the 20th century most major Australian sports were transformed – by money. Professionalism in sport was a phenomenon of the second half of the century, though it had earlier beginnings in some sports.[1] Rugby League, for example, developed at the beginning of the century out of the amateur game Rugby Union, and was a professional sport from the outset, while golf had long had separate competitions for its professionals. But it was not until well after World War II that the rewards from professional circuits and sponsorship became sufficient to allow the top international tennis players and golfers to devote themselves full-time to their sport.

In Australia professional sport was transformed after Kerry Packer's Channel Nine network launched the breakaway World Series Cricket in 1977, catching completely unawares a conservative and complacent cricket establishment in Australia and elsewhere. Packer persuaded most of the world's best cricketers to sign contracts with World Series Cricket, brought them to Australia and then redesigned one-day cricket to meet the needs of television. Borrowing heavily from American baseball, Packer changed the way the players dressed and the way the game was played. As well as coloured clothing he changed the colour of the ball (to white) to aid another innovation, night cricket. He also pioneered the use of helmets and drop-in cricket pitches (the latter because he was unable to access most of the traditional cricket arenas). He also paid players as professionals, at a rate about twice what they were previously receiving.

Packer's gamble paid off, and not just for his television station which built its audiences and advertising revenue covering the sporting fad that he had created. His innovations were adopted (and developed) by the whole cricketing world. The amount of cricket played internationally expanded, feeding the media (particularly television) with a product they could sell to the public and advertisers. Packer's success was so striking that the official cricket authorities had to take him back into the fold, rewarding him with long-term contracts for his television network. The players benefited greatly, and not just at the elite (national) level: while State competitions had difficulty attracting customers into cricket grounds, the flow of money from television contracts and sponsorship allowed authorities to pay them reasonable salaries.

In 1995 News Limited emulated Packer and took on the Rugby League establishment by creating its own Super League competition. A two-year battle resulted in a few innovations (a video referee and night-time final) and to a change in control, with News Limited taking half-ownership of the newly created National Rugby League (NRL). Significantly, however, there was a large injection of money into the game during the two years the battle between the rival competitions flourished and later through substantially increased amounts received for television rights, from which ultimately the players were to benefit.

Rugby Union, the poor and essentially amateur code, also underwent a conversion. Through cooperative arrangements with the South African and New Zealand Unions it developed a regional competition based on State and provincial sides (Super 12, and later Super 14) alongside a tri-nation competition. Again the driver was television, and again the rewards meant vastly increased financial rewards for the players.

Australian Rules Football did not have the advantage of international competition: its innovation was to expand its reach and turn the Victorian competition into a national one with clubs from all States except Tasmania. And yet again, it was the demand of the commercial free-to-air television networks for popular sporting product that provided a financial bonanza for the game and its players.

At about the same time the major spectator sports began to harvest riches from television and sponsorship, the Federal Government and the State Governments were slowly deciding that they too should be providing financial assistance for sport, developing or improving sporting venues, providing specialist assistance for sports development and even directly subsidising participants and coaches. The Federal Government had always provided some funding to help the various organisations responsible for fielding teams competing in Olympic and Commonwealth Games and to attract the hosting of the Olympic Games in Melbourne in 1956. The first moves to create an enduring Federal Government support system for sport were taken during the Whitlam Government from 1972 with the appointment of a Minister for Tourism and Recreation and the provision from 1974 of grants to subsidise travel for athletes and provide support for coaches and sports management.[2] While the Fraser Government disbanded the program at the end of 1975, an extremely poor performance by Australia at the Montreal Olympics in mid-1976 prompted its eventual revival and expansion. At Montreal, Australia won just 5 of the 613 medals that were awarded and finished 32nd on the medal table. However it was not until 1980 that the government finally agreed to establish the Australian Institute of Sport (AIS) in Canberra, a proposal that was on the Whitlam Government's agenda in 1975. The creation of the AIS prompted the States and Territories to establish their own institutes and sports academies over the following 15 years.

Funding of sport

Money began flowing into sport from the government after the election of the Hawke Government in 1983. Existing programs were expanded and new ones created, extending far beyond the elite sports that had been favoured originally. Funding was increased by about 25 per cent immediately – to almost $20 million – and $10 million was pushed into further buildings and equipment for the AIS. Two years later the government made another substantial increase in its funding, and continued to increase budget allocations for sport for the next 10 years. In 1986 the Federal Government spent $32 million supporting sport, but this was relatively trivial compared with the funding provided for sport in some countries mainly in Eastern Europe, but also in some Western European countries. While Australia was spending about $2 per head on sport, East Germany and Czechoslovakia were spending 10 times that amount, while most West European countries and the US were spending two to three times as much, on a population basis, as Australia.

Ten years later, in 1996, the Federal Government allocated $90 million to sport. By 2005 the allocation to the Australian Sports Commission (ASC) was $168 million, covering the budget for the AIS and for a range of other programs. In 2006-2007 the ASC was allocated more than $204 million, of which $125 million was for high performance sport. In the 2006 budget the government committed itself to providing an extra $55.7 million over four years for elite sport preparation and support services. Almost $5 million of this was to establish a national talent identification network, $8.8 million to identify potential and athletic skills in the indigenous community, particular for track and field, $7.2 million to promote regionally significant sports and $4.6 million to train and retain elite coaches. There was also additional money for sports science and for sports excellence at the AIS.

State governments have also provided increasing funding for sport, spending collectively more than twice the amounts provided by the Federal Government. Local government is an even larger contributor to Australian sport, mainly through its provision of venues, grounds and facilities, and their upkeep. And business has become a major contributor to sport, mainly through sponsorship.

Some of the funding provided by government is devoted not to particular sports but to fostering healthier recreational and sporting lifestyles for children. In 2004, for example, the Commonwealth began a three-year pilot study, at a cost of $30 million, to get primary school children involved in sport after school. Its aim was to reach about 150,000 children in 3250 primary schools. This initiative was intended to overcome in part the problem that children don't have the mobility skills most Australian children once had. A generation earlier, sport and physical education were part of the ordinary school curriculum, in primary and secondary schools, both public and private. In many schools these were squeezed out of the school day by more academic, 'essential', requirements. The ASC's response has been to develop a school-based program, that is put it in place after the end of the normal school day.

National sports policy

Since the mid-1980s, national sports policy has been mainly in the hands of the ASC, which in 1989 took the AIS under its wing. The AIS remained responsible for elite sport, but the ASC set general policies that affected the role of the AIS – for example, deciding in 1989 to select seven sports that would receive $10 million to prepare for the 1992 Barcelona Olympics. Gradually the policy role of the ASC expanded, to the point where it began to seek to ensure coordination between the AIS and the various State institutes (rather than them competing) and to push its own policies onto national sporting organisations (NSOs), the latter in return for either direct funding or the provision of special assistance for participants in the relevant sport, for coaching and for administrative guidance and help.[3]

By 2005 the ASC had funding and service level agreement with all States and Territories except Queensland, with which it had a close understanding. It had agreements with 75 national sporting organisations covering funding and services that required NSOs to implement various policies developed by the ASC. Those NSOs were able to access the ASC's initiatives in such areas as coaching and officiating, Indigenous, disability, junior, women and club development. In return for funding and support, the NSOs were helped to meet their obligations in the areas of member protection, risk management, corporate governance, financial management, participation and high performance success. The ASC's anti-doping policies were formally adopted by 70 of those organisations.

Under the agreements between the ASC and NSOs, the sports organisations are responsible for the overall elite athlete pathway in their sport. However, as agreed between each NSO and the AIS, the AIS may conduct a special elite or senior international program (23 sports in 2004-2005) or run a pre-elite or development program (12 sports in 2004-2005).

At the 2004 Athens Olympics 289 current or former AIS athletes were selected to represent Australia in the 20 Olympic sports in which the AIS had conducted a sport scholarship program. This represented 72 per cent of the total team in these sports. They won 32 medals, and 70 per cent of the total medal tally was in sports where the AIS offers scholarships. As well as providing full training and other facilities for scholarship holders, the AIS provides sports science and sports medicine services to 22 national teams, on a commercial basis.[4]

The AIS in 2005 had scholarship programs covering 26 sports. However while the Australian team performed well at the Athens Olympics, winning more gold medals than ever before and holding fourth place on the overall medal tally, some 77 per cent of the medals were won in just two sports – swimming and cycling. The ASC and AIS have expressed concern that Australia's successes in recent years have encouraged other countries to copy its policies and spend increasing amounts on developing high performance sport. According to Mark Peters, executive officer of the Australian Sports Commission:

Figure 11.1: Disbursement of the budget across the Australian Sports Commission 2005-2006

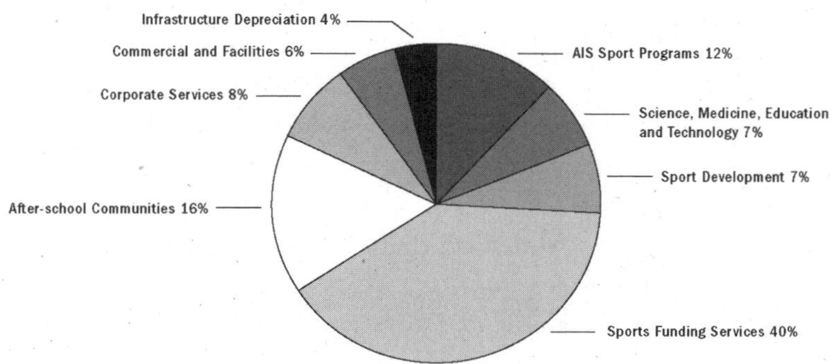

Source: ASC.

> Australian sport is under pressure from its international competitors, the likes of which have not been seen for some decades. They say imitation is the best form of flattery, but in Australia's case that imitation brings with it the need to constantly improve in order to stay ahead.

He claims countries around the world have seen Australia's success and adopted its model for the delivery of high performance coaching based on the Australian system of sports institutes, academies and intensive training centres, which in turn were underpinned by sophisticated sports science, sports medicine and vocational support services to elite athletes.[5]

Top sports

For the past 20 years Sweeney Sports Reports, a commercial organisation, has been assessing Australia's most popular sports. It calculates 'interest' in 50 major sports covered by the media, combining participation in each sport, attendance, television viewing, radio listening and print media readership. Its survey conducted from October 2005 to March 2006 found the sport in which most Australians were interested was swimming (61 per cent of capital city adult population). It had the highest participation rate of all sports (42 per cent – the next highest at 35 per cent were bushwalking/hiking and gym workout). Swimming rated third highest for television viewing (41 per cent, behind Australian Rules football on 51 per cent and cricket on 49 per cent) but it had low rankings with radio and print media and for attendance.

The most popular of the football sports was Australian Rules (54 per cent), followed by soccer (50 per cent) Rugby League (42 per cent) and Rugby Union (40 per cent). Cricket rated 54 per cent, tennis 52 per cent and motorcar racing 36 per cent.

An earlier survey of television viewing by Sweeney Sports found that during the winter of 2005, 55 per cent of Australians watched Australian Rules football, its best result for a decade, putting it eight points ahead of tennis and cricket, and at least 15 points ahead of other football codes.[6]

The Australian Bureau of Statistics (ABS) also conducts regular surveys of Australian sport. In 2002 it found the most popular physical recreation activity for both males and females was walking for exercise. The participation rate was almost 33 per cent for females and about 17 per cent for males. For children the most popular organised sport was soccer (with almost 20 per cent) while for girls it was netball (18 per cent). About seven million adults attended at least one sporting event during 2002, the most popular being Australian Rules football (21 per cent of men and 13 per cent of women) and horseracing (15 per cent of men, 11 per cent of women). The next most popular sporting venues were motor sports, Rugby League, cricket, soccer and Rugby Union.[7] Between 1995 and 2002 there was a large increase in the number of people going to watch Australian Rules (up from 1.7 million to 2.5 million and Rugby Union (up from 330,000 to 673,000) but a fall in cricket attendance (down from 1.1 million to 866,000).

The 2001 census found that the main job of just over 83,000 people was in a sports and physical recreation occupation, more than one-fifth higher than the number recorded in the 1996 census. But people in these occupations were more likely to be working part-time and more likely to have a lower income the people in the general working population. More than 8 per cent of the adult population – a total of 1.1 million people – undertook voluntary work for sports and recreation organisations in a 12-month period prior to interview in 2000. This was a greater number than for any other type of organisation.

Perhaps the most comprehensive survey of the participation of Australians in recreation and sport is conducted annually by the Australian Sports Commission, in conjunction with State and Territory agencies. The 2005 Exercise, Recreation and Sports Survey (ERASS) found that the top five organised sporting activities (by number of participants) were aerobics/fitness (over 1.5 million people), golf (over 590,000), tennis and netball (both over 500,000) and soccer (431,000). Between 2001 and 2005 there had been an increase of over 50 per cent in the number of people involved in fitness/aerobics. The largest fall was in the number playing golf (down almost 10 per cent). In the top 10 sports the only significant change was in those involved in Australia Rules (rising from 272,000 to 387,000, from 11th place to sixth.). Measuring the top 10 activities

– organised and otherwise – ERASS found walking ranked number one, with almost 6 million people involved, followed be aerobics/ fitness (almost 3 million), swimming (2.3 million) cycling (1.6 million) tennis and running (both 1.2 million) and golf 1.1 million.

Australian Rules Football

Australian Football (or Australian Rules) is the most attractive sport for Australian television. It is the most popular of the football codes in Australia (overwhelmingly in all States except NSW and Queensland, but enjoying significant support even in those two States where the rugby codes predominate). That is demonstrated by the size of the contracts the Australian Football League (AFL) has been able to extract from television networks in recent years, deals that have been bitterly contested by rival television interests. The AFL rights were worth about $150 million for the 1996-2000 period, and about $500 million for 2001-2006. The deal for 2007-2011 cost Channel Seven and Channel Ten $780 million, some of which they expected to recoup by selling a package of live games to Foxtel or some other pay-TV operator. The AFL also sold to Telstra for about $60 million the right to show limited footage of matches in 2007-2011 on mobile phones and the internet. Television rights provide about 60 per cent of the revenue received by the AFL.

The players are paid 25 per cent of the total revenue of the AFL. A collective bargaining agreement between the players and the AFL sets out minimum pay rates – for rookie players, $25,700 a year. Each club has to abide by a salary cap set by the AFL, of more than $6 million. That has to cover, on average, 43 players. The average salary paid to players in 2005 was $185,000. However a few senior players may receive close to the $1 million mark, while most of the better players receive around $600,000 a year.

Rugby League

Rugby League players receive somewhat less, on average, than the AFL players, at about $135,000 a year. Again, there is an official salary cap – in 2005, $3.25 million for the 25 highest paid players, an average of $130,000 a player. The cap is actively policed. One club lost four competition points in the 2006 season after the National Rugby League (NRL) discovered the cap had been breached in earlier years. Media deals and other arrangements allow the top players to earn around a million dollars a year. However the average payment for senior players is around $400,000 a year.

Players expect the salary cap (and their earnings) will benefit from the latest sale of television rights. It is not as lucrative as that achieved by the AFL, not least because of Rugby League is centred on just two States, New South Wales and Queensland, though there are also teams based in both Melbourne and New Zealand. The new television contract, with Channel Nine and Fox Sports, is $500 million for a six-year deal beginning in 2007. This was a 65 per cent increase in the annual amount paid under the previous television contract covering Rugby League.

Rugby Union

The Rugby Union matches attractive to television have a (mainly) international flavour. Since 2006 the main competition in which Australian teams were involved was Super 14, in which teams from New Zealand and South Africa were involved along with Australian teams. In addition the three nations play a three-round round robin involving their national teams. In 2004 News Limited acquired the broadcast rights for all these matches for five years for $419 million, of which the Australian Rugby Union (ARU) was to receive slight less than one third (the deal also covers the domestic competitions in South Africa and New Zealand).

While not as lucrative as the television deals for the AFL and NRL, the ARU's share and its other income allows it to pay senior players more than those in the other codes because there are fewer of them. In 2006 the collective bargaining agreement with the players required the ARU to allocate 26 per cent of gross player revenue to the players, with a minimum amount of $25 million (increasing by $750,000 a year). That was to be divided among 132 professional players, with an average of just over $190,000 a player. Regular members of the national squad would expect to receive over $600,000 a year.

Soccer

Soccer has never achieved in Australia anything like that ranking that might be expected of the 'world game', the name by which it was promoted at the time of the World Cup in Germany in 2006. Its international standing perhaps explains its attraction to SBS television, which broadcast the World Cup and won the rights to the next two. But SBS was financially able to win the rights to soccer only because none of the commercial television networks wanted it. However it was News Limited, through its subsidiary Fox Sports, that won the rights to broadcast the new domestic soccer competition, the A-League, and all international matches in which the Australian Socceroos would be involved other than World Cup finals, for seven years, at a cost of $120 million. These matches would only be shown on pay television.

Local soccer players cannot expect anything like the financial rewards of the other football codes, at least not in Australia, in the near future. The best of them head overseas, where they may win extremely lucrative contracts with British or European clubs. But in Australia soccer has struggled. Its post-World War II history was based on predominantly southern European ethnic-based clubs that failed to capture support in the wider community. Between 2000 and 2002 the national organisation lost $65 million.[8] It was transformed in 2003 when the Federal Government decided to financially support a bail-out of the former Soccer Australia, replacing it with the Football Federation of Australia (FFA), headed by one of Australia's richest men, Frank Lowy. The government agreed to give the FFA $9 million over three years, and a loan of up to $6 million, but only on condition that soccer implemented the recommendations of a review by businessman David Crawford. It took the ASC 18 months of pressure, taking on an administration that did not want to budge, before the old board agreed to step down to allow the sport's constitution, structure and management to be completely overhauled. It was a defining moment not only for soccer but also for the ASC, which succeeded in making the sport accountable to the government for the handouts on which it relied.

The new FFA inaugurated an initial eight-team competition, one-team-one-city model, with teams based on the areas where the game was strongest: Sydney, Melbourne, Adelaide, Queensland, Newcastle, the NSW Central Coast and Perth together with a New Zealand team. Although it had intended to keep this format for five years, the success of the first year of the competition was such that John O'Neill, former FFA chief executive, thought it would become a 12-team competition well within that time.[9] Another major change made by the FFA was to change its international relationship by moving from the Oceania grouping to the much stronger Asian Confederation. Australian soccer's recovery was boosted by its success in qualifying for the World Cup (for the first time since 1974) and reaching the final 16. Its success followed the FFA's decision to invest more than $1 million hiring, for just one year, one of the world's most successful coaches. In painting an optimistic picture of soccer's future in Australia O'Neill points out that it is already the largest participation team sport in Australia, with more than 700,000 players in organised competition in clubs and schools affiliated with FFA. Excluding schools soccer in 2006 had 450,000 registered players. The next largest team sport was netball (328,000) followed by Australian Rules (308,000) and cricket (274,000).

Cricket

Just as Australia's poor performance at the Montreal Olympics persuaded the Federal Government to substantially increase funding and support for national sport, Australian cricket's 'mediocre' results in the late 1970s and early 1980s prompted the creation of the Cricket Academy, now known as the Commonwealth Bank Centre of Excellence. According to Cricket Australia CEO James Sutherland, it was a bold step but the proof of its success is reflected in the fact that almost every member of the Australian Test squad that played in the 2005 Ashes Test Series held in England was an academy graduate, as were nearly all the contracted Australian players in 2006.[10]

Sutherland says the Australian initiative to identify and develop young talented cricketers has now been copied by other countries. England, he says, is going even further and through money provided by a national sports lottery is spending tens of millions of dollars on its academy and facilities. To try to help Australia maintain its recent dominance, Cricket Australia decided the Centre of Excellence should move from Adelaide, where it was established initially, to Brisbane, for the better climate. He says the Centre has developed 'very much as a winter program, enjoying the benefits of Queensland's weather, where players can practise on turf and play matches'.

Australia's senior players are now enjoying the rewards of higher television rights contracts. Since the mid-1990s, and following protracted and sometimes acrimonious negotiations, the players became what Sutherland calls 'partners' in the game. The memorandum of understanding with the players' organisation signed in 2005 and five for a four-year period, entitles players to 25 per cent of Cricket Australia's gross cricket-related revenue. The 25 Australian players receive 55 per cent of the pool, while the remainder goes to State players. The minimum retainer for national players for 2006-2007 was $150,000. They would also receive $12,250 for each test match and $4900 for a one-day international. The senior players are paid in excess of $500,000 not including sponsorships and media contracts. For State players the minimum payment under the agreement was $36,000 and the maximum $100,000. Rookie State players could be paid between $10,500 and $23,500. The match fee for the Pura Cup was $3300 and for one-day ING matches, $1,150. These payments were up to 50 per cent higher than in the previous contractual period.

While changes to the rules in one-day cricket are made regularly, Sutherland denies these are driven by television. One-day cricket, he insists, is still a very young game and still evolving. 'The changes that are made are to try to enhance the game and make it better for everyone, players and spectators'.

He is optimistic about the way cricket has retained its appeal. 'Whichever way you look at it, our television numbers have held up very well. There would appear to be continued growth in the worldwide audience, which is really encouraging for the game'.

Attendance at international matches in Australia has also held up, but is very low at Pura Cup matches, where almost no one goes to watch the State players. Sutherland says:

> It's disappointing from our perspective that it doesn't have as much support as it might deserve in terms of the quality of cricket being

> played. It is certainly not economic. But we recognise it is a loss leader for us. It has such an important development function and we don't want to compromise the competition because of the great service it provides through to the next level of competition. It really is that final stepping stone into international cricket. It really is a genuine advantage that (Australia) has that we have a highly competitive system where we have six teams and literally the top 60 to 80 players in the country are going hammer and tongs in both one-day and four-day cricket.

Golf

The Australian Golf Union and the Australian Ladies Golf Union were quite happy going their separate ways. But the Australian Sports Commission disapproved and used the kind of argument that tends to be successful – financial pressure. It told both organisations they would be cut off from any federal funding unless they amalgamated. The two groups thought about the threat for a few years, before eventually succumbing. Golf could not afford to reject the help the AIS had been providing since 1996, in the form of scholarships for full-time, year-long, residential training in Melbourne for six boys, two girls and two Professional Golf Association trainees.

The two Associations were also conscious of the fact that although golf attracts at least as many players as any other sport in Australia, the membership of golf clubs is in decline. According to statistics compiled by Golf Australia and surveys by the Australian Bureau of Statistics, after peaking at half a million in 1998, membership had fallen back to just over 450,000 in 2005. About one fifth are women. However a total of almost 1.3 million people (including members) play golf socially each year.[11] Persuading more social golfers to join clubs is the biggest problem facing the organisation in Australia. The main difficulty is the cost. According to a survey conducted for Golf Australia by Ernst & Young in 2003, the fees for most golf clubs range from $500 a year to $1500, while around a quarter pay more than $1500 a year.

Athletics

With a few notable exceptions such as Cathy Freeman, Australia's athletes have not performed outstandingly at the Olympic Games in recent decades. At the last five Olympic Games, Australia's track and field team produced medal tallies of two, two, two, three and three. According to Mark Peters, chief executive officer of the Australian Sports Commission, Australia's record in unlikely to improve much in Beijing in 2008. In fact he says Athletics Australia, the ASC and the AIS are working on a seven to 12 year program 'before you see the results of anything happening'.[12] Athletics Australia tells the same story. It says a joint review carried out by it and the ASC found that its existing high performance system was not working. The review said, 'There is no shared vision for high performance, structures and roles are unclear, resources are spread too thinly (across 250 athletes) and performance outcomes have been unsatisfactory'. It says bluntly:

> We cannot afford to keep doing what we've done in the past. Our objective is to build a focussed and transparent system for high performance that delivers exceptional outcomes in a cost effective manner by 2012. There are two core strategies for achieving high performance:
>
> 1. Establish a network of event-focussed national high performance centres to provide coaches and athletes access to the best infrastructure within the (state institutes and academies) framework.
> 2. Create a national junior development program to identify and nurture talented young athletes[13]

The study pointed out that Australia came 15th in athletics in the Athens Olympics, though it had the unrealistic and unachievable aim of being a top five nation. It now has no expectations of a quick turnaround in its fortunes. Its objective is to increase its medal count by just one (to four) in Beijing, but it wants to win five medals in London and become one of the top nations in athletics at the 2012 Olympic Games.[14]

Peters says the response of Athletics Australia to the review was 'really positive'. He admits that by investing more money in athletics the ASC might be thought to be rewarding failure. 'There have been suggestions we should be investing less'. However he says athletic skills are a basis for every other sport. 'Its important we have kids involved. The more numbers that come through little athletics into a national program – that's better for all sports, including athletics'.[15]

As part of its development program the ASC opened a European-based training centre, half an hour outside Milan, to benefit a number of sports including athletics. 'Athletes can be based there, competing regularly in Europe where most of the competition is, and in a proper environment with their coach and supported by sports medicine people'.

Peters has another explanation for the relative failure of athletics to produce many champions:

> One of the struggles they have in athletics is that you might have a really fantastic young athlete, 15 or 16, and you say to them 'if you train really hard then in four years time you might have a chance of being in the Commonwealth Games, or in four to eight years in the Olympic Games'. But then one of the professional sports comes along and says 'if you sign a rookie contract, here's x number of dollars and we'll put you in the business program'.[16]

The result is, Peters says, that:

> most of our best athletes are running around on football fields or ovals, or netball courts. Athletics has always had this problem and about how you keep the talented young athletes in the sport when there are lots of other options they have. Athletes that are well-built and quick are in great demand. And there is the immediacy of reward against a long-term promise of representation in the Commonwealth or Olympic Games.[17]

Peters says some athletes go on to earn a good living, but most don't:

> But they want to represent the green and gold, they want to represent their country. We need to support them more. We keep arguing to all governments that we need more money because we are not seeing much money from the corporate sector going to the non-professional sector.[18]

Racing

The 'sport of kings' is unlike any other major sport in Australia. While most have prospered from television rights and commercial sponsorship, racing has largely missed out. This is despite the fact that racing is the second most popular sport after the AFL (measured by attendances) and the fact that the Melbourne Cup and the AFL Grand Final are the two greatest sporting events on the national calendar.

Racing is distinguished in a number of important ways from other sporting activities. On the positive side, it is on any measure except attendances, the largest – so much so that it is perhaps best described as an industry, rather than a sport. According to a study prepared for the Australian Racing Board in 2001, in the year 2000 a total of 249,000 people were employed full-time, part-time or casual in the thoroughbred racing industry, with the equivalent full-time employment of 77,000 people. The direct participants included more than 6500 trainers, 1500 jockeys and apprentices and over 4000 bookmakers and their assistants. Two-thirds of all jobs were in non-metropolitan areas. It estimated that $5.5 billion was spent by the industry, $2.4 billion on land, buildings and breeding stock and $3.1 billion on people and running expenses. There were more than 133,000 registered owners of racehorses. The survey calculated that the racing industry had a direct economic benefit of $7.74 billion to the Australian economy and made a taxation contribution of $1.46 billion to the State Governments and Federal Government. In 2003-2004 almost 2800 race meetings were conducted in Australia, offering prize-money of more than $344 million. In the same year, sales of over 4500 yearlings at auction totalled more than $221 million. Australia has more racecourses (479) than any other country, is second only to the US in the number of individual horses staring in races, and offers the third largest amount of prize-money in the world.[19]

A second distinguishing feature of racing is its lack of central control. According to Tony Hartnell, a member of the Australian Racing Board Advisory Council and chair of the NSW Thoroughbred Racing Board since 2000, racing in Australia is affected by State politics, and is different in every State, sometimes with good results, sometimes with bad. 'The big debate is whether you want a powerful regulator who runs racing in the interests of the whole industry, or a bitsy regulatory system', he says:[20]

> The sport needs to be regulated and run at a national level. The horse-racing industry claims to be the fourth largest industry in Australia. We should see the whole of Australia as one single industry. Failing to run it that way results in economic leakage internationally and between states and territories.

Finally, the racing industry is reliant on gambling for its prosperity and success to a greater extent than any other sport. In 2003-2004 the gambling turnover on thoroughbred racing in Australia was more than $11.15 billion, of which almost $700 million was distributed back to the racing industry, mainly the race clubs. Harness racing and greyhound racing accounted for another $3.86 billion of the gambling turnover. Betting on all other sports (particularly the various football codes and cricket) totalled just $1.42 billion. These figures may be compared with the betting on Lotto and Tattslotto ($3.01 billion), turnover in casinos throughout the nation of $17.27 billion, and just over $90 billion that was put through poker machines.[21]

Notes

1 The 'phenomenon' is explored in a High Court judgment, *Commissioner of Taxation v Stone* [2005] HCA 21, a case dealing with the liability of an athlete to pay tax on various subsidies, prizes and sponsorships.

2 A detailed history of sport in Australia is provided in John Bloomfield (2003), *Australia's Sporting Success*, UNSW Press, Sydney.

3 Bloomfield 2003: 136-143, 162-174.

4 ASC 2005.

5 Peters 2005; and 2006: 3.

6 Sweeney Sports 2006.

7 ABS 2004.

8 O'Neill 2006b.

9 O'Neill 2006a: 112.

10 Sutherland 2005.

11 Golf Australia 2006.

12 Peters 2005.

13 Athletics Australia 2005: 2.

14 Athletics Australia 2005: 3, 4.

15 Peters 2005.

16 Peters 2005.

17 Peters 2005.

18 Peters 2005.

19 Australian Racing Board 2005.

20 Hartnell 2005.

21 Australian Racing Board 2005.

12

International foundations

Immigration is and always has been fundamental to Australia's growth, to its development as a nation and to its future prosperity. But the nature and extent of immigration has often been controversial and frequently an important political and social issue.

Since Governor Phillip established the first British outpost at Sydney Cove in 1788 the content and numbers of who would be required, permitted or encouraged to join this convict outpost created problems for decision-makers and sometimes aroused the concerns of those who were already present in the colony.

The arrival of free settlers from the last few years of the 18th century created difficulties, not least in the relationship between them and the emancipists (the convicts who had served their time or otherwise freed from their servitude), but the newcomers were necessary for the viability of the settlement. Later, the discovery of gold provided a huge boost to the population of the colonies of New South Wales, Victoria and later Queensland and Western Australia. And it led to the first attempts (in the 1880s) to restrict immigration – the imposition of special taxes on ships that brought Chinese into the colonies. There was widespread agreement with the motto adopted by the new weekly magazine, *The Bulletin* – 'Australia for the White Man'.

When, in the 1890s, the politicians began discussing the possibility of the federation of the colonies to form the new nation, Australia, they were near unanimous in the view that the Commonwealth should be given power to make laws about immigration, and equally convinced that the power would be used to control and restrict non-European immigration.

Among the first laws passed by the Commonwealth when it was created in 1901 were laws restricting immigration (through the imposition of a dictation test, to be administered in any European language – a device to exclude Asians who might speak English) and another to repatriate most of the South Pacific Islanders who had been brought to Queensland to work in the cane fields.

It was another half a century before the next problems emerged over immigration, and they were social rather than political, and flowed from a change in the composition of the migrants. After World War II there was a significant increase in migrants attracted to Australia from southern Europe, particularly Greece, Italy and Yugoslavia, and from northern Europe, in addition to the traditional source countries, Britain and Ireland.

As was to be expected, there had been a huge fall in immigration during the two World Wars and the Depression. This is demonstrated in the statistics concerning the proportion of the population who had been born overseas. In 1901 almost one in every four Australians (24 per cent) had been born overseas. By 1945 this had fallen to one in 10.

While there have been some fluctuations in policies adopted by various governments since 1950, mainly reflecting the state of the national economy at the time, the main thrust of those policies has been to encourage immigration and to permit migrants from an increasingly diverse number of countries. By 2001, the percentage of Australians born overseas was restored to almost the same as it had been a century earlier – about 25 per cent.

After the end of World War II the Labor Government decided Australia needed to substantially increase its population, for economic and defence reasons. At the time the population was just over 7 million. The government decided it would use immigration to boost the population by one per cent each year, to match a similar 'natural' population increase. The policy initially relied on persuading Britons to migrate, effectively giving them free passage. In addition, about 300,000 displaced (by Hitler and the war) persons from eastern Europe were also accepted as migrants.

These policies were continued by the Coalition Government that was elected in 1949 but there was some social discontent which grew as the number of people with an Anglo-Celtic background fell in relative terms, and the program was widened to include (in the 1950s) people from southern Europe and then (in the 1960s) people from parts of eastern Europe and the Middle East. Until 1971 the immigration rate remained high, averaging about 0.9 per cent of the population, but it slowed through the 1970s and despite some later boosts never returned to post-war levels.

The next important policy change affecting immigration was the decision by the Holt Government in 1967 to begin breaking down the White Australia Policy. That historic decision was deliberately played down by the government, which feared a political backlash.

Figure 12.1: Settler arrivals by region of last residence, Australia – 1947-1999(a)

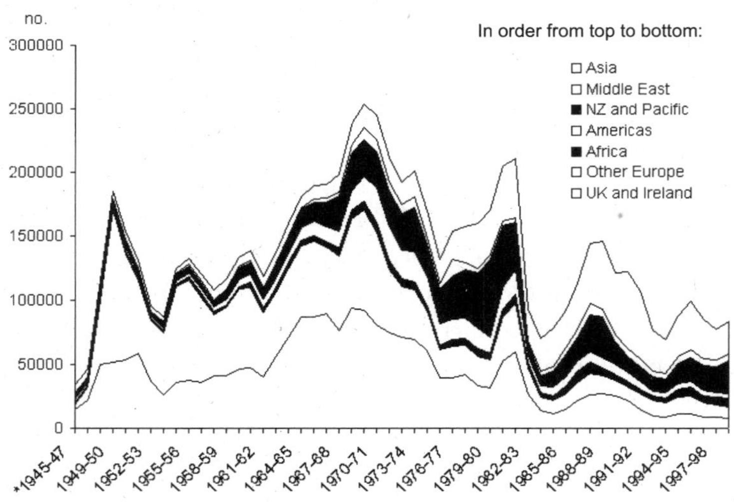

(a) The first marker shown related to the period July 1945 to June 1947. Thereafter the markers represent years July to June.

Source: ABS.

Its decision was conveyed to the public merely as a means of allowing highly qualified people to migrate, and indeed that was the way the policy was initially administered. Five years after the abolition of the White Australia Policy the official migration target was 140,000, including 90,000 European migrants whose fares were (still) highly subsidised. The number of non-Europeans was about 9500, and included a large number of people with qualifications Australia then needed – doctors and teachers. By this time the Labor Party had also officially abandoned its support for the White Australia Policy replacing it with a policy of non-discrimination. But the Liberal-Country Party Government of William McMahon maintained that its policy was to maintain a 'predominately homogenous society' despite predictions from Don Chipp, then a Minister, that by the 1980s Australia could become a multiracial society.

Migrants and population growth

Demographer Professor Graeme Hugo points out that until recently the United Kingdom remained the largest single source country of Australian migrants while the bulk of the remainder of settlers until the late 1960s were from elsewhere in Europe:[1]

> But with the dismantling of the White Australia Policy there was a diversification of origins. The twentieth century saw a transformation of Australia from an overwhelmingly Anglo-Celtic, homogenous population in which 95.2 per cent had been born in Australia, the United Kingdom or Ireland, to one of the world's most multicultural societies by 1996 when 16.2 per cent had been born elsewhere. Moreover, 19 per cent were Australian-born persons with at least one parent born overseas and 8 per cent had at least one parent born in a country in which English is not the main language.

Hugo describes the impact of immigration on post-war population growth as 'enormous'. He says of the growth of 11,501,442 people between 1947 and 1999, 'some 7 million can be attributed to the net gain of immigrants, their children and grandchildren'. He quotes research and estimates that Asian-origin population had increased from 0.3 per cent in 1947 to 6.4 per cent in 1999 and was expected to increase to around 10 per cent in 2030 if trends in the late 1990s were continued.

'Immigration', he says, 'has impinged significantly upon most aspects of Australian life and society'.

The debate about the composition of migrants resumed in the late 1980s and remained alive under Pauline Hanson through the turn of the century, mainly questioning the increasing number of people from Asia who were being admitted to the country. After its election the Howard Government tried to change the focus of the debate by increasing the proportion of skilled migrants. Excluding humanitarian commitments, in the first nine years of the Howard Government, skilled migrants increased from 29 per cent of the program to 62 per cent, while in the 2005-2006 the plan was for 70 per cent of the total migration program, or 98,000 people, to be in the skilled category.

To try to inject a significant degree of rationality into the debate, the government asked the Productivity Commission to conduct a study into the impacts of migration and population growth on both productivity and economic growth. In an issues paper the Commission pointed out that 5.9 per cent of recent migrants had higher degrees compared to 1.8 per cent of the population, while 73 per cent had Year 12 or equivalent schooling compared to 42.5 per cent for the population generally. It said recently arrived migrants tend to be better qualified and younger than the population. It pointed out that of the present population 43 per cent were either born overseas or had at least one parent born overseas, and over 200 languages are spoken.[2]

The Productivity Commission made the obvious point that migration was likely to be an important factor influencing the size of Australia's population and the size and composition of the workforce. It pointed out that the Australian migration experience was part of a global context in which there has been a large increase in both the scale and complexity of international population movements, driven by the globalisation of labour markets, increasing levels of education, the proliferation of social networks, information and transportation revolutions, the expansion of trade, economic change and the development of what it calls 'an immigration industry'.[3]

In its research report the Productivity Commission concludes that the overall economic effect of migration appears to be positive but small, and says this finding is consistent with previous Australian and overseas studies. It says positive effects from additional skilled migrants arise from higher participation rates (in the workforce), slightly higher hours worked per worker and the up-skilling of the workforce. But it says it is unlikely that migration would have a substantial impact on income per capita and productivity because the annual flow of migrants is small relative to the stock of workers and population, and migrants are not very different in relevant respects from the Australian-born population and, over time, the differences become smaller.

The Productivity Commission points out that in the past few decades the international flows of migrants has increased and their characteristics have changed, with an increasing diversification of countries of origin, increased temporary flows of migrants and increased skilled migration. Immigrants from China and other Asian countries have increased significantly as a proportion of total arrivals in Australia. It points out that while in 1981 English-speaking countries (Britain, New Zealand, the US and South Africa) accounted for around 40 per cent of long-term arrivals, by 2004 these accounted for only 21 per cent. While in 2004 Britain remained the largest single source of migrants (almost 45,000 people), as a proportion of total migrants it had fallen by more than half in 23 years from 23 per cent to 11 per cent. By 2004 China had replaced New Zealand as the second largest source of migrants (about 11 per cent) with India supplying six per cent (about the same as New Zealand) Malaysia just under four per cent, followed by Hong Kong, Indonesia, Japan and South Korea (between three and two per cent).

The report also puts the Australian migration program into an international context, pointing out that Australia, the United States, Canada and New Zealand were among the few countries in the world that admit immigrants for permanent settlement.[4]

Increase in skilled migration

The report highlights the substantial increase in skilled migration in recent years, jumping from around 30,000 in the mid-1990s to over 90,000 10 years later. By 2005-2006 skilled migrants were to be 65 per cent of the planned migration program. Candidates for this form of migration have to satisfy a points test that rates them according to their occupation, experience, age (points decrease as age increases) English language skill, Australian qualifications, willingness to live in regional Australia, and spouse skills. According to Professor Glenn Withers, Professor of Public Policy at the Australian National University and an advisor to the Department of Immigration on the migration program, the points cut-off for migrants is twice the score an average Australian would score and 'not a single member of the Federal Cabinet in the Australian Government would pass the test as a migrant'.[5]

Although the skilled migration program has raised some concerns that the government is using it to avoid tackling the need to improve the skills of young Australian workers, the general immigration program at the beginning of the 21st century was uncontroversial. What was a matter of political concern was the humanitarian program – or rather, that part of it covering asylum seekers arriving by boat, who had not passed through the government's offshore processing and approval system for refugees. In 2001 several groups arriving from Indonesia were involved in two incidents – the detention of one group aboard the *Tampa*, and the 'children overboard' accusations – that resulted in the government introducing drastic new measures to try to exclude 'illegal' boat people, including arranging that they be detained in other countries (the 'Pacific solution') and excluded from access to Australian judicial review after their claims for asylum are evaluated by departmental officials. The total humanitarian program was fixed at about 13,000 through most of the Howard Government's first nine years in office and of these fewer than 1000 a year (on average) were granted to on-shore applicants.[6]

In the mid-1990s governments decided to introduce a different means of attracting skilled people to work in Australia. The Keating government approved, and the Howard government soon after introduced, a new class of visa – a 'temporary (long stay) business visa' – known as a 457 visa. This visa allows employers to sponsor skilled workers for periods of from three months to four years. Visa holders may apply for a permanent skilled migration visa: many do (successfully), and most apparently intend to do so.

Initially around 30,000 visas in this category were issued, but this jumped to almost 50,000 in 2004-2005 and over 70,000 the following year.[7]

Although Queensland and Western Australia were the States most expected to benefit from the 457 visas (because of their high growth rates) in fact most of the visa holders were destined for New South Wales and Victoria. This may be because State governments were among the main users of the visas, recruiting (in particular) doctors and others involved in providing medical services (the largest single industry sector). Despite the bipartisan origins of the 457 system, it later created controversy: unions claim it is being used by some employers to recruit workers on rates and conditions that are well below those that would apply if Australian residents were employed and are intended to undermine existing rates and conditions for Australians.

Australia had previously resisted the notion of importing 'guest workers'. The 457 workers are different: they are relatively highly skilled (the government designates what skill levels are required) and there is a high chance that the workers (and their families) will become permanent residents.

The British connection

For a long time – probably till quite late in the 20th century – a vast number of Australians happily referred to England (or another part of the British Isles) as 'home'. A generation ago – certainly until the early 1970s – thousands of young Australians would head for London after completing their studies for a look at the old world, before returning to Australia to begin a career and family life.

It still happens, but London does not have the unique attraction it once had for Australians. Australians have changed, their horizons have broadened. Emotionally and politically, the relationship between Australia and Britain has been transformed.

There remains a constitutional link. The Queen of the United Kingdom is also the Queen of Australia. Her heir, the Prince of Wales, will succeed also to the Australian throne, unless Australia decides to change its Constitution and become a republic.

The ties that once bound Australia to Britain are remarkable. The country that emerged from its days as a dumping ground for the mother country's convicts did not harbour a grudge about its origins. For most of those who were transported, a much better life was possible in the Australian colonies than would have been possible had they remained at home. And almost all still had ties with the old country – bonds of family, culture, religion and race.

Race was very important. As late as World War II Prime Minister John Curtin, who at the outbreak of the war in the Pacific acknowledged Australia's dependence on the United States for its survival, spoke in 1944 in London about the 'consanguinity' of the British race. Even in his speech after the attack on Pearl Harbor in December 1941 Curtin said Australia would be preserved as a citadel of 'the British race'.

Yet immediately after that war was concluded, Britain decided that British citizenship would no longer extend to the people of its Dominions, including Australia. However no-one who witnessed the Queen's first visit to Australia in 1954 would have questioned the strength of the bonds between Australia and Britain. Two years before television reached Australia, millions of people turned out in force to watch, witness and celebrate the progress of their Queen (and Britain's) through Australia. They were captivated. Even in 1962 when the Queen made her second visit, the crowds were substantial and demonstrative, and relatively few winced when Prime Minister Sir Robert Menzies intoned the words of a 17th century poet, 'I did but see her passing by, and yet I'll love her till I die'.

Menzies was, as he proclaimed, British to the bootstraps, but his retirement in January 1966 left the political leadership of the country in the hands of a succession of leaders more anxious to promote Australia's independent identity and (in the case of most of them) intent of reducing Australia's direct legal and constitutional links with Britain. The legal system was given independence progressively until appeals to the Privy Council were eventually eliminated completely in 1986. After Menzies the practice (of Liberal Governments) of appointing superannuated British generals and politicians as the Governor-General of Australia was abandoned and it became unthinkable that anyone other than an Australia could hold the position (though Prince Charles lobbied the Fraser Government seeking the post for himself). The honours system was given an Australian flavour by the Whitlam Government when the Order of Australia was created (with the Queen at its head. No longer would Australians be rewarded for their community service with an Order of the British Empire). The final formal cut resulted from the passage of the *Australia Acts*, which came into effect in 1986, when the Parliaments of Britain, the Commonwealth and all of the States voted for measures which ended the ability of the British Parliament to make laws overriding those of the Australian Parliaments.

Yet many people would have been surprised by several High Court decisions that established that in the eyes of the law, Britain was no different from any other foreign country. One of those decisions came in 1999 when the High Court decided that because a One Nation candidate held dual (Australian and British) citizenship she was disqualified from election to the Federal Parliament because, for constitutional purposes, Britain was a 'foreign power'.[8] Additionally the High Court held in a number of cases that people with British citizenship, even those who had migrated to Australia as children, were liable to be treated as 'aliens' and could be deported.[9]

So officially, legally, Britain is a foreign country. Given the changes in migration patterns in the past half century that change in status reflects a real change in the feelings of most Australians towards Britain.

The American alliance

The American alliance, given formal expression in 'The Security Treaty between Australia, New Zealand and the United States of America (ANZUS)', is 'one of the fundamental institutions of our national life' according to Professor Hugh White of the ANU

Department of Strategic Studies. This is an assessment that relatively few Australians would contest – even among those who oppose the way it currently operates. As White points out, even when individual policies are unpopular with the public (as with the war in Iraq) or when US leaders are unpopular (as in the case of President George W Bush) Australians 'still have a very high regard for the alliance as a whole. Australians are smart enough to see the difference between individuals, or even the Administration, and the influence of the US as a whole'. He points out that at the time of the 2004 US election around 80 per cent of Australians thought the alliance with the US was important, but 70 per cent did not want Bush to be re-elected.[10]

However there are some vocal critics of the alliance and the way it is working, including former Labor Leader Mark Latham, and a small number of people who are defiantly anti-American in their views. In his published diaries Latham describes the US alliance as 'just another form of neo-colonialism' and that if the Australian people preferred being 'an American colony under Howard, that's a nation not worth leading'. He points out that New Zealand quit ANZUS almost 20 years ago. '(New Zealand) have their foreign policy right and it's the safest country on earth. Labor should be the anti-war party of Australian politics'.[11]

Former Liberal Prime Minister Malcolm Fraser is not anti-American but he does not believe it is in Australia's interests always to follow where the US leads – particularly into international military engagements. He now doubts the wisdom of the reasoning behind Australia's commitment to the Vietnam war (he was Minister for the Army and later Minister for Defence during that conflict). He says Sir Robert Menzies committed Australian troops there to secure America's involvement in Asia, 'not realising that America was going to be involved anyway'.[12] 'Anyway' he says, 'what we did was immaterial and inconsequential'.

Similar views about the relationship between John Howard and the Bush Administration abound. For example Bruce Grant, a former Australian High Commissioner to India wrote:

> The Americans under George W Bush are too entranced with their exceptional virtues and global military reach to pay attention to the voice of a marginal player, and we under John Howard are too

> concerned with our need for American protection to raise our voice … The result has been a deep division of opinion in both countries, weakening the alliance.[13]

And political scientist Professor William Maley, writing before the 2004 election, said the alliance needs to be reappraised. 'There is room in a mature alliance for critical as well as supine or obsequious partners and, in the long run, a new generation of leaders will have the opportunity to explore these possibilities'.[14]

According to Peter Costello, who as Federal Treasurer discussed the issue of anti-Americanism in a 2005 address to the Australian American Leadership Dialogue Forum it is common to come across Anti-American sentiment in Australia, like so many others. 'It is always there but it rises at times of Australia's military engagement in coalition with the United States. Most recently Australia's engagement in Iraq has raised these sentiments'.[15] Costello's view is backed by surveys conducted in 2005 and 2006 for the Lowy Institute.[16] The surveys found that Australians had very positive feelings about many countries with which Australia has had longstanding relationships: New Zealand (94 per cent in the 2005 survey); the United Kingdom (86 per cent in 2005, 74 per cent in 2006); Europe (85 per cent in 2005); Singapore (83 per cent in 2005, 65 per cent in 2006); Japan (84 per cent in 2005, 64 per cent in 2006) and China (69 per cent in 2005, 61 per cent in 2006). But only 58 per cent of those polled had positive feelings about the United States in 2005, though 62 per cent had that positive attitude in 2006. The 2005 survey reported:

> 68 per cent of Australians think we take too much notice of the views of the United States in our foreign policy … Only 29 per cent think we take 'the right amount of notice' and a mere 2 per cent that 'we take too little notice'.

Those figures were virtually unchanged a year later. The 2005 survey found that of the 58 per cent of Australians who had positive feelings towards the United States, half thought Australia paid too much attention to Washington's views. Of those with a negative view of the US, not surprisingly 94 per cent thought Australia paid too much attention to Washington. There was a striking finding from the question in the 2005 survey 'How worried are you about the following potential threats from the outside world?' Unfriendly countries developing nuclear weapons, and global warming were almost on a par at the top of the list (71 and 70 per cent) followed by international terrorism and international disease epidemics (63 and 61 per cent). But next, on 57 per cent, came Islamic fundamentalism and US foreign policies. In 2006, with the question phrased slightly differently to ask people about possible threats to Australia's vital security, international terrorism topped the list of concerns (73 per cent) followed by unfriendly countries becoming nuclear powers (70 per cent), global warming (68 per cent) and Islamic fundamentalism (60 per cent).

The ANZUS pact

However suspicious Australians are about the dangers US foreign policy might pose, and however concerned they are that Australia's Government takes too much notice of what Washington wants, they remain convinced of the importance of the ANZUS pact. (See previous page and below.) Overall, 72 per cent of those surveyed believe the alliance to be very important or fairly important in 2005, 70 per cent in 2006. Even among those with negative feelings about the US, some 53 per cent think the alliance very important or fairly important. Again, however, as with the war in Iraq, the survey shows there are limits to how far the alliance should take us. In 2005 only 21 per cent of those surveyed believe the alliance should lead to Australia being involved in a war with China over Taiwan.

The ANZUS alliance has been in existence for well over half a century, so it is unsurprising that Australians regard it as important. It was the first formal alliance Australia negotiated with a foreign power. According to Professor Hugh White Australian politicians had been seeking to establish a regional security pact since at least the mid-1930s, but without success. In 1951 two events created the opportunity for ANZUS. The first was the war in Korea, under United Nations auspices, in which the US led the resistance to North Korea's invasion of the South, and in which Australia was an early participant. The second was America's desire to ensure support for a peace treaty with Japan involving its wartime allies. White says 'If it had not been for Korea it seems to me very unlikely that we would have succeeded in using the leverage of the Japanese Peace Treaty to get ANZUS'. And if the treaty had not been signed then, the chances were low it would have happened later. 'America only went through one big period of treaty-making'.

But he says ANZUS did not emerge fully-born as the institution in the mental make-up of Australians that it has become 'because we still had a big focus on the British in those days'. In fact Australia's primary focus was on the Middle East and Malaya (as it then was). While people may remember the West was engaged in a cold war with the Soviet Union from shortly after the end of World War II, few people today would realise there was a threat of a full-scale hot war. In 1951 that was the message Sir Robert Menzies tried to tell the Australian people – there could be a war with the Soviet Union within three years. And the government certainly took its own warnings seriously. It virtually doubled its defence spending and it came to an agreement with Britain about what its responsibilities would be in the event of a new world conflict. Australia would send its main army and air force units to the Middle East, and to prepare for this possibility it actually based some RAAF squadrons in that area. Australia's defence ties with Britain also helped dictate the kind of equipment it bought for its armed forces. It was another 10 years, towards the end of the 1950s, that Australia began to standardise on American rather than British hardware. White says it was not until the mid-1960s and the Vietnam commitment, following the British withdrawal from what it described as 'East of Suez' in 1968, that ANZUS emerged with the saliency it now has. But he points out that the original political concept of Australia – to maximise US engagement in the Pacific area – has never changed.

New engagements

The Lowy Institute poll suggests there has been a major change in the way Australians view their place in the world in the last half century. As the second half of the twentieth century began, Australia was still 'White Australia' and many of the countries of Southeast Asia were in the process of winning independence from their European colonial masters and Australians still feared the possibility that a re-armed Japan would again threaten the country's very survival. Politicians led a reluctant nation to approve the Japanese Peace Treaty and six years later signed a trade agreement with Japan. Political efforts to improve relations with Asian countries, particularly through the Colombo Plan, made little impact on Australians who were still more interested in what was happening in Europe and the Middle East than in their own neighbourhood. No-one would have predicted that in 2005 Australians would rate Japan among the nations of the world about which they held the most positive feelings or that China would rate higher than France, or Malaysia and Papua New Guinea would outrank the United States.

The polling results stand easily alongside policies adopted by recent Australian governments that tie Australia much closer to the countries of its region. Whether dictated by security, trade or other national interest calculations, Australia has sought closer ties with the Association of South East Asian Nations (ASEAN) collectively and individually, it actively supported the emergence of the new country, East Timor, with military and economic aid both before and after it achieved independence. It has also provided crucial assistance to the Solomon Islands to rescue it from anarchy in the hope of preventing it from becoming a 'failed state'. Since 2004 it has also increased the aid it has provided to Papua New Guinea since it gave that country its independence in 1975, and also provided police and administrative personnel to help it cope with mounting internal disorder. And these developments all have the support of a very solid majority of Australians.

In his paper on immigration and population policies referred to earlier in this chapter, Professor Glenn Withers wrote:

> Until the 1980s, Australia was an inward looking welfare state: directed at protecting ourselves from change. Our economic landscape included high tariff walls, a centralised industrial relations system with high minimum wages, many state owned enterprises and women were obliged to resign public service positions if they married. But since 1983, a reform program was put in place designed to make us a much more globally oriented and globally integrated, outward looking, more self confident economy and society, able to cope so much better with the emerging trends and changes in the world.

These reforms were necessary because Australia had become a sclerotic society. As Paul Keating put it, we were on the way to becoming a 'Banana Republic' or, as Lee Kuan Yew put it, we were becoming seen as 'the poor white trash of Asia'. These remarks, among other things, initiated a revolution in our economic affairs that has had significant positive effects.[17]

Notes

1 Hugo 2002.
2 DIMIA 2005: paras 28, 31.
3 Productivity Commission 2005a: 7.
4 Productivity Commission 2006a: Media release.
5 Withers 2006: 13.
6 Parliamentary Library 2005b: 2.
7 See the Research note issued by the Parliamentary Library on 21 January 2007.
8 *Sue v Hill* (1999) 199 CLR 462.
9 The first such case was *Nolan v Minister for Immigration & Ethnic Affairs* (1988) 165 CLR 178.
10 White 2005.
11 Latham 2005: 393.
12 Fraser 2005.
13 Grant 2004.
14 Maley 2004: 19.
15 Costello, P 2005a: 2.
16 Cook 2005 and 2006.
17 Withers 2006: 2.

13

Conclusion: Evolving institutions

Most of Australia's significant institutions have undergone remarkable – but often unremarked – changes in the past generation or so. Some of the changes flow naturally and inevitably from Australia's strong population growth and its growing prosperity. But many have occurred as a result of very deliberate decisions and actions by senior federal ministers, bureaucrats and administrators, wealthy businessmen and a few High Court justices.

In the past 20 years Australia's formal, constitutional structure of government has not been altered. In 1999 the Australian people, voting at a referendum, rejected proposals to change the Constitution to establish a republic, headed by a president selected by our political leaders, to replace the existing monarchy, headed by the Queen of the United Kingdom (and Australia). Nevertheless, many changes have occurred during those two decades that affect the way Australians are governed, the way they work or do business and the way they are informed and entertained.

Australia's national government and the governments of the States and Territories have become increasingly presidential, both as a matter of style and substance. Prime Ministers and Premiers are no longer just the first among equals – the traditional term used to describe their role in the Cabinet system of government inherited from Britain. Increasingly they function like an American President, but without most of the checks and balances that restrain the president's powers in the United States' system. Parliament has been degraded as an institution, or at least down-graded in importance. The Prime Minister and his ministers are no longer 'responsible' to Parliament, and are rarely called on to account for their actions. When the Howard Government gained a majority in the Senate, that Chamber ceased to exercise any independent review of the government's activities.

As governments have become less accountable they have increasingly resorted to using public funds to promote their partisan political interests, and have begun tampering with the electoral system to improve their prospects of retaining office, signalling a return to a much earlier period when malpractices such as gerrymandering and blatant weighting of some electoral districts and votes (generally rural ones) were common.

At the same time, political power has increasingly been centralised in the national government, reflecting in part the emergence of a strong national economy. The federal system enshrined in the Constitution has been distorted and the States have increasingly found themselves administering policies determined by the Federal Government, even in areas such as education, health and transport where the Constitution appears to give no direct power to the Commonwealth Parliament. Federal governments have achieved this transformation of the federal system using their control of the tax system and the States' dependence on federal money to deliver essential services.

Another aspect of government that has changed is the way the public service operates. It has become increasingly 'responsive' to the demands of the government of the day. The 'permanent heads' who formerly ran departments have been replaced by men and women on relatively short-term contracts, directly responsible to the Prime Minister. They can be dismissed with relative ease if they run foul of the minister to whom they report. Public servants must also respond to the burgeoning numbers of political apparatchiks who staff ministerial offices, and act in the names of their ministers to secure the political and administrative aims of the minister and the government.

It is debateable whether the public service is as good at offering ministers independent, frank and fearless advice as it was when it was supposedly less 'responsive' to the political agenda of government.

Institutions outside government have also undergone change in recent years. The universities were transformed by the Dawkins revolution of the late 1980s, when dozens of colleges of advanced education merged with existing universities or were transmogrified into new ones. In turn the new university sector then had to adapt to a funding revolution that has seen the proportion of university budgets provided by the Federal Government halve, to around 40 per cent. Universities have coped mainly by increasing their intake of full-fee paying students, mainly from overseas, but this presented them with new problems and risks. Australian students meanwhile were burdened with increasing debts they must pay off when they obtain employment.

The trade union movement has also had to cope with a difficult new environment. This partly resulted from a fall in union membership and changes in the composition of the workforce and the way it operates, all of which lessened the power of unions to represent their members' interests. A more demanding challenge came from the Howard Government's Work Choices law, that centralised control of workplace relations and further reduced the ability of unions to influence the pay and conditions of employees. The unions responded to what they perceived to be a direct threat to their continuing existence by raising substantial levies to fight against the changes and to campaign against the government's re-election.

Another institution that underwent massive change was sport. Its very nature was radically altered as it become increasingly professional at elite levels. This flowed partly from a substantial contribution to many sports by the Federal Government, which imposed its own policies on those sports most dependent upon the aid it provided. However even more important for the mainstream sports such as cricket and the four football codes, were the vast sums television networks were prepared to pay for exclusive coverage of domestic and international competitions. Those competitions and sometimes the sports themselves were created or recreated by television – most notably in the case of one-day cricket, by Kerry Packer. Senior players were able to obtain lucrative contracts, unimaginable a few decades earlier.

Externally also, changes were occurring in Australia's institutional relationships. The long-standing ties between Britain and Australia slackened further as Australia affirmed its national independence. The relationship was affected also by the changing make-up of Australia's population, as it became genuinely multicultural. This resulted from a decrease in migration from the British isles and a substantial increase in those coming from Asia, South America and Africa. A further factor was Australia's increasing reliance for defence and security on the United States, in place of its previous dependence on Britain.

Australian institutions have been influenced also by globalisation and its forces, impacting on the development of its economy and also affecting its security. The terrorist attacks on the United States in 2001 and in Bali the following year resulted in a revamping of the defence, security and police forces to meet new threats, external and internal.

Australia's institutions continue to evolve, some more rapidly than others. The challenge is to determine whether the institutions are appropriate and effective and to discover whether any changes they are undergoing are appropriate and beneficial or need to be reviewed. They should not be ignored.

Bibliography

Many of the primary and secondary references used in this book can be accessed through the Internet. Speeches by politicians, public servants, academics and judges are routinely listed on the websites maintained by the government. Media organisations allow access to their news archives, though some charge fees to access them. Almost all the references to speeches by government officials can be located through the relevant government website, and those of Commonwealth politicians and officials through <www.aus.gov.au>. All the independent authorities, such as the Reserve Bank and the Productivity Commission, have their own websites. All are easily located and relevant speeches, and reports are readily available.

Reference is made to some High Court and Federal Court cases. Where access to the relevant authorised reports (such as the Commonwealth Law Reports) is not possible, the text of the judgments can be accessed through <www.hcourt.gov.au> for the High Court (speeches by the judges are also available), and through <www.austlii.edu.au> for all courts.

For references to the Commonwealth Grants Commission (2006), a history and its current activities can be found on the Commission's website <www.cgc.gov.au>.

The author conducted tape-recorded interviews with more than 50 people and those interviews were transcribed. One interview, with Dennis Richardson, was not recorded as it took place in ASIO headquarters where a tape-recorder was not permitted. Instead, extensive notes were taken.

Abbott, T (1997) 'How to win the constitutional war: and give both sides what they want', in *Australians for Constitutional Monarchy*, Wakefield Press, Adelaide.

Abbott, T (2004a) 'Labor's now a party of apparatchiks' *The Age*, 17 August, p 11.

Abbott, T (2004b) 'Responsible Federalism', in Hudson, W and Brown, AJ (eds), *Restructuring Australia*. Federation Press, Sydney.

ABS (Australian Bureau of Statistics) (2004), *Sport and recreation: a statistical overview, 2003*, ABS, Canberra, <www.abs.gov.au/AUSSTATS/abs@.nsf/mediareleasesbyReleaseDate/664ACEA167C1CA4BCA256DDD007FB416?OpenDocument>.

ABS (2007) *Employee Earnings, Benefits and Trade Union Membership, Australia, August 2006*, <www.abs.gov.au/AUSSTATS/abs@.nsf/Lookup/6310.0Main+Features1Aug%202006?OpenDocument>.

Advisory Committee to the Constitutional Commission (1987) *Executive Government*, Canberra Publishing and Printing Co, Canberra.

AIJA (Australian Institute of Judicial Administration) (2001) *Litigants in person management plans: issues for courts and tribunals*, AIJA, Melbourne, <www.aija.org.au>.

Aitkin, D (2004) 'Teaching-only model is all too familiar', *Australian Financial Review*, 11 December.

Aitkin, D (2005) Interview with the author.

Akerman, P (2004) *Daily Telegraph*, 10 October, quoted by Dennis Glover, 'Is the media pro-Labor', in Manne, R (ed) (2005), *Do Not Disturb*. Black Inc Agenda, Melbourne, p 202.

ALRC (Australian Law Reform Commission) (2006) Media release, 'Support for anti-violence measures, not "sedition": ALRC', 13 September, <www.alrc.gov.au>.

Andren, P (2004) 'Level Democratic Playing Field – You Must Be Joking', Democratic Audit, Australian National University Press, Canberra.

APC (Australian Press Council) (2006) *State of the News Print Media in Australia*, October.

Arnison, P (2003) Speech to the Australasian Study of Parliament Group (Queensland), 8 September, Parliament House, Brisbane.

ASC (Australian Sports Commission) (2005) *Annual Report, 2004-2005*, <www.ausport.gov.au/publications/annualreport2005/docs>.

ASC (2006) *The 2005 Exercise, Recreation and Sports Survey*, (ERAS), ASC, Canberra.

ASIC (Australian Securities and Investments Commission) (2005a) *ASIC Annual Report 2004-2005*, <www.asic.gov.au/asic/asic.nsf/byheadline/annual%20reports?openDocument#05>.

ASIC (2005b) *ASIC Strategic Plan 2005-10*, April 2005, ASIC at a glance.

Athletics Australia (2005) 'Achieving High Performance 2005-09 – Executive Summary', <http://athletics.telstra.com/insideaa/pdfs/hp_executive_summary_webversion.pdf>.

Australian Government (1972) Cabinet papers, National Archives of Australia.

Australian Government (2006a) Commonwealth Budget, Budget Paper No 3, <www.budget.gov.au>.

Australian Government (2006b) *Meeting the digital challenge* Discussion Paper on Media Reform Options, March, <www.dcita.gov.au/__ data/assets/pdf-file/37572/media_consultation_paper>.

Australian Government (2006c) *Protecting Australia against Terrorism* and the *Flood Report*, <www.dpmc.gov.au>, and *The Australian Intelligence Community*, Australian Government, Canberra, 2006.

Australian Public Service Commission (2005), State of the Service Report 2004-05, AGPS, Canberra.

Australian Racing Board (2005) *Australian Racing Fact Book 2003-2004*, ARB.

AVCC (Australian Vice-Chancellors' Committee) (2004) *Achieving the Vision for Australia's Universities*, AVCC, Canberra, November.

AVCC (2005) *Statistical Highlights*, AVCC, Canberra.

AVCC (2006) *Australian University Handbook*, AVCC, Canberra.

Bacevich, A (2006) 'This is not World War Three – or Four', *The Spectator*, 22 July.

Bagehot, W (1967) *The English Constitution*, Oxford University Press, London.

Banks, G (2005) 'Structural reform Australian style: lessons for others' Chairman's speech, Productivity Perspectives Conference March 2006.

Barratt, P (2006) 'Who minds the minders?' *New Matilda*, 15 March.

Beattie, P (2006) in Allen, Lisa 'Get rid of Senate's party hacks: Beattie' *Australian Financial Review*, 12 October 2006, p 8.

Blainey, G (2004) 'Why every major region should be its own State', in Hudson, W and Brown, AJ (2004) 'Reform of the Nation State', in Hudson, W and Brown, AJ (eds), *Restructuring Australia*, Federation Press, Sydney.

Blewitt, N (2005) Interview with the author.

Bloomfield, J (2003) *Australia's Sporting Success*. UNSW Press, Sydney.

Brenchley, F (2003) Allan Fels – A Portrait of Power. Wiley, Brisbane.

Brenchley, F (2006) 'ACCC denies it is holding back', *Australian Financial Review*, 1 August, p 3.

Brown AJ (2005) (lead author), *Chaos or Coherence? Strengths, Opportunities, and Challenges for Australia's Integrity Systems*. Griffith University, Brisbane.

Burrows, S (2005) Interview with the author.

Button, J (2002) *Beyond Belief - What Future for Labor?* Quarterly Essay, Black Inc, Melbourne.

Cabinet Secretariat (2004) *Cabinet Handbook* (Fifth Edition), AGPS Canberra.

Callinan, I (1994) Address to the Queensland Bar Association, 1 July, Gold Coast.

Carlton, JJ (2005) Interview with the author.

Chubb, I (2005) Interview with the author.

Coaldrake, P (2005) Interview with the author.

Coleman, P (2007) 'No wonder state Liberals are confused', *Australian Financial Review*, 7 March, p 63.

Comrie, N (2005) *Inquiry into the circumstances of the Vivian Alvarez Matter*, Report No 03/05, Commonwealth Ombudsman, Canberra.

Cook, I (2005) *The Lowy Institute Poll 2005*, Lowy Institute for International Policy, Sydney.

Cook, I (2006) *The Lowy Institute Poll 2006*. Lowy Institute for International Policy, Sydney.

Costello, M (2004) 'Let's re-create bureaucrats' independence' *The Australian*, 7 May, p 15.

Costello, P (2005a) Address to The Australian-American Leadership Dialogue Forum, 20 August.

Costello, P (2005b) Transcript of *7.30 Report*, ABC TV, 9 March.

Costello, P (2006) Address to the Bulletin Top 100 Most Influential Australians Luncheon, 26 June.

Cowen, Sir Z (1985) 'The Office of Governor-General', in Graubard, SR (ed), *Australia: The Daedalus Symposium.* Angus & Roberston, Sydney.

Craven, G (2004) 'The Developing Role of the Governor-General: The goldenness of silence', *Federal Law Review,* Vol 32.

Craven, G (2006a) 'A lighter hand on the leading rein', *The Australian*, 14 June, p 33.

Craven, G (2006b) 'IR threat to unis' vital role' *The Australian*, 25 January, p 32.

Craven, G (2006c) 'The New Centralism and the Collapse of the Conservative Constitution', in *Democratic Experiments, Lectures in the Senate Occasional Lecture Series 2004-2005,* in Papers on Parliament Number 44, The Department of the Senate, Canberra.

Craven, G (2006d) 'Struggle ahead for the states', *The Australian,* 16 November 2006, p 10.

Creighton, B and Stewart, A (2005) *Labour Law,* Federation Press, Sydney, Fourth edition.

Davis, G (2005a) 'Control stifles competition', *Australian Financial Review*, March 19, p 16.

Davis, G (2005b) Interview with the author.

Davis, G (2005c) 'It's a whole new playing field', *The Australian*, 20 April.

de Jersey, P (2003) 'Legal Educators State Conference Keynote Address' 13 August.

de Jersey, P (2005) Interview with the author.

Dent, C and Kenyon, A (2004) 'Defamation law's chilling effect: a comparative content analysis of Australian and US newspapers' *Legal Studies Research* Paper No 94.

Department of the Parliamentary Library (1996) *The Constitution Papers.* AGPS, Canberra.

DIMIA (Department of Immigration, Multicultural and Indigenous Affairs) (2005) 'Economic impacts of migration and population growth', Submission to the Productivity Commission inquiry on Economic Impacts of Migration and Population Growth.

Downes, G (2006) Overview of Tribunals Scene in Australia, presented at International Tribunals Workshop, Canberra, 5 April, <www.aat.gov.au>.

Drummond, M (1998) 'Statistical Research', published as Appendix 1 in Hall, R *Abolish the States!* Pan Macmillan, Sydney.

Drummond, M (2005) *Australian Financial Review*, 14 March, p 5.

Evans, C (2006) A not so humble anniversary: a year of government Senate control, address to the ACT Branch of the Fabian Society, 28 June.

Evans, H (1992) 'Parliament: An unreformable institution?' *Parliament: Achievements and Challenges*, Papers on Parliament No 18, The Department of the Senate, Canberra.

Evans, H (2000) 'Accountability versus Government Control', in Costar, B (ed), *Deadlock or Democracy? The future of the Senate*, UNSW Press, Sydney.

Evans, H (2002) 'Senate inquiries: who can be called', *The Canberra Times*, Public Sector Informant, April, p 10.

Evans, H (2005a) 'Executive and Parliament', in Aulich, C and Wettenhall, R (eds), *Howard's second and third term governments*. UNSW Press, Sydney.

Evans, H (2005b) Interview with the author.

Evans, H (2006a) 'Government advertising – funding and the financial system', Parliament Matters, No 15, p 1.

Evans, H (2006b) 'The Australian Parliament: Time for reformation', Speech to the National Press Club, 24 April, Canberra.

Faine, J (2005) 'Talk Radio and Democracy', in Manne, R (ed), *Do Not Disturb,* Black Inc Agenda, Melbourne.

Flood, P (2004) Report of the Inquiry into Australian Intelligence Agencies, Commonwealth of Australia, Canberra.

Foley, M (2005) Interview with the author.

Fraser, JM (2005) Interview with the author.

Gleeson, M (2004) Summary of remarks at conference opening, Supreme and Federal Court Judges' Conference, Auckland 27 January.

Gleeson, M (2005) Interview with the author.

Gleeson, M (2006) *Australian Financial Review*, 10 March.

Golf Australia (2006) 'Statistics', <www.golfaustralia.org.au/site/_content/document/0005776-source.pdf>.

Goot, M (2002) 'Distrustful, Disenchanted and Disengaged? Polled Opinion on Politics, Politicians and the Parties: an Historical Perspective', in Papers on Parliament No 38, The Department of the Senate, Canberra.

Grant, B (2004) *Fatal Attraction: Reflections on the Alliance with the United States*, Black Inc Agenda, Melbourne.

Hall, R (1998) *Abolish the States!* Pan Macmillan, Sydney.

Halligan, J and Horrigan, B (2005) 'Reforming Corporate Governance in The Australian Federal Public sector: From Uhrig to Implementation', *Corporate Governance ARC Project*, Issues paper series No 2.

Hamer, D (1994) *Can Responsible Government Survive in Australia?,* The Department of the Senate, Canberra.

Hartigan, J (2004) Media release, 'Newspapers up, television down.' 12 August.

Hartnell, A (2005) Interview with the author.

Hasluck, Sir P (1979) The Office of Governor-General. MUP, Melbourne.

Hasluck, Sir P (1995) *Light that time has made*, National Library of Australia, Canberra.

Hawke RJ (2005) Interview with the author.

Hay, J (2005) Interview with the author.

Hayden, W (1996) *Hayden, An Autobiography*, Angus & Robertson, Sydney.

Henderson, G (2007) 'Fragile union, even with a Labor win' *Sydney Morning Herald*, 10 April, p 11.

Herman, J (2005) Interview with the author.

Heydon, D (2003) 'Judicial Activism and the Death of the Rule of Law', *Quadrant*, January-February.

Hindess, B (2004) 'Corruption and Democracy in Australia', Democratic Audit, ANU, Canberra.

Howard, J (2003) Quoted in Starick, P, "MPs need life experience', *Adelaide Advertiser*, 13 December, p 34.

Howard, J (2004a) Address to The Australian Strategic Policy Institute, 18 June.

Howard, J (2004b) Foreword to *Protecting Australia Against Terrorism*, Department of the Prime Minister and the Cabinet, Canberra.

Howard, J (2005) <www.pm.gov.au>.

Howard, J (2006a) Media Release, 'A stronger AFP: Responding to regional challenges', 25 August, <www.pm.gov.au>.

Howard, J (2006b) Media Release, 'A Stronger Army: Two more Battalions', 24 August <www.pm.gov.au>.

Howard, J (2006c) *Australian Financial Review*, 1 June, p 10.

Hudson, W and Brown, AJ (eds) (2004) *Restructuring Australia*, Federation Press, Sydney.

Hughes, CA and Costar, B (2006) *Limiting Democracy – The Erosion of Electoral Rights in Australia*, UNSW Press, Sydney.

Hugo, G (2002) 'A Century of population change in Australia', in *Year Book Australia.*, Australian Bureau of Statistics.

Hurford, C (2004) 'A republican federation of regions: Re-forming a wastefully governed Australia', in Hudson, W and Brown, AJ (eds), *Restructuring Australia.* Federation Press, Sydney.

IMF (International Monetary Fund) (2005) *IMF Survey*, 31 October, Vol 34 No 20.

Jaensch, D, Brent, P and Bowden, B (2004) 'Australian Political Parties in the Spotlight', Democratic Audit, ANU, Canberra.

Keating, M (2004) *Who Rules? How government retains control of a privatised economy*, Federation Press, Sydney.

Keating, M (2005) Interview with the author.

Keating, M, Wanna, J and Weller, P (eds) (2000) *Institutions on the edge? – Capacity for governance*, Allen & Unwin, Sydney.

Keating, M and Weller, P (2000) 'Cabinet government: an institution under pressure', in Keating, M, Wanna, J and Weller, P (eds) (2000) *Institutions on the edge? – Capacity for governance*, Allen & Unwin, Sydney.

Keelty, M (2005) Interview with the author.

Kelly, N (2006) 'MPs incumbency benefits keep growing', Democratic Audit, ANU, Canberra.

Kirby, M (2004) Industrial Conciliation and Arbitration in Australia – A centenary reflection, opening plenary session paper presented at The Centenary Convention – Conciliation and Arbitration in Australia, 22 October, Melbourne.

Kryger, T (2004) 'Casual employment: trends and characteristics', Research Note No 53, 24 May, Parliamentary Library, Canberra.

Kryger, T (2006) 'The incredible shrinking public sector', Research Note No 29, 24 March, Parliamentary Library, Canberra.

Laker, J (2003) Evidence to the Senate Economic Legislation Committee, 6 November.

Laker, J (2004) Evidence to the House of Representatives Standing Committee on Economics, Finance and Public Administration, 10 May, *Hansard.*

Latham, M (2005) *The Latham Diaries*, Melbourne University Publishing.

Lavarch, M (2005) Interview with the author.

Liberal Party of Australia (2006) *Federal Platform*, Liberal Party of Australia, Canberra.

Lynch, A (2006a) On-line opinion, 6 April 2006. <www.onlineopinion.com.au>

Lynch, A (2006b) Submission by Dr Andrew Lynch and others, Centre of Public Law, University of NSW, to the UN Study on Human Rights Compliance while Countering Terrorism, <www.gtcentre.unsw.edu.au>.

McDonald, D (2005) Address to the National Press Club, Canberra, 1 June.

McHugh, M (2004a) 'The Constitutional Jurisprudence of the High Court: 1989-2004', Speech at the Inaugural Sir Anthony Mason Lecture in Constitutional Law, 26 November, Banco Court, Sydney.

McHugh, M (2004b) 'The strengths of the weakest arm', Keynote address, Australian Bar Association Conference, Florence, 2 July.

McHugh, M (2004c) 'Women Justices for the High Court', Speech to the WA Law Society, at the High Court Dinner, 27 October.

McKeown, D and Lundie, R (2005) 'Crossing the floor in Federal Parliament 1950-August 2004', Research Note No 11, Parliamentary Library, 10 October.

McKinnon, K (2006) in Sally Jackson, 'Papers can withstand net growth' *The Australian* 12 October.

McKnight, D (2005) 'Murdoch and the Culture War', in Manne, R (ed), *Do Not Disturb,* Black Inc Agenda, Melbourne.

McMillan, J (2005) Interview with the author.

Macfarlane, I (2005a) 'Global Influences on the Australian Economy', Address to Australian Institute of Company Directors, Sydney, 14 June.

Macfarlane, I (2005b) *The Australian*, 14 December, p 6.

Macfarlane, I (2006) Quoted in Uren, D, 'Bank chief hits at campaign rates vow', *The Australian*, 11 September, p 6.

Macintyre, S and Marginson, S (2000) 'The University and its Public', in Coady, T (ed), *Why Universities Matter.* Allen & Unwin, Sydney.

Maley, W (2004) 'Australia's defence and strategic priorities', *Strategy*, October, Australian Strategic Policy Institute.

Manne, R (2004) 'The Howard Years: A political interpretation', in Manne, R (ed), *The Howard Years*, Black Inc Agenda, Melbourne.

Mason, Sir A (2003) Speech to the Constitutional Law Conference Dinner, NSW Parliament House, Sydney, 21 February.

Mason, Sir A (2005) Interview with the author.

Mayer, H (1964) *The Press in Australia,* Lansdowne Press, Melbourne.

Menzies, Sir R (1967) *Central Power in The Australian Commonwealth*, Cassell, London.

Metcalf, A (2006) Speech on improving DIMIA's departmental performance, 2 May, Canberra.

Miskin, S and Lumb, M (2006) 'The 41st Parliament: middle-aged, well-educated and (mostly) male', Research Note No 24, 24 February, Parliamentary Library.

Mitchell & Partners (2006) Submission to the Federal Government discussion paper on media reform options, South Melbourne, <www.mitchells.com.au>.

Moore, D (2001) 'Judicial Intervention: The old province for law and order', Address to the Samuel Griffith Society, 2 September, Melbourne.

Moore, J (2000) 'Executive Summary', *White Paper Defence 2000*, Department of Defence, Canberra.

Murdoch, R (2005) 'The challenges of the online world', Speech to the American Society of Newspaper Editors, 13 April, Washington, DC.

Murdoch, R (2006a) 'The Dawn of a New Age of Discovery: Media 2006', Address to The Annual Livery Lecture at the Worshipful Company of Stationers and Newspaper Makers, 13 March.

Murdoch, R (2006b) 'Murdoch pushes for competition across spectrum', *The Australian*, 29 June.

Murray, A (2006) Media statement, 4 July, Canberra.

Nash, C (2005) 'Freedom of the Press in Australia', Democratic Audit, ANU, Canberra.

Nelson, B (2005) Letter from Education Minister Dr Brendan Nelson to State Ministers, 30 March.

OECD (Organisation for Economic Cooperation and Development) (2006) Economic Survey of Australia 2006, OECD, Paris.

OECD (2005) OECD Factbook: economic, environmental and social statistics, OECD, Paris.

O'Neill, J (2006a) 'A-League aiming to kick on', *The Courier-Mail*, 19 August.

O'Neill, J (2006b) Speech to the National Press Club, 26 July, Canberra.

Owen, N (2003) The HIH Royal Commission, <www.hihroyalcom.gov.au>.

Palmer, M (2005) 'Report to the Commonwealth Ombudsman on the Rau affair', Commonwealth Ombudsman, Canberra.

Parliamentary Library (2005a) 'Australia's Corporate Regulators – the ACCC, ASIC and APRA', Parliamentary Library Research Brief, No 16 2004–05, 14 June.

Parliamentary Library (2005b) 'Australia's humanitarian program', Research Note, No 9, 9 September, Parliamentary Library, Canberra.

Peters, M (2005) Interview with the author.

Peters, M (2006) 'Budget brings unprecedented level of funding to Australian sport', Ausport, June, Australian Sports Commission, Canberra.

Podger, A (2004) 'Managing the interface with ministers and the parliament', Speech to SES Breakfast, 23 April.

Podger, A (2005a) 'Ethics and Public Administration', November, Democratic Audit, ANU, Canberra.

Podger, A (2005b) 'Parting remarks on the Australian Public Service', *New Matilda,* 17 August.

Police Federation of Australia (2006) *Submission to the Joint Parliamentary Committee of Foreign Affairs, Defence and Trade*, May..

Prescott, V (2000) 'The Need to Reform the Constitution of Australia' *Public Law Review*, Vol 11, June.

Print, M, Saha, L and Edwards, K (2004) 'Youth Electoral Study, Report 1', Australian Electoral Commission, Canberra.

Productivity Commission (2005a) *Economic Impacts of Migration and Population Growth,* Issues Paper, 10 August.

Productivity Commission (2005b) *Review of National Competition Policy Reforms,* Productivity Commission Inquiry Report, No 33, 28 February.

Productivity Commission (2005c) *Trends in Australian Agriculture,* Productivity Commission (2006a) *Economic Impacts of Migration and Population Growth,* Report and Media release, 24 April.

Productivity Commission (2006b) *Report on Government Services,* AGPS, Canberra.

Productivity Commission (2006c) Media release, 'The role of non-traditional work in The Australian labour market', 25 May.

Quiggin, J (2006) '2006 Budget – Market failure', *Australian Policy Online,* 15 May, <www.apo.org.au>.

Richardson, D (2005) Interview with the author.

RMIT, Journalism Program (2005) 'How Journalists View the Media', in Mills, J (ed), *Barons to Bloggers: Confronting Media Power,* Miegunyah Press.

Roy Morgan Research (2005) 'How Australians View the Media', in Mills, J (ed), *Barons to Bloggers: Confronting Media Power,* Miegunyah Press, Melbourne.

Ruddock, P (2005a) 'Ruddock pushes for standards across states', *Australian Financial Review,* 11 April, p 3.

Ruddock, P (2005b) Closing Speech to the LawAsia Conference, March 24, Gold Coast.

Rundle, G (2005) 'The Rise of the Right', in Manne, R (ed), *Do Not Disturb,* Black Inc Agenda, Melbourne.

Samuel, G (2005a) Interview with the author.

Samuel, G (2005b) 'Media convergence and the changing face of media regulation', Speech to 2005 Henry Mayer Lecture, 19 May, University of Queensland.

Samuel, G (2006a) 'Australian Infrastructure Reform: Where to from here?', Speech to South Australian Centre for Economics corporate lunch, Adelaide, 18 May.

Samuel, G (2006b) 'The Regulation of Commerce and Public Authorities in Australia', Speech to Western Australian Law Society Summer School, 24 February.

Saul, B (2006) 'Preventive detention of terrorism suspects', 3 July, International Society for the Reform of Criminal Law, Brisbane.

Sawer, M (2004) 'Election 2004: How democratic are Australia's elections?' Democratic Audit, ANU, Canberra <www.democratic.audit.arw.au/search_keyw_frm.htm>.

Sawer, M (2006) 'Damaging democracy? Early closure of electoral rolls' Democratic Audit, ANU, Canberra.

Scalmer, S and Goot, M (2004) 'Elites Constructing Elites: News Limited's Newspapers, 1996-2002', in Sawer, M and Hidness, B (eds), *Us and Them: Anti-Elitism in Australia,* API Network.

Senate Legal and Constitutional References Committee (2004) *The Road to a Republic,* The Department of the Senate.

Shergold, P (2006) Address to the National Press Club, 15 February, Canberra.

Solomon, D (1971) 'Commonwealth/State relations', in Harris, M and Dutton, G (eds), *Sir Henry, Bjelke, Don Baby and friends.* Sun Books, Melbourne.

Solomon, D (1976) *Elect the Governor-General!,* Nelson, Melbourne.

Solomon, D (1999) *The Political High Court,* Allen & Unwin, Sydney.

Spigelman, J (2004) Graduation address at Charles Sturt University, 29 October.

Spigelman, J (2005) Interview with the author.

Stephen, Sir N (1989) 'Depicting a nation to its people', *The Weekend Australian,* 7 January.

Sutherland, J (2005) Interview with the author.

Sweeney Sports (2006) *Sweeney Sports Report,* Melbourne, <www.sweeneyresearch.com.au>.

Tanner, L (2005) 'Abolish the States', *New Matilda,* 23 November.

Thomson, E (1980) 'The "Washminster" Mutation', *Politics,* Vol 15, No 1, p 50.

Thomson, M (2006a) *The Cost of Defence: ASPI Defence Budget Brief 2006-07,* Australian Strategic Policy Institute (ASPI), Canberra.

Thomson, M (2006b) *Your Defence Dollar: The 2006-07 Defence Budget,* Australian Strategic Policy Institute (ASPI), Canberra.

Tiernan A (2006) 'Advising Howard', *Australian Journal of Political Science,* Vol 41, No 3, p 309.

Tiffen, R and Gittins, R (2004) *How Australia Compares,* Cambridge University Press.

Varghese, P (2006) Australia's strategic outlook: a longer term view, Speech to The Australian Strategic Policy Institute, 28 June.

Veit, R (2005) 'Australia and counter-terrorism' *AQ,* Sept-Oct.

Walker, G de Q (2001) 'Ten Advantages of a Federal Constitution – And How to Make the Most of Them', The Centre for Independent Studies, Summer 2000-2001.

Warren, M (2004) 'The Growth in Tribunal Power', Speech to the Council of Administrative Tribunals, 7 June.

Weller, P (2000) in Keating, M, Wanna, J and Weller, P (eds), *Institutions on the Edge?* Allen & Unwin, Sydney.

Weller, P (2003) 'The Australian Public Service: Still Anonymous, Neutral and a Career Service?' Department of the Senate Occasional Lecture Series, 30 May 2003, in Papers on Parliament No 40, The Department of the Senate, Canberra.

Weller, P (2005) Interview with the author.

White, H (2005) Interview with the author.

Wiltshire, K (2004) 'The Price of Nationhood', *Australian Chief Executive,* April, p 14.

Wiltshire, K (2005) *The Courier-Mail,* 21 May, p 32.

Winterton, G (2003) 'Lessons from the Hollingworth affair' Democratic Audit, ANU, Canberra, 17 June.

Withers, G (2006) 'A curate's egg? Australia's immigration and population policies', Asia Pacific School of Economics and Governance Discussion Papers, Speech at National Museum of Australia, 2 May.

Wood, J (2005) 'The Commonwealth Ombudsman – Time for Independence?', Democratic Audit, ANU, Canberra.

Wright, DI (1970) Shadow of Dispute – Aspects of Commonwealth-State Relations 1901-1910. Australian National University Press.

Yerbury, D (2005) Interview with the author.

Young, S (2003) 'Democracy, communication and money', Democratic Audit, ANU, Canberra.

Young, S (2004) *The Persuaders: Inside the Hidden Machine of Political Advertising*, Pluto Press, Sydney.

Zines, L (2000) 'The present state of constitutional interpretation', in Stone, A and Williams, G (eds), *The High Court at the Crossroads: Essays in Constitutional Law*, Federation Press, Sydney.

Index